THE SPLENDOUR
OF
TIPHARETH

Omraam Mikhaël Aïvanhov

THE SPLENDOUR
OF
TIPHARETH

New Translation from the French

2ⁿᵈ edition

Complete Works – Volume 10

EDITIONS PROSVETA

Editor-Distributor

Editions PROSVETA S.A. – B.P. 12 – 83601 Fréjus Cedex (France)

Distributors

AUSTRIA
MANDALA
Verlagauslieferung für Esoterik
A-6094 Axams, Innsbruckstraße 7

BELGIUM
PROSVETA BENELUX
Van Putlei 105 B-2548 Lint

N.V. MAKLU Somersstraat 13-15
B-2000 Antwerpen

VANDER S.A.
Av. des Volontaires 321
B-1150 Bruxelles

BRITISH ISLES
PROSVETA Ldt
The Doves Nest

Prosveta
The Doves Nest
Duddleswell
Uckfield
East Sussex TN22 3JJ

CANADA
PROSVETA Inc.
1565 Montée Masson
Duvernay est, Laval, Que. H7E 4P2

GERMANY
URANIA – Steinsdorfstr. 14
D 8000 München 22

HOLLAND
STICHTING
PROSVETA NEDERLAND
Zeestraat 50
2042 LC Zandvoort

HONG KONG
HELIOS
31 New Kap Bin Long Village
Sai Kung N.T., Hong Kong

IRELAND
PROSVETA IRL.
84 Irishtown – Clonmel

ITALY
PROSVETA ITALIE
19-2 Via Ennio 20137 Milano

LUXEMBOURG
PROSVETA BENELUX
Van Putlei 105 B-2548 Lint

NORWAY
PROSVETA NORGE
Postboks 5101
1501 Moss

PORTUGAL
PUBLICAÇÕES
EUROPA-AMERICA Ltd
Est Lisboa-Sintra KM 14
2726 Mem Martins Codex

SPAIN
EDICOMUNICACION, S.A.
C/ de las Torres 75-77
08033 Barcelona

SWITZERLAND
PROSVETA
Société Coopérative
CH - 1808 Les Monts de Corsier

UNITED STATES
PROSVETA U.S.A.
P.O. Box 49614
Los Angeles, California 90049

Prosveta S.A. – B.P. 12 – 83601 Fréjus Cedex (France)

ISBN 2-85566-421-7

édition originale : ISBN 2-85566-352-0

By the same author
(translated from the French)

'Complete Works' Collection

Revised edition forthcoming

Brochures :

New Presentation

Forthcoming

Omraam Mikhaël Aïvanhov

TABLE OF CONTENTS

*The reader is asked to bear in mind
that the editors have retained the spoken style of
the Master Omraam Mikhaël Aïvanhov in this presentation
of the Teaching of the Universal White Brotherhood*

Chapter One

Surya-Yoga — The Sun, Centre of our Universe — All that Exists on Earth Exists Etherically in the Sun

I am sure you have already noticed that in the morning, when the sun first appears over the horizon, a deep hush falls over the whole of nature ; every living creature is silent and attentive, as though it were deeply recollected, waiting to receive something from the rising sun. For the space of a few minutes, the earth, animals, insects and trees, even the birds, are silent and peaceful. The birds are awake, flying about and singing joyfully, long before the sun gets up, but just as it is about to appear they pause in their song and keep quiet for a few moments. Only men continue to make a noise ; they are the only ones who have not understood what is happening, and they go on with their noise, talking and shouting as though this event which affects the whole universe were of no importance. It is in things like this that one sees how ignorant and lacking in respect human beings are ; they don't know how to benefit from the presence of the sun.

And what about you ? Why do you come up here, to the Rock, at sunrise every morning ? Some come because they want to be like everybody else ; others for the aesthetic pleasure they get out of it. How many of you come for the sake of the infinitely noble work that you can do here, or to understand the sun a little better ? Very few ! And this is why I want to talk to you about what the sun means and how important it is, and about all the possibilities, all the treasures it can give us ; for it will help you enormously if your ideas on the subject are clearer. Then you will be able to do some really valid, important spiritual work.

These days, yoga has become a popular subject of discussion. In fact, I have sometimes talked to you myself about all the different types of yoga that have come to us, principally, from India and Tibet, but also from China, Japan, Egypt and Persia. All religions have their own form of yoga, even Christianity. Yes, Christians have always practised adoration, prayer, contemplation, devotion and love of God ; in fact, these are the foremost characteristics of the Christian religion, and in India this is known as Bhakti-yoga, the yoga of devotion, adoration and spiritual love. But this form of yoga suits certain temperaments better than others ; some people have different gifts and qualities and need to express and develop them in other ways. The paths that lead to the Creator are without number and, although Christians have limited themselves to one way (and we must not criticize it, for it is a very wonderful way), the Hindu tradition is richer in that it teaches many different methods.

For those who are given to study and philosophical reflection, who like to work with the mind, there is the yoga of knowledge : Jnana-yoga, the way to God through the use of one's intelligence.

Others have no philosophical or scientific bent nor do they feel the slightest desire to fall on their knees in adoration or contemplation, but they have will-power and abundant energy and the desire to work and serve others with selflessness. For them there is Karma-yoga, the yoga of good works, of achievements on the physical plane, of duty to be done without hope of payment or reward. Karma-yoga is the yoga of gratuitous, disinterested service.

For those who want to control themselves and master their instincts and impulses and the tendencies of their lower nature, there is Raja-yoga : through concentration and self-control, they too seek to lose themselves in the Almighty. They become the kings (*raja* means king) of their own inner kingdom.

Kriya-yoga is the yoga of light. This is the yoga of the great Babaji and consists in thinking of light, of getting to know and understand light and colours, and of drawing them into oneself and projecting them all around. It is a magnificent way to work.

Hatha-yoga is for those who want physical exercise, who enjoy adopting the postures or *asanas* as they are called : they twist and turn and roll themselves into balls, stretch out, lie flat on their stomach, stand upright, fold their legs behind their heads and so on. These exercises are based on a detailed knowledge of the psychic centres which are activated by the different postures, and they require a great deal of will and perseverance. Hatha-yoga is the type of yoga most widely known in the West. Unfortunately, however, Westerners don't have the same temperament or constitution as Orientals, nor do they have the necessary conditions of calm and silence to practise Hatha-yoga correctly, with the result that it often leads to a physical or psychic breakdown. Many, many people have told me that they had abandoned the practice of Hatha-yoga because they felt that it was making them unbalanced ! If you want to practise it you must go about it with great prudence and care ; I have never recommended this type of yoga for Westerners.

Agni-yoga is the yoga of fire in which one thinks of fire, works with fire and kindles the fire within. Since fire is at the origin of the whole of creation, Agni-yoga is yet another path to God.

Shabda- or Mantra-yoga is the yoga of the Word. It consists of pronouncing certain formulas or *mantras* at certain specific moments, a certain number of times, with a certain degree of intensity. The Word possesses power, and he who knows how to use that power can obtain beneficial results.

And now, I want to talk to you about a form of yoga which surpasses all others : the yoga of the sun. This form of yoga was well known in the past : the Greeks and Egyptians practised it, as did also the Persians, Aztecs, Mayas and Tibetans. But nowadays it is almost abandoned, especially in the Western world. The name 'Surya-yoga' comes from the Sanskrit word for sun :

Surya. This is the type of yoga I prefer above all others, for it includes and sums up all others. Yes, why not combine all the different types of yoga into one ?

A disciple of the Universal White Brotherhood must break out of the narrow-minded, limited ways of the past ; he represents the new man who must grow and develop in every domain. He must act with absolute disinterestedness, and this is Karma-yoga ; he must love, seek and adore God, and this is Bhakti-yoga ; he must meditate and practise concentration so as to rule over himself and his population of cells, and this is Raja-yoga. When he is sitting perfectly still and meditating on the Rock or executing the movements of our gymnastics or the Paneurythmics, he is practising a form of Hatha-yoga. When he mentally surrounds himself with light and colour and works to build up a brilliant, luminous aura, he is practising Kriya-yoga. When he fixes his mind on fire, calling on it to burn away all his impurities, this is Agni-yoga. By striving to control every word he utters and be constantly on his guard not to say anything that might cause divisions amongst men or infect them with doubt or despair ; by endeavouring, on the contrary, to use his faculty of speech to create new life, he practises Shabda-yoga. And, finally, when he focuses all his attention on the sun, loving it and seeking to unite with it, seeing it as the gateway to Heaven, the manifestation of Christ, God's representative, he is practising Surya-yoga. A disciple who practises Surya-yoga spurns none of the other kinds of yoga ; on the contrary, he uses them to become a whole being and fulfill himself in every way.

What I have described to you is the new ideal, the new model for mankind which the Universal White Brotherhood is creating : human beings whose ideal is to develop every possible quality and virtue. For Surya-yoga includes it all : adoration, wisdom, power, purity and activity, selflessness, light and the sacred fire of divine love. This is why I am going to spend the next few days talking to you about Surya-yoga, the yoga of the sun, and I hope that you will then have a clearer idea of what it is and of all the benefits to be gained from being present at the sunrise every morning.

Each of the other types of yoga helps to develop one particular aspect of oneself, whereas Surya-yoga activates every one of our psychic centres. By uniting ourselves with the sun we are bound to get results, for we are uniting with the central power that governs and animates all the planets of our universe. This is why I say that all the other kinds of yoga, which were once considered so wonderful — and which are, indeed, still wonderful — will one day be replaced by Surya-yoga which surpasses them all, for when you work with the sun you are working with God Himself. There are people who have worked successfully with this yoga, and you cannot imagine the light and lucidity they have gained from it, the sense of wonder that fills their lives ! In fact, I can tell you that the sun has revealed things to me that no one else could ever have taught me ; no book can give you what the sun can give if you learn to relate to it in the right way.

This is very easy to understand ; let me give you a simple example. Suppose that you are reading a book, one of the very best books, the Bible, the Vedas or the Avesta, for instance, but it is winter and you catch cold and have to go to bed. Well, the best book in the world cannot warm you, can it ? Or imagine that it is evening, and the light fades until you can read no longer : here again, even the most inspiring book cannot give you light to read by ! And, finally, suppose you have become anaemic from reading too much, here again, your books cannot restore your vitality. Whereas the sun can give you heat, light and life : it is obviously the most beneficial of all books !

Nobody realizes how important the sun is. Oh, of course, scientists interest themselves in the sun, but only for utilitarian purposes : they would like to bottle and sell it ! People only think of the material, commercial advantages ; they are a million miles from seeking any spiritual advantages from it ! Even religious people — I should say, religious people especially — are quite unaware of this aspect. And it is precisely this spiritual aspect that I want to explain to you : how to grow spiritually by getting to know the sun, by learning how to look at and contemplate it and even how to enter into it mentally.

The sun is the source, the father of everything, the Prime Cause ; it is he who engendered the earth and the other planets. This is why we find the same elements on earth and in the sun, the only difference being that, on earth, they are condensed and solidified. The minerals, metals, precious stones, plants and gasses, all the dense or subtle bodies to be found in the ground, water or air, or on the etheric plane, come from the sun. Yes, all medicines or quintessences extracted or manufactured by chemists, come from the sun. And shortly, you will see what this means for a disciple, the possibilities that it opens before him and how, by focussing all his powers of concentration on the sun, he can capture and draw into himself, in all their original purity, all the elements needed to ensure his health and equilibrium.

Nowadays, people stuff themselves with medicines ; they are ready to swallow wholesale quantities of drugs in the hopes of curing their ailments. But they never think of rising to a higher plane, of seeking purer, more effective remedies from subtler regions : they are content to look for remedies on the physical plane. But where do those remedies come from in the first place ? From the sun ! And this being so, would it not be better to get them directly from the source ?

You will better understand this notion if I tell you that the universe was formed by a gradual condensation. In the beginning was fire. Little by little, fire emanated a denser substance, air, and the air, in turn, emanated water. The air, you see, wanted to go back to its father, fire, but its father said, 'No, no. I've had enough of you. You're very well-off where you are, so stay there !' And the air began to weep and shed floods of tears, and this made the rain ! No doubt you will say that this is nonsense and no explanation at all ! Well, let's just say that it is a home-made explanation ! But the fact remains that water rejected the denser elements it contained, thereby forming earth. Incidentally, we now have scientific proof that all life on earth came from water. Each element, you see, is a condensation, a solidification of the next subtler element : air comes from fire, water from air and earth from water. But beyond and above the fire that we know there is another kind of fire, the light of the sun, which is the source of everything and which contains, in a subtle, etheric state, all that exists on earth.

Perhaps you are wondering what made all these elements condense ? Simply the fact that they moved away from the centre : the sun. When elements which originally existed in the sun began to move out towards the periphery, they condensed and became opaque and heavy. And the same thing happened to man : when man moved away from the Centre, from the bosom of the Lord, he lost his transparency and became heavy and unwieldy. If we want to recapture our purity and light we have to return to the centre.

You will soon see how the precepts of all religions converge in this quest for the centre or, to put it symbolically, the quest for the sun. As soon as a man decides to return to the centre something begins to change. You will remember my descriptions of the 'rotor' that I saw, years ago, at the Luna Park fairground. People would climb onto this circular platform, which would then start to spin and, gradually, as it spun faster and faster, the centrifugal force became stronger and stronger so that those who were far from the centre lost their balance and were thrown out towards the outer edge, whereas those who were standing close to the central axis, remained safely in place, laughing at the plight of the others. This is an excellent illustration of what happens when one moves away from the centre : the further away from the centre you are, the less able you will be to stand up to the chaotic forces of disorder and, little by little, you will lose your inner balance and peace. When you move closer to the centre, on the other hand, the movement is different and you find yourself inundated with a great sense of peace, calmness and joy.

It is through observations of this nature that Initiates have reached extraordinarily advanced states of awareness which have enabled them to establish their science and their philosophy and methods. And their discoveries and the fruits of their researches have been handed down to us, and today I am handing them on to you for your edification and fulfilment. The only thing is that you must understand me correctly : I have been given the privilege of being able to explain things in a very clear, almost childishly simple language, whereas most books by theologians or philosophers are so abstract and difficult to understand ! Why shouldn't the greatest truths be expressed in simple accessible language ? Why shouldn't we make them so clear and easy that even children can understand them ? This is a quality that God has given me : the capacity to present things clearly and simply.

When we go out in the morning to contemplate the sun and draw strength from it, when we try to enter into it and, at the same time, draw it into us, we are moving away from the outer fringe, back towards the source, in peace, light, liberty and oneness with God. The sun is the centre of the solar system and the planets move harmoniously in orbit around it, and it is this harmonious movement of the planets round the sun that must be duplicated by our own cells. But before this can be, we have to discover our own centre : the sun, God, the spirit within us. When we achieve this, every particle of our being moves in rhythm with universal Life, and the sensations and states of consciousness that this produces in us are unutterably glorious. What I am giving you today is the philosophical aspect of this question of the centre : but you do not yet know the practical, magical aspects of the question which are of the utmost importance. We shall talk about them later.

Perhaps you feel like asking, 'Is it really necessary to go out and watch the sun rising ? Wouldn't it come to the same thing if I prayed at home ?' Of course, you can pray at home in your own room, you can seek your centre and unite yourself to God, and you can experience the same results and the same rapture at home. True ! But if, while you are praying and meditating, you are breathing pure, fresh air and benefiting from the sunlight at the same time, you will not only be achieving union with God intellectually, by means of your thought, but also physically, through your communion with air and light : in this way, your prayer will be more complete. When you are up here at sunrise, there are many potent factors to help you : the pure air, an almost tangible peace, wide horizons and splendid warmth and light ! What more could you ask for ? You see, my dear brothers and sisters, if we learn to put things in their proper place and appreciate them for what they really are, they will help us to find better, more direct and more effective ways of approaching the source of life that we all need.

Every single being without exception needs to return to the source. And every single being understands this differently, of course, but the fact remains : they all seek God. Those who spend their time eating and drinking, those who have an insatiable appetite for sex, those who are only interested in money, power or knowledge, are all looking for God. This may shock some devout and religious people because they are often narrow-minded and prejudiced. They will say, 'It just isn't possible for anyone to seek God in such warped, roundabout ways !' But they are wrong, it is possible ; all creatures seek their Creator. The only thing is that they all seek Him in their own way. If one knew exactly where He was and how to find Him totally and perfectly, it would, of course, be better ; but there is something of God in all these things : food, money and the love of men and women. Yes, for the sensations of delight, fulfilment and wonder found in human love were put there by God. And those who hunger for power and authority, are they not reaching for attributes that belong to God ? And the desire to be beautiful, even to the point of wasting all one's money on beauty salons, face lifts and goodness knows what, is also a desire to partake of God's own beauty. Even gluttons who spend their days making pigs of themselves, find delight in their food only because it contains something of the Lord ; if it were not so, food would give no pleasure to palate or stomach. There is nothing good, beautiful or delectable on earth which does not contain some tiny particle of God. However, I am not recommending any of these ways of finding God ; they are far too unclean, deplorable and costly ! No, if you really want to find the Lord, I can show you the best path which will take you directly to Him.

The very first thing to do is to realize how important the centre is and what great changes will begin to occur within you, even without your knowing it, as soon as you start to seek the centre. The nearer you get to the sun in spirit, soul and thought, with your heart and will, the nearer you will be to God for, on the physical plane, the sun is the symbol and the tangible, visible representative of the Deity. All those abstract, remote names by which men designate God : Source of Life, Creator of Heaven and Earth, Prime Cause, Almighty God, Universal Soul, Cosmic Intelligence, can all be summed up in the one concrete, familiar reality of the sun. Yes, the sun can be seen as the summary and synthesis of all those sublime, abstract ideas which are beyond our comprehension. The sun is the gateway, the physical link, the medium through which we can unite with the Lord.

Take what I have said today, think about it and meditate on it. Above all, don't say, 'Oh, I know all that ; I've already heard or read it.' That may well be true, but even if it is, behave as though you were hearing it for the first time, otherwise you will never evolve. The trouble with most people is that they try to show their superiority by hiding behind that reaction : they have heard it all ! Whatever you tell them, their answer is always, 'Yes, I know.' Well, if they know, why have they never done anything about it ? Why are they still so weak and ill and so hidebound ? If they really possessed true knowledge they would already have overcome every difficulty and obstacle. True knowledge enables us to overcome everything that stands in out way ! But these people have never achieved anything, never conquered even the slightest weakness, they are always in the same sorry predicament ! In these conditions how can you expect me to have any faith in their superiority ? It is vitally important that you change your attitude and stop thinking you know everything. Your pride clouds your intellect to such an extent that it prevents you from evolving. So drive out pride, be more humble and react to what I have just been saying as though it were the first time you had heard it : 'Oh, but this is marvellous ; it's a real discovery, a revelation !' If you have this attitude you will be amazed at the progress you make. Oh, yes, I know very well what is preventing you from evolving.

Take what I have said about the sun today, and treasure it as an extremely important truth ; make a note of it, meditate on it and never forget it, because the more you work with this new form of yoga which is still unknown or despised, the more effective you will find it. It will give you a much better grasp of many things and will help you to fit your actions to your new understanding. Try to realize that by contemplating the centre of the solar system, you will be restoring order to an identical system within you ; you will be reinstating your own inner sun, your spirit, in its rightful place and enabling it to regain command. At present, your inner life is disordered and chaotic ; there is no centre, no government, no one at the helm. Your lodgers eat and drink and live in an uproar ; your thoughts, feelings and desires run unchecked in all directions. How can you hope to solve any of your problems when you live in such a state of anarchy ? It is just not possible ! You have to begin by reproducing the solar system within yourself ; you must have a central core, a strong, warm, luminous core — not a dull, weak, dirty, stupid one as now — and everything else must gravitate round it. So get to work and start spring-cleaning !

One of the first things you will have to do is to call into question all your previous guides, all those who have served as models and examples for you up to now. Whether they be ignorant or learned, intimate friends or historical figures, you must question

them mentally : 'Are you as luminous as the sun ? No ? Then
out you go ! And you, are you as warm as the sun ? No ? You,
too, then : out !' Once you have swept and purified your house,
you can bring in the sun and give it the place of honour. And
you may be sure that once it is back in the centre of your being,
truly present and alive within you, it will demonstrate its power.
At its approach, all your inhabitants will recognize their leader,
their Lord and Master.

I have often given you the example of how children behave
in the classroom when the teacher is absent : they spend their time
fighting and getting up to mischief. But as soon as the teacher
arrives they scurry back to their desks and listen attentively to
every word he says, looking as though butter wouldn't melt in
their mouths ! Or take the example of a group of choristers or
a troop of soldiers : when their leader, the choirmaster or sergeant-
major, is absent, they all go their own way, but as soon as he
arrives they get back into place and begin working as one. At
present, man's heart has descended to where his belly should be,
his belly has usurped the place that belongs to his head and his
brain has dropped down to the level of his feet ! Yes, that is what
I see : everything in man is upside down : his legs are up in the
air and his head down on the floor !

Let me give you just one more example : suppose a friend
whom you love and respect knocks on your door, just as you and
your family are in the middle of a violent quarrel. What do you
do ? Why, you try to forget your grievances and look as though
nothing were amiss : 'Oh, do come in. How lovely to see you !
How are you... etc., etc.' You do whatever you can to make him
feel welcome ; you even start smiling at each other so that he may
never guess that anything was wrong. Well, why not make use
of the same law within yourselves and bring the sun, the warmest,
most luminous, most vibrant visitor you could ever imagine, into your home ? If you do this, all your fragmented, quarrelsome
inhabitants will instinctively, magically, slip into place, because
they would be ashamed to be rude and unruly in front of such

an eminent friend. When a riot breaks out inside you, therefore, and your inhabitants start arguing and pulling in different directions, you can get them to calm down immediately if you begin to pray with all your heart, and peace and joy will flood into you because you will have brought in a friend whose mere presence is enough to shame them into silence ! Haven't you already experienced this for yourselves time and time again ? And if you pray to that friend even more fervently and persistently, and ask him to stay with you and never leave you again, to dwell permanently at the core of your being, peace and light will reign within you for ever.

Human beings live as though they were in a huge cave lit by one solitary candle : they can see just enough to get along, but they don't even know where they are. Then, all of a sudden, the sun appears and illuminates everything, and they realize that they have been living in surroundings of unimaginable splendour and wealth but that, not knowing it, they had never even tried to approach the treasures all round them. Or, again, it is as though they were standing up to their necks in water without knowing it : they are convinced that they are dying of thirst. 'Water ! Water !' they plead, unaware that they already have all the water they could possibly want. When the sun enters into your soul and spirit you will be able to see all the riches you already possess.

The presence of the sun brings light, but it also brings warmth. Human beings shiver with cold all their lives. They complain : 'I'm dying of cold. No one loves me ! I need friendship and affection !' and they look to each other for the warmth they need. The poor creatures think they will be warmer if they have another human being in their arms ! But they will never find true warmth in that way, for as soon as they let go they feel the cold even more and start shivering all over again.

No, my dear brothers and sisters : that is not the way to find warmth. If you want true warmth you must let in the sun. And when the sun comes in it will be so hot that you will begin to sweat and have to take off all your clothes ! Of course, I am

speaking symbolically ; I mean that you will know truth. You
have heard the expression 'the naked truth'. At present people
are so cold that they are all wrapped up in furs, like Eskimos,
with only the tips of their noses to be seen. How can they possibly
get to know each other in these conditions ? How can they see
each other's beauty and manifest their love ? It is too cold, there
is no warmth, that is to say, no love. When there is no sun, that
is, no love, it is too cold. But when the sun appears, it will heat
and vivify human beings to such an extent that, symbolically
speaking, they will have to undress ! Then they will be seen as
they really are, in all their beauty and splendour ! They will be
free. For that is what freedom is : to be fully alive.

Be grateful for the splendid conditions you enjoy here : for
the chance to stand in the presence of the rising sun, every morning, and drink to your fill, for the chance to warm yourselves
in its rays and find yourselves becoming light and free. Yes, to
my mind, Surya-yoga is superior to any other form of yoga
because it enables you to practise them all at once at sunrise, when
you can benefit from warmth and light and pure air. And even
if you find the other types of yoga too difficult, and don't do
too well with them, you can at least benefit from the sun itself
which warms and caresses you and gives you so much gold. Even
if you have not achieved anything very extraordinary, the sun
has magnetized and healed you and showered its gifts on you.
You have prayed and meditated and breathed deeply and, in addition to all that, you have been helped by the sun !

The Bonfin, 31 July 1967 (morning)

Chapter Two

Obtaining Etheric Elements from the Sun —
When we Gaze at the Sun
our Soul Begins to Resemble it

All the planets have their origin in the sun, they all came from the sun, and this is why everything that exists here on earth in the way of chemical elements or mineral or vegetable substances, exists also, but in a subtle, etheric state, in the sun. The question, then, is to know how to obtain these elements, particularly when we need them to remedy an illness or deficiency. This is important, for men must get into the habit of going to the subtle regions of creation for the remedies they need. If you look for remedies only on the physical plane, without making the effort to rise any higher, you gain nothing on the spiritual level. Quite the reverse, in fact : you will become flabby and lazy, because everything is within arm's reach. You don't even have to go out of the house, you can just pick up the phone or ask someone else to go for you. But it is so much better for you to make the effort and go and look for the elements and quintessences you need on high, on the etheric plane.

Official medicine knows nothing about these etheric elements yet, but they are not only subtler, they are also more effective than those it has discovered so far. The latest medical theory is that it is the endocrine glands which control the functions of the body, but this is not exact ; the endocrine glands are not the most vital factor. They themselves are activated and controlled by other factors which exist on the astral and mental planes. For there must be a reason why an endocrine gland secretes too much or too little of its particular chemical and causes anomalies in the whole organism ; there has to be some external cause. Initiatic Science tells us that we must look for that cause on the level of our thoughts and feelings.

I do not agree with the materialistic medical theory which claims that the health of human beings is determined by the quantity and balance of vitamins and hormones in their diet. There are other, far more potent factors on the astral and mental planes, which either stimulate or disturb our bodily functions, and it is on those levels that we must restore order and harmony, instead of focussing exclusively on the body and looking for the causes of disease only on the physical plane. The astral and mental regions in which our feelings and thoughts originate have not yet been fully explored or brought under control, but this is where those harmful elements come from to wreak their damage in other areas : the endocrine glands, the nervous system, the ganglia, and so on. Both the causes and the remedies of disease, therefore, must be sought on a much higher level and, little by little, science will discover this.

Forty or fifty years ago doctors used to say, 'If you take x units of fat, sugar, proteins, and mineral salts every day, they will be converted into y calories which will supply you with z units of energy.' And everybody thought that nothing more was needed in order to be fit and healthy, until the doctors suddenly started talking about some other, subtler, microscopic elements called vitamins. So then everyone started stuffing themselves with vitamins ! But an Initiate has no need to worry his head over calories or vitamins, for by his spiritual work he rises to higher levels where he finds other, subtler elements more necessary to his body, for they stabilize and harmonize all its functions, including the assimilation of vitamins ! And, in fact, isn't the very fact that medicine has discovered the existence of endocrine glands and the mystery of their functioning, a sure sign that there are other, still subtler regions to be explored.

So now you can see why I insist so much on the quality of your thoughts and feelings, for thoughts and feelings are forces which trigger the activity of certain subtle centres. These centres, in turn, influence the endocrine glands and the nervous system and, through them, all the other physiological systems, thus upsetting or maintaining and restoring the order and balance of the whole organism. There are a few researchers who are working in this direction, today, but nobody listens to them. But this will change before too long ; official medicine will be obliged to recognize their findings, and then research will concentrate only on these subtle elements : thoughts and feelings. New branches of study will be created, with new and appropriate laboratories and special techniques, and everybody will recognize that, from the beginning, Esoteric Science has always been based on very solid, truthful foundations. In the meantime, though, it is an object of derision.

Now, let me tell you how you can harvest the etheric particles that pour from the sun in such profusion every morning. Actually, it is extremely simple ; it is not even necessary to know what elements you need to improve your health ; that is not important. You simply have to rise mentally to the subtlest regions and, once there, maintain an expectant, receptive attitude and wait. Yes, just wait ! And your soul and spirit, which are highly skilled doctors and chemists who know the exact nature of every etheric substance, will choose those you need and leave aside all the others. Your role is simply to concentrate and wait in a spirit of submission, joy and trust, and very shortly after, when you come back, you will feel that something in you has been healed, pacified and strengthened.

It does not matter if, for the time being, you do not know the exact nature of these subtle elements. It is enough for me to tell you that they are to be found in the Prana. Prana is a living force, the outpouring of vitality from the sun that we breathe in with the air and absorb into every cell of our body. Prana is like a pure stream, cascading down from the mountain heights, its waters charged with every kind of element for the nourishment of the fishes swimming in it, as well as for the animals and men living along its banks. Prana is a torrent flowing from the sun and, by respiration and meditation, we can obtain from it all the elements we need.

Those who choose to make no more effort than it takes to open their mouths and swallow a pill, are perfectly free to do so, but they should be aware that, in the long run, this is not the best solution. Any physical relief they get in that way can never be more than temporary and superficial ; it will never give them a deep-seated, lasting cure. But, above all, it is a solution that does far more harm than good, for it prevents them from developing their will-power. Don't misunderstand me : I am not saying that you should not take medicines. I am simply saying that you must not do so without, first of all, absorbing the living, spiritual elements contained in Prana, because the effort that this demands of you, both psychically and spiritually, strengthens your will, puts you onto a higher plane and vivifies, stimulates and activates certain centres within you. And the activation of these centres prepares the terrain so that, when you do take your physical remedies, their effect is more potent and longer lasting. What I recommend, therefore, is a combination of both : the chemist's remedy and the spiritual remedy ; but I give priority to the spiritual dimension. Obviously, as I have already said, medicines contain mineral and vegetable substances which come, originally, from the sun, and if God has placed these elements in nature it is because they were intended for our use ; there is no doubt about that. But to believe that they contain everything we need and that only a physical remedy can do you any good is contrary to the teaching of Esoteric Science. If this were so, what would be the use of thought, feeling and will-power ?

So you see, my dear brothers and sisters, it is not entirely pointless to gaze at the sun with love, comprehension and gratitude. You will object, perhaps, that the particles we get from the sun are so small as to be imperceptible. That is true ; they cannot be seen, weighed or measured, but they constitute the vital quintessence that the sun sends out into the universe. Besides, the fact that homoeopathic medicine uses an extremely diluted dose because it is far more potent than one that is highly concentrated, demonstrates the truth of what I am saying. Why not take highly diluted, weightless particles, these extremely subtle kinds of vitamins brought to us by the sun's rays ?

In the future, the sun will be our principal source of energy. Already, many years ago, I told you that all the other sources of energy, such as oil and coal, would one day be exhausted and that, when that happened, men would use water and, above all, the sun, for the sun is an inexhaustible reservoir in which we can find everything, absolutely everything. Modern technology has already taken the first steps in this direction. But we, who go to the sun to find vitality and health as well as love, wisdom and peace, are several centuries ahead of the rest of mankind. In fact, some people recognize this ; they have often said to me : 'Your ideas are several centuries ahead of your time.' That is true : the whole of mankind will be thinking as we do in the future.

And now I would like to talk to you about another aspect of the sun. This morning, when I was talking about the importance of the sun as the centre of our universe, I said that when we watched the sun rising in the morning, we naturally, almost automatically, drew closer to our own centre. You wonder, perhaps, how this happens. Well, do you know what happens when you look at something : a picture, a face, a bird, a mountain or the sun ? Do you know what happens when your eyes see something ? No act is vaster, more profound or more full of meaning than the act of seeing. It may seem to be very simple and totally without mystery, but examine it more attentively and

try to decipher it, for in this simple act you will see the whole
universe unfolding before you. It is magic of a very high degree.

Nobody realizes, when they look at an object, that it always
represents either a danger or a blessing that is lying in wait for
them, depending on the nature of the object, its form and its radiations, and also on their own inner state, for their whole being
takes on the shape, dimensions and attributes of that object. You
will object, 'But human beings don't change shape !' No, of
course they don't, not outwardly, anyway. But inwardly, on the
psychic level, a human being identifies with what he looks at. This
is a biological law of nature.

You know that certain animals, the chameleon, for instance,
or the praying mantis, butterflies, frogs, snakes and even bears,
have lived in a certain natural habitat for so long that they have
come to resemble it ; they have taken on the shapes and colours
of their environment to such an extent that, at times, they blend
into it. Look at polar bears, for example : they are as white as
the snow they live in. Nature has been at work in them to make
them resemble the surrounding whiteness. And a praying mantis : you can hardly distinguish it from the little twigs or branches it perches on. And, one day, I saw an octopus which changed colour according to the colour of the sand on the sea bed :
it was extraordinary to see how it changed from pink, to green,
blue or grey in harmony with the varying colours of the sand.
Naturally, you will say, 'That is a question of camouflage ; it
is dictated by strategy, economics or politics.' True ; this is
Nature's way of preserving the different species : she has given
them these safety devices so that they can hide from predators.

But none of that changes the undeniable fact that imitation
is a natural law from which man himself is not exempt. If he lives
in dirty, dark, drab surroundings, his thoughts and feelings will
gradually become sad, morose and pessimistic. It is not his
physical body that changes, but a kind of osmosis takes place
in which his external surroundings permeate his soul and his

psyche. In another setting, made beautiful by flowers, greenery and streams, poets, painters and musicians will make their appearance, influenced by the charm and the light and colours of their surroundings.

When we gaze at the sun, therefore, even if we don't know it, our soul assumes the same shape and becomes a luminous, incandescent sphere. It is the law of imitative magic that is taking effect : we look at the sun and our whole being begins to resemble it. Simply by looking at something, we create an association, an alliance between ourselves and the object or being we are looking at, our vibrations adjust to its vibratory rate and, quite unconsciously, we imitate it. When we see someone laughing, making funny faces or gesticulating, don't we have a tendency to imitate him ? Young children, particularly, are just like monkeys, they spontaneously imitate every gesture they see you making ! And when you see someone suffering, don't you begin to feel some of their pain and distress ? It is contagious. And mediums are even more vulnerable than others : when they go into a trance they feel exactly the same pain as the sick or unhappy people who consult them. Sometimes, in fact, they suffer too much and have to be roused from their trance.

In varying degrees, therefore, according to one's sensitivity, the level of development of one's psychic faculties or one's capacity for mediumship, we all acquire the illnesses, pain or weaknesses, or the qualities and virtues of those we look at. This law is true and absolute, and it means that when we gaze at the sun the law becomes operative and we begin to resemble what we are looking at. All of you who watch the sun rising will one day resemble the sun ! Yes, but only if you know how to do so correctly ! If you want to be like the sun you must gaze at it with great love and trust. In this way you will become warmer and more luminous and better able to pour life into others ; in their midst you will be like a sun, radiating light, warmth and life. Yes, if you keep up this practice for years, consciously reaching out towards the sun, the law will manifest itself with real power, and you will become a veritable sun.

So now you can see how important it is, when you go to watch the sunrise in the morning, to do so with a clear awareness of the meaning and worth of what you are doing. Above all, remember that since the sun is the centre of the solar system, when you look at it you are drawing closer to your own centre which, although you have lost touch with it, is still there, within you. The sun, being itself a centre, uses its magic influence on your centre to awaken it and restore it to its rightful place. And when you have found your centre again, all the different currents which flow through you, today, in disorder, will begin to fall harmoniously into place round it.

So, there you have the explanation of the usefulness of attending the sunrise. And if you continue to come up here each morning, with great love and devotion, you will begin to understand that the sun is really someone wonderful ! Yes, yes, I assure you : he is very distinguished, very well-dressed, very rich and completely disinterested. He's perfect in fact ! Do you think that it is very peculiar to talk of the sun like that ? I am sure you do ! But I am ready to use whatever comparisons are necessary to get you to understand me.

Did you know that the sun even practised yoga ? Yes, he practises all the different forms of yoga. Take Karma-yoga, for instance, the yoga of disinterested service : the sun never stops doing this form of yoga. He never stops giving, and he never asks to be paid or even to be thanked : it is all absolutely free. In fact, it was the example of the sun that caused the Initiates to discover Karma-yoga, for they saw that the sun gave everything without asking for anything in return, that he made plants germinate and grow, that he nourished the whole world and that his own generosity was the source of his happiness. And now it is our turn to practise this great and excellent form of Yoga, Karma-yoga ! The sun also practises Jnana-yoga, the yoga of knowledge.

He sees and observes and knows everything : nothing is hidden from him, for his rays are like a beam of light from a projector, a very extraordinary projector whose rays travel more than ninety million miles, and he can see us here, on earth.

And he also practises Bhakti-yoga, the yoga of love and devotion, for he adores his Creator by doing his work well. He is constantly in such a state of effervescence and adoration that torrents of light and love and gratitude to the Almighty, bubble up and pour from him travelling out through space until they reach us.

As for Kriya-yoga, where could you hope to find the yoga of light more excellently practised than in the sun ? Kriya-yoga consists in being luminous and radiant and projecting light in all directions, and the sun does nothing but that ! And since he has become so proficient and acquired such a perfect mastery of the art, why not go and seek instruction from him ?

And Agni-yoga, the yoga of fire ? But the sun is fire itself ! It is he who distributes fire to all those who want to light their hearts, their candles from his flame. He is the perfect incarnation of Agni-yoga.

The case of Shabda-yoga is even better, for the sun is the Word ! Nobody has understood this yet, but the fact is that the sun sings. Yes, the sun sings and talks and explains things to us even though we cannot hear him yet. It is only recently that scientists have begun to try and decipher the sound waves emitted by the sun ; they have already heard certain sounds, but they still have not understood them. There is music coming from the sun, the most beautiful music that exists ; the sun sings, speaks and creates, and one day astronomers will record the music coming from the sun and the planets.

You will ask, 'What about Hatha-yoga ? Doesn't he practise Hatha-yoga ?' Well, it seems to me that this is one kind of yoga he neglects. He leaves it to human beings : if they want to bend and twist and fold themselves in two, that is their business ! Although, of course, we do say that he gets up and goes down.

He does not do it very rapidly, of course, but still, you could say that that is a form of Hatha-yoga !

That is what I wanted to tell you today, my dear brothers and sisters : it was not long but it is very important. When you gaze at the sun your soul begins to resemble it and becomes the same shape. Soon I intend to explain how you should look at it, and also, exactly what it is. For it is a whole, vast world that contains living beings, dwellings, palaces, trees, cities and oceans — a world with a culture that is beyond anything you can imagine ! It is the loveliest of lands, the Land of the Living spoken of in the Bible, which says, 'I will walk before the Almighty in the Land of the Living.' 'The Living' are the immortal, eternal beings who dwell permanently in light. The sun is their home and it is they who send us light. The sun is the most marvellous of worlds, peopled with angels, archangels and divinities who go to and fro to do their work in each one of the planets and help the creatures who inhabit them before returning once more to the sun. It is all very highly organized and, in fact, some of these extremely beautiful, intelligent and powerful beings often come to visit us on earth.

You think that the universe is an absurd piece of machinery, without soul or intelligence, but you are very, very wrong ! Everything in the universe is intelligent, everything is alive, meaningful and beautiful. How do I know ? Well, I don't have the gifts of a clairvoyant or a fortune-teller, so I cannot say what you have in your pockets, how many illegitimate children you have or how much money you owe. It's no good expecting me to tell you that because I cannot 'see' these things and they do not interest me. But, what I can see is a universe inhabited by countless beings of great beauty, intelligence and power. They come and go throughout creation, bringing messages or help, and wherever they are, be it in the stones, plants or animals of the earth, in the waters or in the stars, they are constantly at work.

Little by little, you will begin to have an idea of what Surya-yoga, the yoga of the sun, is. If you really practise it with all your heart you cannot help but benefit from it, for the sun is the most substantial and most indispensable nourishment for our times. In the future, everyone will go to the sun for strength, warmth, love and courage. Other sources of energy will be abandoned because they are already beginning to run out, and men will turn to the one inexhaustible source. Solar energy will light our cities and heat our houses, and our means of locomotion will be powered by the sun. We shall even be nourished by sunlight, foods will be made from it.

Have a happy afternoon, my dear brothers and sisters, and try to think about the sun, rather than about all those things that drag you out towards the periphery where you will always be bitten and trampled on. Turn your steps towards the sun, towards unity, simplicity and light !

The Bonfin, 31 July 1967 (afternoon)

Chapter Three

Our Higher Self Dwells in the Sun

It is vital that you realize that we are on this earth in order to evolve and, consequently, that there is nothing more important than to work at our own improvement and perfection : our success, our future and our happiness are all based on this. It is no good hoping to make progress or get ahead in any other way.

And today, since we have been dealing with the question of the sun, I want to add a few words to what I have already told you. I have often told you that you should prepare yourselves in advance for the sunrise. You must be careful not to eat too much or go to bed too late the evening before, and you must avoid doing anything that might trouble or torment you the next morning. In other words, try to do whatever has to be done in such a way as to feel free, with a mind that is crystal clear and a heart at peace, and no loose ends to settle, regret or repair. This is important.

Then, in the morning, rested and in peace, you can start your meditation, slowly and gently, without concentrating intently on the sun too abruptly. Start by glancing inwards to see if all your inhabitants are at peace, and if they are making a noise or being rowdy and rebellious, try to calm them down and restore order and balance, for you cannot project yourself out towards the sun

until peace and harmony reign within you. Once you are in a state
of inner peace, then you can project your thoughts out to the
sun and imagine it as a glorious world inhabited by the most
perfect, absolutely luminous creatures who live in sublime intelligence and absolute love and purity ; think that up there, in
the sun, an order, a culture, a civilization exists that is perfect
beyond description.

The day before yesterday I told you that there were mountains and palaces and whole towns in the sun, and you were dumbfounded and horrified : 'That's ridiculous ! How could anything
living exist in such heat ?' But what do you know about all the
different ways in which life can manifest itself and the conditions
it needs in order to develop ? Life exists everywhere throughout
the whole universe ; why should it not also be in the sun ? Obviously it is impossible for human beings to imagine any form
of life in the conditions that prevail in the sun, so nobody will
believe me yet. They will just have to find out for themselves.
Yes, you must prepare yourselves to go and find out, for everyone
is going to have to do it for himself. You must no longer believe
what other people say or listen to all their fairy-tales, you must
equip yourself for your own excursion to the sun ! 'How can I
do that ?' you will ask ; 'There are no aircraft or even spacecraft
that can take me to the sun.' That is true, but the Lord has given
us all the machines and instruments we need : haven't we got formidable powers of thought and imagination ? These are the
vehicles we can use to travel directly to the sun : thought and imagination.

And what would be your reaction if I told you that, without
realizing it, you were already in the sun ? You cannot feel it, but
there is a tiny part of yourself, a very, very subtle element, which
already dwells permanently in the sun. Science has not really
studied man yet ; it does not know the tremendous wealth nor
the breadth and depth of a human being. As you already know,
the visible part, the physical body, is not the sum total of man.
He has other bodies which are made of increasingly subtle mat-

ter. And I have told you the same thing about the earth : the earth is not only that part of it that we can see. Round the globe is an atmosphere many miles deep, and science divides this atmosphere into several different layers, each with its own name. But what science does not know is that within each of these layers there lives an infinite number of elements and entities, and that beyond the atmosphere lies the earth's etheric body which stretches all the way to the sun : in fact, it actually touches the sun.

The etheric body of the earth, therefore, mingles and melts into the etheric body of the sun, for the sun, too, has an etheric body which reaches far beyond its own sphere, as far as the earth and beyond, all the way to the other planets. This is why sun and earth touch and are already united. And, as man is built in the image of the universe, he too possesses this subtle dimension of emanations from which he projects rays which reach as far as the sun. In this way we can say that man, in his higher, sublime, divine dimension, actually lives in the sun already. He is not aware of it, of course, because he only uses his brain, and the brain is built to work within the limits of the physical world.

I know that what I am saying seems quite unbelievable to you, because the conceptions to which your minds are accustomed are so narrow and down-to-earth that they prevent you from understanding and accepting anything like this. And yet, these are truths which you must know and study. When someone begins to study in the Divine School of the Universal White Brotherhood, he gradually moves out of the limited field of a purely sensorial and physical consciousness, to the higher regions of superconsciousness. And this immense region of superconsciousness has thousands of different levels through which he must travel until he feels that he really is an inhabitant of the sun, that he already dwells in the sun.

That entity, that subtle being that is part of ourselves and that dwells in the sun, is our higher Self. It is evident that our higher Self does not live in our physical body, otherwise it would constantly make itself felt with its prodigies. No, it comes to visit us from time to time, manifesting itself to us through a brief contact with our brain. But our brain is incapable of sustaining the intensity of its vibrations ; it cannot get onto the same wavelength as the higher Self, so the higher Self goes away again. But our higher Self is working to prepare the brain, and when it is ready and fit to be its dwelling place, it will abide within us permanently.

Our higher Self is none other than God Himself ; a part of God. This is why we can truthfully say that in the higher regions of our being we *are* God, for nothing exists apart from God. God manifests Himself through creation and creatures, and this means that we are a tiny part of Him ; we have no existence apart from God. The only real illusion is to believe that we are separate entities. When the sages of India speak of *maya*, illusion, they are not referring to the material world. The material world is not an illusion, it is our lower self that is the illusion, because it gives us the impression that we exist as separate entities, independently of the Deity. The world is a reality ; matter, too, is a reality, and even lies and Hell itself are reality. The only illusion, I repeat, comes from our lower self which constantly urges us to see ourselves as separate beings. As long as we remain on too low a level, on the level of our lower self, we shall continue to live in error and illusion, unable to perceive the one, universal life, the Cosmic Being that fills the universe ; our lower being prevents us from perceiving its presence or understanding it. And this is, precisely, what we are trying to do here, at sunrise in the morning : our work with the sun, our meditations and prayers, are all aimed at restoring communications, at building a bridge between our lower self down here, and our higher Self in the sun. When the bridge is built and communications restored, we shall once again be united with that higher Self that dwells with God in constant happiness and bliss and boundless freedom. Yes, part of ourselves already dwells in God, in a state of indescribable bliss.

This is something that you really must understand. I know very well that you have been brought up with conceptions that are completely foreign to these truths, and that it is very difficult for you to accept them. But if you continue to live exclusively in the awareness of your separateness, in the conviction that you are not a part of collective, universal life, then you will continue to live in illusion, error and untruth. You will continue to struggle, strive and suffer without any hope of attaining peace, because peace is absolutely impossible for one who is in this state of separateness. Whereas if you abandon that philosophy or, at least, make an effort in that direction and try to free yourself from it, you will begin to feel universal life flowing within you, too, and you will begin to dwell consciously in eternity and infinity. This experience is so extraordinary that, to begin with, one does not understand what is happening ; but the only thing that is happening is that one has, at last, come back to reality, to divine life.

Thousands of people have already achieved this state of consciousness, so why shouldn't you ? It is very simple and very easy, but it cannot be done if you cling to this notion of separateness, if you continue to think of yourselves as entirely extraneous and foreign to others, if you think that others are not you, and that you can cheat or injure or harm them with impunity. When you injure others you are unwittingly injuring yourself too, for you are a part of them. But this is something that you cannot yet understand. One day, when you begin to come closer to your higher Self who lives not only in the sun but also in the other planets, in the earth, trees, oceans and mountains and in every other being, you will feel that the suffering you inflict on others is your own suffering ; when you hurt them it is you, yourself, who feel the hurt ; in inflicting pain on others you are inflicting it on yourself. Yes, I know that I am talking to you about things that are not often mentioned, but they are absolutely true and they have been known to Initiates for thousands of years. This great light has come down to me from the furthest reaches of time ; I am simply handing it on to you.

Know, then, that the sun can be the most enormous help in bridging the gulf that separates us from our higher Self. Without

this help, men might well spend thousands of years more sunk
in the philosophy of separateness and never find the fulfilment
they seek. The time has come to adopt the philosophy of universal unity, the point of view which enables us to feel our oneness
with the Creator and with all the entities of light, angels, archangels and divinities. With this philosophy to point out the
'shortcuts', man can find his way back to the Source far more
rapidly and effectively.

Now, let me explain a method which can help you : when you
go up to the Rock in the morning for the sunrise, imagine that
you are up there, in the sun, from where you can see that creature
down here : that creature that is you yourself ! You project
yourself out of your body and amuse yourself, watching and smiling at yourself sitting down here : 'Oh, look at that funny creature
down there ; to think that it's me ! How small and puny he looks !
But I'm going to help him ; I will ! I'll give him all the help he
needs !' If you do this very simple exercise every day, you will
already be starting to rebuild the bridge. Nobody can tell you how
long it will take to complete the job, for you are not building
with iron, steel or concrete, but with another, far subtler matter,
matter from the mental plane. Every one of you has been invited
to do this work, but I wonder how many of you are ready to go
this far.

And once you have reached the sun, you can imagine that you
go and pay a visit to the Archangel who rules the sun : you see
yourself talking to him, he puts his arms round you and tells you
many of his secrets, and then he gives you some of his light so
that you can send rays of it down to that little creature sitting
on the Rock ; that creature who thinks he is you, but who is not
really you ! Little by little, you will begin to feel your consciousness expanding, heavenly peace floods into you, and revelation after revelation unfolds before your mind. In this way you
will be cultivating new faculties of comprehension, and gradually, even though you continue to be just like everybody else outwardly, inwardly you will no longer be the same, you will become

someone quite exceptional, thanks to the new possibilities that you have developed.

Obviously, one cannot concentrate on the same subject every day, so I will give you other methods, and you can use them turn and turn about. Each day you can think of the sun, but in a different way ; there is such a variety of choices, in fact, that you will never be bored. One cannot do exactly the same exercise every day ; it seems that the mind is built on exactly the same pattern as the stomach : it needs a varied diet. If we try to give it the same food every day it ends by refusing to eat, digs in its toes and stops functioning altogether. What should you do when your mind refuses to concentrate on the subject you were working on the day before ? You must look for another subject. Anything will do as long as it is a 'vegetarian dish' (symbolically speaking), that is to say, something spiritual. Yes, look through the menu of subjects and find something that tempts your appetite : 'Pears ? No. Eggs ? No. How about a lemon ? Ah, yes. I think I'd like a lemon.' And there you are. And the following day : 'What will it be ? A sweet pepper ? Yes, that just fits the bill'. And so on, each day ; there is an endless variety of subjects to choose from. In the spiritual life, you see, you need experience, you need to know the psychological factors involved, otherwise you will never make any progress. And that is what I am here for : to show you different means and methods that will make your work easier, but always, of course, with the same goal in mind. Vary your methods as much as you like, as long as you always go in the same direction, that is, towards the centre, towards the Creator, towards light, freedom and glory.

The facts I have revealed to you about your higher Self should give you a great deal of hope and courage. You have no reason to feel lost, helpless and insignificant any more. The higher Self of every one of you without exception dwells in the sun. The only difference is that some of you will link up with it sooner than others, for this depends on many different factors, amongst which is the state of your physical health. Those of you who have already

worked for a long time to prepare your body, brain and lungs
for the encounter with these truths, will reach self-fulfilment much
sooner than others. But what I have been telling you should banish
all shadow of discouragement or bitterness, and fill you with absolutely invincible hope for your future. Yes, one day, every single
one of you will reach harbour.

Your wishes will, one day, be fulfilled. I cannot tell you when,
but it will happen, for it is written in the laws of living Nature
that man shall obtain all that he fervently and perseveringly wishes
for. So continue to wish for all that is best. He who desires beauty,
for instance, will one day be so beautiful and expressive that,
wherever he goes, people will gaze on him in wonder and exclaim,
'Lord God, today I have seen and contemplated You. I have felt
Your presence. How beautiful You are, Lord !' He who desires
power, the power that renews, heals, soothes and ameliorates men,
the power that brings harmony in its wake, will one day obtain
it, and when they see him, men will murmur, 'Lord God, I felt
Your strength brush by me today. I feel so happy ! I want to
follow You, to be with You.' And he who wants knowledge and
intelligence will one day project light in all directions ; his revelations will lead men and women to their Creator. He who wishes
for love will incarnate the warmth and perfume of divine love ;
wherever he goes, kindness, warmth and affection will pour from
him into the hearts and souls of others. He who loves purity will
become a fountain of crystal-clear water, washing away all stains
and impurities. Wouldn't it be wonderful to become like a river,
a waterfall, a lake ?

So choose the virtue which attracts you most strongly and work
on it, concentrate on it. Later, one by one, you will work on all
the other virtues, for we have to become perfect as our Heavenly
Father is perfect ; we have to become beings of purity, light, intelligence, love, kindness, power and beauty.

It is really worthwhile, isn't it, coming up here at sunrise in
order to reach up with all your strength and energy towards such
a lofty ideal ? Look at the ideals other people try to tempt you

with : money, pleasure, revolution... Whereas here you are on the road towards glory, total fulfilment and true wealth. If you abandon the treasures to be found here in order to follow all kinds of rubbishy philosophies it will not say much for your discernment !

Eat and drink your fill of this heavenly nourishment ! And when you come up to the Rock at sunrise, say 'thank you' ; never stop saying 'thank you' for the golden opportunities that are put before you, for such marvellous conditions, for all this peace, purity and fresh air. A tremendous work of cleansing and purification is taking place within you, and it is this purification that attracts all the other divine qualities.

I will also give you an exercise with the four elements, by which you can learn to work with fire, air, water and earth.* You would be truly amazed if you knew all the work done by the earth and, in particular, by the Rock we are sitting on at this moment ! I have not talked to you about that yet, but this Rock is a living, intelligent creature who is here for our service. It absorbs a great many of our impurities, swallowing them up and sending them down towards the special factories in the centre of the earth where workers transform them into subtle, crystalline matter. Perhaps you did not know that ? I love this Rock dearly ; so often it has relieved us of our fatigue and impurities. But you have to know how to talk to it ; it will not necessarily help everyone ; you have to be very attentive and show it great respect.

Believe me, there is so much work to be done ! But those who are entirely absorbed in their humdrum, worldly concerns cannot devote themselves to this work ; in fact they have no inkling that it even exists. You have to be free in order to devote yourself to this work. When I talk to you about exercises like this, I am not inventing anything new : I have being doing them myself for years. Normally I do not talk about the exercises I do ; I wait for the Invisible World to tell me when to talk about them. You have no idea of all the work I have been doing for years and years !

* See *Complete Works,* vol. 7, Part Three.

Be grateful to Heaven ; ask yourselves what you have done to earn the privilege of receiving such revelations. People forget to thank the Lord for all the good things they receive ; when disaster strikes they are ready enough to complain and say, 'What have I ever done to deserve such bad luck ?' Actually, there is no need to ask ; the answer is very clear : they have been too stupid, or too wicked or too weak. No other explanation is necessary !

Am I torturing you by keeping you up here in full sunlight ? It is just as well that there is a nice, cool breeze from time to time. But don't worry, we'll go down, now, and go on with this another time. For the moment, I want you to remember just one thing : when you come up here in the morning, forget about everything else. Tell yourself that the sun is the only thing that matters ; concentrate on the sun, look for yourself in him and start building that bridge !

The Bonfin, 1 August 1967

Chapter Four

The Creator Sows Seeds in us and the Sun Makes Them Grow — The Sun Reflects the Blessed Trinity

To begin with I want to come back to the idea we were talking about yesterday : the need to vary the subject of one's meditation in order to avoid mental staleness or indigestion. As with food, you must vary your diet. This means that I must give you many different methods by constantly explaining other aspects of the sun so that, when you meditate, whether up on the Rock or anywhere else, you will always be able to find something to suit you for that day.

If you want to get the most out of the methods I give you, however, I advise you to take notes and make yourself a list that you can consult, like a cook who has her list of possible menus. Each day you can look at your list, 'Now, let's see, that doesn't tempt me ; how about this ? Yes, that's exactly what I need, to-day.' And then you will enjoy yourself because your meditation will be a success. And as there is no guarantee that the same exercise will be what you need the next day, you can change your menu and choose a new subject of meditation. In this way, little by little, you will run through the whole cycle of marvels, and will evolve much more rapidly than if you always clung to the same method.

Besides, if you persist in trying to use the same method every day you will give yourself a headache ! Sometimes you try to con-

centrate on a well-worn topic and you don't realize that your brain
wants nothing more to do with it for the moment. It needs a
change ; you must find another subject. Some would perhaps
think, 'Ah, I need a change ? Well, as I've been chaste and sober
for so long, I'll give myself a change by eating and drinking or
finding someone to seduce !' and he goes on a spree ! No, as I
said yesterday, you have to stick to a 'vegetarian' diet ; you must
not go any lower than the diaphragm and all that it symbolizes.
There is an infinite variety of paths to choose from, but you must
not go below the 'horizon', the dividing line of the diaphragm.
Often, when people feel the need of a change, they don't know
how to get it without running into danger : instead of exploring
the vast space above the horizon, (surely a range of 180 degrees
gives you plenty of scope ?), they plunge down into the lower
regions, setting off reactions within themselves which are very
detrimental both to their peace of mind and to their evolution.
In this Teaching one learns what direction to take when one needs
a change.

What else can I tell you about the sun ? I have already spoken
of it as the centre of our solar system and explained how important this centre is in our lives and how it contains all the elements
we need in an etheric state. I have also revealed the fact that our
higher Self dwells in the sun. And today, if you have no objec-
tion, I have a few things to say about agriculture.

Let's look at how a farmer works : he ploughs the soil, sows
the seed and then leaves it alone, waiting for the warm weather.
With the coming of spring, the sun warms the ground, and the
seeds, lying buried in silence beneath the surface, feel the caress
of its warmth calling to them to rouse themselves and begin work.
'That's all very pretty', you will say ; 'But germination and growth
are purely automatic, unconscious mechanisms in plants...' Of
course, I know that ; but let me poetize a little if I want to !
Besides, there is a secret life slumbering in every seed, and it does
begin to stir when the sun warms it. And, as the seeds thrust their

shoots up through the ground and begin to grow, men are happy because they know that there will be a rich harvest and plenty to eat.

You are disappointed because you think that this is nothing new : you have known it all for ages. I have no doubt that you do know it, but I am saying it all the same, because I want to show you that although you know it, you have never really understood it. Knowledge and understanding are quite different things. You all know so many things, but what good has all that knowledge done you ? None at all ! If you had understood, you would have realized that you, too, contain seeds that must be made to grow.

The Creator has sown seeds in the soul, spirit, heart, mind and physical body of every human being : the seeds of gifts and virtues, of magic powers and of all Heaven's splendours, and only the light and warmth of the sun is capable of awakening these seeds and making them grow. The day man understands this and decides to draw nearer to the spiritual sun, all the seeds lying dormant in him will begin to sprout and grow and produce flowers and fruit.

I hope that these few words will give you an even greater desire to go and look at the sun. Expose yourself to its rays and let it do its work, and you will feel a mass of tiny buds and seedlings beginning to grow within you. Of course, you are going to have to water them, otherwise they will wither away. The sun can contribute light and warmth but it cannot water your plants : that is your job, for the water they need is in you. The sun does part of the work and we have to do the rest ; the sun warms our plants, but it is up to us to water them with our love, faith, trust and enthusiasm. The sun expects us to lend a helping hand ! If you leave it all to the sun, letting it warm you, and doing nothing to help, the results will not be up to much : the shoots that spring up thanks to its warmth will die from lack of moisture.

But how do you actually do this ? When you are sitting up here in the light of the sun, you must respond actively to its action ; that is, you must meditate, pray and contemplate and be grateful to the Lord, or pronounce a few words. In this way you will be watering your seeds with all the love of your heart, and encouraging their growth. You must learn to cultivate your own plot of land. Nothing will grow without sunlight ; that is why you have to put yourself consciously in the presence of the sun and expose yourself to its rays, and let it awaken the seeds and germs which God has sown in your soul. This is all quite clear and simple : the sun can awaken all your dormant qualities and virtues.

You were scandalized when I said that there were towns, palaces, mountains and rivers in the sun, because you had never heard anything of the kind before. Besides, science tells us that the sun is an incandescent ball of fire, a world in a state of fusion in which life is impossible ; so what I told you is totally unscientific. But Hermes Trismegistus says 'That which is below is like to that which is above.' In other words, the things that we see in this world (rivers, mountains, lakes, rocks, trees and animals, etc.) could not exist if the models on which they were based did not already exist on a higher plane. Hermes Trismegistus was saying that there was a world above which was the model for our world, and that in that higher world there were mountains, rivers, animals and men, made of another matter and with other forms.

Hermes Trismegistus did not say that that which was below was *identical* to that which was above, but that it was *like* it. The things we see here, on earth, are no more than a reflection, a repetition, an imitation of another world, just as the shadow of a tree resembles the tree, but is not the tree itself ; or as a man's reflection in a mirror resembles him, but is not him. The Initiates have always spoken of the world as a shadow, an illusion, the reflected image of a higher, divine world ; as a reflection which points the way to that higher reality which, indeed, it resembles but which is infinitely more glorious.

The sun is the world 'above' and the earth is the world 'below'. The sun represents Heaven (or rather, the heavens) and it is teeming with life : its inhabitants have houses just as we do, and they eat and drink, are born, love and make love, but divinely. And there are towns, too, in the sun : towns, mountains, rivers and a tremendous variety of plants, but the matter of which all these things are made is quite different from that which exists on earth.

If none of this existed, both Hermes Trismegistus and Jesus would have been speaking nonsense. When Jesus said, 'Thy will be done on earth as it is in Heaven', he was praying that that which was on high : harmony, order, beauty, light, perfection, love, strength, power and eternal life, be brought down to earth so that the inhabitants of earth might live in the same harmony, abundance and joy as those of Heaven. If Jesus had not been familiar with the perfect structure of the world above, he would never have formulated this prayer.

And since the sun symbolizes and is the image, the reflection and reproduction in miniature of Heaven, what else can we learn by looking at it ? We see its light, we feel its heat and we receive the life emanating from it. The sun is vibrantly, exuberantly alive ; it warms all creatures, and lights up the whole world. This trinity of light, heat and life, is spoken of in the sacred scriptures of all religions. It is, in fact, the Blessed Trinity revered by Christians, but Christians see the Trinity as a cold, abstract notion, very remote from everyday life, and their theologians refuse to speak of it in simple terms for fear of defiling it. Whereas we feel free to rejoice in the presence of this Blessed Trinity ; we frequent it, greet it and communicate with it every day.

The Blessed Trinity is an essential element of Christianity and yet it has been hidden away out of sight ; it is mentioned in books but it is not seen as a reality that Christians can relate to and communicate with in their daily lives. They are told that it is a 'mystery', which means that no one has the right to discuss it ! Try telling Christians that the Blessed Trinity is accessible and even tangible and they will reply that you are blaspheming. The average Christian envisages the Deity as being necessarily hidden and remote ; God cannot be seen or contemplated, He is utterly unapproachable. Is it any wonder that men have so completely lost touch with God, that they no longer feel His presence, that He no longer dwells in them and that, as a result, they indulge in every form of insane and immoral conduct ?

In the new morality, the new philosophy, which is coming ever nearer and which will soon sweep through the whole world, spiritual realities will become so close and accessible, so tangible, that men will understand and experience them in their daily lives and become one with them ; every day, men will absorb such extraordinarily luminous nourishment that they will be obliged to transform themselves. For it is only by absorbing a totally different kind of nourishment on every level that man can really be transformed.

The Trinity exists, under different names, in all religions : it can be found in Egypt and India, in the Cabbalah and in Tibet ; the only exception is the religion of the Persians who were dualists. But how can we understand the Trinity ? In the beginning there is always one being, and this original being engenders a second who, in turn, engenders a third. In Christianity they are called Father, Son and Holy Spirit. I have mentioned the different names they go by in other religions before, in other lectures, but today let's just speak of the Father, the Son and the Holy Spirit. The Father is the life that flows through the universe, the Source of all creation. The Son can be said to be light, for Christ said, 'I am the light of the world' ; but this is no reason why we should not also see Him as the manifestation of love. And the Holy Spirit who descended in the form of tongues of fire, represents heat or love ; but here, again, this does not prevent us from seeing Him as the light which illuminates the minds of men and enables them to prophesy, to speak in tongues and to know and understand the mysteries. Actually, it does not matter whether we see the Holy Spirit as love and the Son as wisdom or vice versa for, in reality, they are one ; they have the same powers and each can transform Himself into the other.

The essential thing to understand is that these three principles, Father, Son and Holy Spirit, can be found in the life, light and heat of the sun. Perhaps you will ask, 'But have we got the right to see a correspondence between these infinitely exalted Entities and light, heat and life ?' Yes, indeed we have ! In fact the enormous practical advantage of doing so is that this correspondence enables us to contemplate and communicate with the Blessed Trinity every morning, and to create bonds through which we can receive Its blessings. It is a promise of resurrection and life.

Why are Christians so reluctant to understand that the greatest truths are there, for all to see, in nature ? Everybody can understand this except Christians, who will go on saying, 'Oh, the sun isn't important ; even if it didn't exist we would only have to go to Mass to be saved !' Perhaps they have never realized that if the sun did not exist there would be nobody to say Mass and that they themselves would be dead, frozen and turned to stone ages ago ! No group of people is quite so unaware of the living bond that binds man to nature as Christians.

I can hear you protesting, 'But, what have you got against Christians ?' No, no, I have nothing against them. I am a Christian, too. If I shake them up from time to time, it is simply because I want to get them to open their eyes and use their intelligence a little more and understand that God manifests Himself everywhere, in everything that exists. Everything is a manifestation of the Divine : flowers, birds, trees, mountains, lakes and stars, and even human beings. In different forms and different degrees it is always God Who is manifesting Himself. Wherever there is a living creature there is God, for there is no life which is not in God.

God alone disseminates life throughout the universe. He alone is the Source of life, He alone can create or distribute it. Man can do no more than serve as a conductor through which it flows ; life itself comes from a much higher source. It would be utterly false for a Father to tell his child that it was he who gave him life and that he, therefore, had the right of life and death over him. Life is created by God ; man is simply a channel through which it is passed on to his children. If man were capable of creating life would he not be able to add a few years to his own life when death approached ? If he is not even capable of prolonging his own life, is that not proof enough that it was not he who created it ? Each man has been allotted a fixed span of years and he cannot lengthen this span by even one hour. Life flows through man, but God is the Source from whence it flows.

Wherever life appears it is a manifestation of the presence of God. And as all life on earth comes from the sun, surely it is obvious that God manifests Himself more perfectly through the sun than through any other creature. Is there any being other than the sun who is capable of nourishing the whole of mankind and giving life and growth to wheat and to the vine ? Others write a few books or make a few speeches, but when all is said and done they all disappear without a trace, whereas the sun is always there to give life, light and warmth to the entire world.

When the world above created the world below, it left its seal and signature on all things, so that man would be able to find his way back to it. Cosmic Intelligence, the Trinity, has no desire to remain totally hidden and inaccessible ; It manifests Itself in the sun so that men may have the possibility of finding It. In reality, the Blessed Trinity is not wholly present in the light, heat and life of the sun ; It is far greater than the sun. But through that light, heat and life which pours into our world every day, we can reach out and touch the Trinity : we can talk and communicate with It, love It and draw It into ourselves. And since each one of us is created in the image of God, each one of us is also a trinity. Through our mind, heart and will we are a trinity which thinks, feels and acts. Of course, at the moment, this little trinity is cold, lacklustre and numb, but progressively, as it spends more time with the sun, it will become warmer, brighter and more alive. So, once again, we can see the point of being present at sunrise :

gradually, the little trinity that each of us represents becomes as bright, warm and life-giving as the sun ; gradually it draws nearer and nearer to the Supreme Trinity of Father, Son and Holy Spirit.

Christ said, 'You shall be perfect, just as your Father in heaven is perfect.' But if we have never seen the Father, where can we find an example of His perfection ? Here, in the sun, we have the model we need. God is very far above us, very far away, but in His mercy He has given us the means of finding Him ; He has left tracks, a vital lead, and if we follow it, it will take us all the way through the sun to the Father. The sun points the way.

Every day this reflection, this sublime, perfect image of the Holy Trinity, is before our eyes, and if we learn how to work with it and model ourselves on it, our own little trinity can also become holy. It is all very well to keep repeating Christ's words, 'Be perfect, just as your Father in heaven is perfect', but never having seen the Father, how can we have any idea of how He manifests Himself, of His vibrations and colours or of His power ; it all remains very theoretical. The sun gives us at least a tiny idea of the Heavenly Father ; it explains, for instance, that Father, Son and Holy Spirit are inseparably one. If we distinguish them one from the other it is only in order to understand them better ; in fact they are one. The three are one. According to the Cabbalah, Three is One and One is Three. In man, too, the three are always united ; mind, heart and will are never separated, they are welded together, they work and advance together as one. The mind makes plans, the heart offers its encouragement and support, and the will races to put the plans into effect. You can see that they run hand in hand ! Sometimes, of course, the order of things is reversed, and a person gets into hot water because their will has rushed ahead, leaving the intellect behind. It can shout itself hoarse, telling the will to wait for it, to warn it that it is going the wrong way ; the will goes on its merry way, replying, 'Shut up, you don't know anything about it !' Oh, yes : the three of them have some terrific arguments. But then, this is not yet a holy trinity !

If we want our trinity to be holy, we must take the sun as our model and try to become as bright, warm and life-giving as the sun. Of course, this is an ideal which we shall never attain, but to work at it is to work towards Initiation. Instead of staying forever on the same spot, marking time to the rhythm of old, outworn notions, it is far better to watch the sun rising every morning and cultivate the ideal of becoming like it. As I have already told you, there is a law of imitation according to which we all end by resembling our environment. If a man looks long and often at the sun, if he understands and loves it and lets its rays sink deep into his being, he will gradually come to resemble it. And, in fact, if he learns how to condense and concentrate the rays of the sun within himself and store them up in his solar plexus and the sympathetic nervous system, he will be able to draw on these reserves all day long and become tireless. There is a great deal to be learned in this area and a long apprenticeship is required, but those who seriously give their minds to it receive great blessings every day.

I think you are beginning to see now, my dear brothers and sisters, just how much the sun can teach us. One day, thanks to all the work you have done by your meditations and contemplations of the sun, you will have the arms you need to attack and drive out the enemies within you, and then the Blessed Trinity will come and dwell in you.

The Bonfin, 2 August 1967

Chapter Five

Every Creature Has a Home —
The Seven Beads of the Rosary

What glorious sunshine today ! It's difficult to drag oneself
away, isn't it ! We are really very blessed.

When I think of the speed with which the sun's rays travel
through space to come to us — they take only eight minutes to
get here — I ask myself, 'Why are they in such a hurry ? What
makes them go so fast ?' And then I find that it is because they
love us. They are filled to overflowing with such extraordinary
love that they are in a hurry to bring us their gifts. If you don't
believe me, go and ask them up there, and find out for yourselves !
I know that I am right : that it is love that impels the sun's rays
to reach us so quickly.

But is there not some other element behind their love ? Yes,
there is : there is the fact that they know ; they have studied the
question and they know and understand that there is nothing
higher or better than love. Wisdom consists in understanding that
love is more important than anything else. If all the studying done
by men has not yet taught them that, it is because their intelligence
is not sufficiently developed. Intelligence that fails to grasp the
fact that love must be given priority, that everything must be for
love, with love and because of love, is not really intelligence at
all. It is high time that men understood that love is at the heart
of everything, and that if they make it the one motive power

behind every aspect of their lives, the intense heat of their love will be transformed into dazzling light and their intelligence will be illuminated. Illumination can only come from love. If the fire of love is lacking, you can study as much as you like, but there will never be enough heat for you to become truly enlightened or intelligent.

Perhaps you will say, 'That can't be altogether true, because I love So-and-so very, very much, but I've never managed to create any light !' Very well ; if you say so. But let's just look at that love of yours : if it is a personal, selfish kind of love, if what you really want is to eat and drink and regale yourself at that person's expense, if it robs your beloved of his or her inner light and wealth and leaves them to disintegrate then, however ardent or impassioned it may be, you will never obtain light from it. Whereas the sun's rays have such an ardent desire to vivify the whole universe, that they detach themselves from the sun, and the disinterestedness of their love transforms them into light. At one time they were simmering in the furnace of the sun, but then they thought, 'We really ought to do something ourselves ; let's go out and help human beings !' and, thanks to this generous thought, they instantly became luminous. Of course, I know that my way of explaining things is a bit unusual ; you never read anything like that in books. But it is all true, nevertheless !

Besides, you have only got to observe your own face ; when you fall a prey to a black mood and feel sad, jealous or vindictive, look at your reflection in a mirror and you will see how sombre and tense you look, and how all the sparkle has gone out of your eyes. It is as though you were in the shadow of a dark cloud. But as soon as you open your heart to a generous impulse or a divine inspiration, your face glows from within and light flows from you. Even very ugly, distorted features can be illuminated in this way. And that is how I came to the conclusion that it was their love that made the sun's rays so bright. How did I understand this ? Well, you all know how primitive people made fire : they rubbed two pieces of wood together. The friction produced heat, the heat produced fire and the fire produced light. So, to begin with there is movement, movement produces heat and heat produces light. If the sun's rays are luminous it is because they have been heated by the sun and, in order to be heated they moved, they moved into the heart of the sun, into the 'furnace'.

For the sun is a furnace (this is an image) and, at the same time, as I was telling you yesterday, it is a marvellous world in which there are cities, houses, palaces, mountains, etc. Of course, I know you are going to find this very difficult to accept, because official science has not yet recognized it, and you are waiting for science to pronounce judgement. But I prefer not to wait ; I don't have time to wait. Science advances too slowly. Do you want me to prove to you that there are houses in the sun ? On earth, all human beings live in houses or shelters of some kind. Everybody feels the need to have some kind of dwelling place, even if it is only a cave. You know this already, but do you know why ? Do you know where the idea comes from ? It is simply that human beings feel impelled to imitate and reproduce what they learned before they reincarnated : for the nine months of gestation they worked with their mother's spirit to build their future home, that is to say, their physical body, which would be a palace or a hovel, depending on their spiritual wealth. Before a human soul reincarnates, it learns that, in order to survive on earth without being battered by poor conditions, strong currents and bad weather, it is going to have to build itself a little house : its physical body. And that is not all : it needs three other houses, as well : one on the etheric plane, one on the astral plane and one on the mental plane (actually, when I say three, this is a simplification. There are really many more).

Every creature, therefore, is obliged to have its envelope or house. Even very exalted spirits have a 'house' which they carry about with them, just as we take our physical body with us ; and it is thanks to their house that they can manifest themselves. Of course, their house is made of extremely subtle matter, but without it they would disappear into the Cosmic Ocean, into Primordial

Light ; they would have no individual existence. A 'pure spirit'
is simply a manner of speaking ; a pure spirit cannot exist on the
level of manifestation or polarization : it melts back into the
Cosmic Ocean. Manifestation requires a body, a vehicle or, if
you prefer, a 'wife'. Does this way of putting it surprise you ?
Don't be surprised : our physical body is our wife ; it is she that
enables us to communicate and exchange with the outside world
and to work and manifest and express ourselves in every possible way. The loftier and more sublime the spirit, the more its body
or vehicle, the matter that envelopes it, is rarefied, subtle and
luminous, so that they are almost as one. And yet, spirit and matter are always opposing poles, otherwise there would be no
manifestation.

There are beings, therefore, whose dwelling is in the sun. But
our sun is not the highest manifestation of the Godhead ; in fact
there are other suns which are far bigger, more powerful and
brighter than ours. But in our 'universe' it is our own sun that
is the biggest and the nearest to God. The sun is a world inhabited
by tremendously powerful spirits ; we cannot even conceive of
such power. These spirits are fire, they are light and, at the same
time, they have a body which is their home. The sun is highly
structured and organized and divided into different compartments,
but everything in it is so subtle and luminous that human beings
cannot see it. If you were clairvoyant though, you would understand that the categories and classifications of the invisible world
are analogous to those of the physical world. In fact the physical
world would not be as it is if it had not originated in and been
modelled on the divine world. And, for us, at the moment, the
divine world finds its best expression, its most perfect image in
the sun : it is the sun that brings us closest to God. Of course,
the divine world is not restricted to the sun ; it is far beyond,
far higher, far vaster than the sun. It is infinite and inexpressi-
ble, but the sun is its most eloquent representative.

You may not be able to understand all that I am revealing
to you, yet ; but understanding will come little by little, and we

shall come back to these ideas again. In the long run you will have a clear, true understanding of all this. Personally, I live constantly in the presence of these truths that Heaven has revealed to me ; I have been given them so that I can pass them on to you and share them with you ; for the new earth that is being created will know a new type of man, with new ideas and a new understanding. Without the knowledge of these great truths, man will never attain the point where he reflects, expresses and manifests the divine world and makes it visible to the eyes of others. This is why you must start building new philosophical systems from new elements and materials. And that is what I am giving you : the new elements with which to build new houses, forge new conceptions and live on a new level of consciousness. When you do this you will feel that you are entering the divine world, a world of splendour, beauty, joy, happiness, intelligence and freedom.

Every human being has at least two dwellings in the physical world : his own body and his house. But he possesses other dwellings on other levels : astral, mental, Causal and so on. Before leaving his disciples, Jesus said, 'In my Father's house are many mansions... I go to prepare a place for you.' Jesus was saying that his Father's house is a vast world that contains many different compartments, or storeys, if you prefer, and that each being, whatever his degree of evolution, is prepared and predestined to dwell in the particular part of that world which corresponds to him. Each one will receive a dwelling place suited to the qualities and virtues that he has developed. One who has worked to become pure, for instance, is predestined to live in a part that corresponds exactly to the extent and the splendour, the beauty of his purity. A person who has always sought knowledge, wisdom and philosophy will live in a part that has libraries and laboratories in which he will be able to reflect and write and conduct research. Yes, yes ! Surely you do not think that Cosmic Intelligence who is always so foresighted and generous would put someone who loved reading and writing in a dwelling where there were no books or pens or paper ! And those who love music, who have always

wanted to play or sing, will not be put in libraries where they
would only be bored : they will be given houses full of music and
musical instruments. And so on, and so on, for painters, dancers
and poets, etc. You must not think that Divine Intelligence is so
niggardly and narrow-minded as to crowd everybody into the same
stable !

This is what Jesus was referring to when he said, 'In my
Father's house are many mansions.' He knew that the divine world
contained a multitude of different dwellings and that they would
be assigned in conformity with the laws of correspondence. The
Father's house is immense, and God plans to give each one of
His creatures plenty of space. So don't worry, you will not have
to put up with noise from the neighbours ! But the first thing
to do is to prepare yourselves, for there will be no question of
your being admitted to such a vast, sumptuous dwelling and of
enjoying surroundings of such grandeur, wealth and beauty if
you are not prepared. If you are not prepared for this world of
beauty, you will find yourself in narrow, cramped quarters where
human beings swarm like tadpoles. Yes, a world as narrow and
constricted as Dante's Inferno ! For space and breadth are attributes of the divine world, whereas narrowness, constriction and
compression are characteristic of Hell.

So Jesus knew that each one of us would receive a dwelling
in keeping with his qualities and the virtues he had worked to
develop. Perhaps, if you have an inquiring mind, you will ask,
'But, suppose someone has every imaginable quality : purity, love,
kindness, intelligence, strength of will, light and peace, etc. Will
there be a special place for him, too ?' Yes, naturally. Everything
has already been planned : Cosmic Intelligence has prepared a
dwelling for such a creature, a place that includes and contains
everything. And anyone who is fortunate enough to go to such
a place will send the good news to others !

'In my Father's house are many mansions.' Now you know
how Esoteric Science interprets and discloses the underlying
meaning of Jesus' words. They have been quoted, repeated and

discussed for the past 2,000 years, but no one has ever explained what these 'many mansions' of the divine world were. But now it should not seem quite so strange and unbelievable when I tell you that there are dwellings even in the sun.

Yes, the spirits who live in the sun, with all their light, all the intensity of their love and all that wealth of life which they dispense in all directions, even they have their own dwelling places. They are not all packed together on top of each other. Each one of them is luminous, warm and life-giving, but they are all different and distinct in their individual expressions, their qualities and activities, and each one belongs to a particular class or category according to his particular function or mission. Together they do extraordinary work on all the planets, uniting to bestow all kinds of blessings on us, but they are all distinct entities : those who send us warmth are not the same as those who send us light or life. But that is not all : the sun distributes currents of energy to the earth and the other planets, of which men know nothing. Man's knowledge goes no further than the light he sees, the heat he feels and the life that flows into him ; in other words his knowledge is still very limited and incomplete and even crude. One day, science will discover that the sun sends us other currents and radiations, other emanations which can be perceived much less easily. Once man begins to realize this he will begin to evolve, for in order to tune in to these subtle energies and blessings, he will have to develop other delicate centres and instruments within himself : the Chakras or Lotuses.

We know very little about the sun, but he too has his ambassadors or representatives : his rays. And each ray is also a little trinity of life, warmth and light ; this is why we must receive them with great love, intelligence and goodwill. Let me illustrate this for you : suppose the postman brings you a parcel containing some rare delicacy : if you don't open the parcel and enjoy its contents you will not get any benefit from it. Similarly, if we want to taste and benefit from all the parcels and gifts that the sun sends us, we have to unwrap them and see what is inside.

In other words, our minds must be awake and conscious of the wonderful gifts that are being showered on us, our hearts must be fired with love so that we hasten to taste and benefit from them, and our wills must be ready to act, to follow a divine impulse, to take a decision. The sun's rays ask to be properly received and welcomed. And if man is unconscious, if he does not have the necessary goodwill, intelligence and love, he will feel nothing and receive nothing, or next to nothing. Of course, our bodies, particularly the skin, are capable of receiving light and warmth, even if we are unaware of it, so that if you sleep through the sunrise you will get at least a little light, but it will be so little compared to what you could get if you were awake and conscious.

You must be aware, therefore, that the sun's rays are a rich gift, a blessing, and it is up to you to receive them with great love, intelligence and goodwill, for then their tremendous potentialities are released and they are capable of carrying you to great heights and revealing many secrets to you.

And now I want to give you a method which could be very useful. I have already explained the symbolic meaning of beads threaded together to make a necklace or rosary. If you asked a member of any religion when the rosaries or chaplets they use were invented and by whom, and why they recite special prayers or formulas as they run the beads through their fingers, do you think he would be able to answer you ? There are all kinds of rosaries in the world, made of a great variety of materials, with beads of different shapes and colours ; some of them round, some oval or square, some large, some small. Some rosaries have 108 beads, some 72, 50 or 12. But the rosary I want to tell you about today has only seven beads. You can make it for yourself, mentally, and the sun has an important role to play in it. You will say, 'What ! Do you mean to say you can punch a hole in the sun and string it on a thread and wear it round your neck ?' Why not ? You can do anything you want by means of your thoughts. You could carry the whole world like a bead on a string round your neck, so why not the sun ? Who is to prevent you ? Especially if it can help you to evolve !

So, now let's make a disciple's rosary. First of all, choose a moment when you are feeling well disposed, and begin by becoming fully conscious of yourself, because you are going to be the first bead on this rosary. 'Aha !' you will say ; 'So now I've got to put myself on a string and pretend I'm a bead !' Yes, why not ? You are still a very tiny bead, but that does not matter ; you will grow ! Yes, in this story beads grow, too.

Next you take your own father. 'Oh, he wouldn't make a good rosary bead', you say ; 'He drinks...' That does not matter ; put him on your rosary anyway. He is necessary. You are the centre of your own kingdom but he is the centre of your family, and even if he is none too wonderful at the moment, he is important symbolically, for he represents our Heavenly Father. Perhaps he drinks, smokes, spits and curses, but that does not matter. He is still your father and the head of the family, and Heaven has given him certain prerogatives. So, think of him as a symbol and put him on your rosary so that he will be linked to you and to the other beads, for this will help him.

Next, you want to find the chief magistrate of your town, the mayor, and thread him on the string too. He may not be any good as a mayor, but that does not matter, either. He is important as a symbol : he is the head of the community, the citizens go to him to express their needs, and when government officials visit your town it is he who receives them. So he has a central position which is symbolically important.

Next you have to find whoever is at the head of your country, the head of government, and string him onto the same thread. He represents a rather bigger bead ! After the head of your country comes the head of the planet, the Regent of the Earth. If you know his name, so much the better, you will be able to thread him onto your rosary all the quicker. He represents a very big bead, for he is far nobler, more intelligent and greater than all the others. Next comes the head of the solar system, the sun itself.

Yes, immense, luminous, hot and perfect as he may be, he must
be threaded onto your rosary !

But you have not finished yet : the last bead on your rosary
is the Lord of the whole universe, God Himself.

There ! Now you have the seven beads of your rosary, with
yourself on one end and the Lord on the other. The next thing
to do is to tie the two ends together, so that there is one con-
tinuous current flowing from God and passing through the sun,
the Regent of the Earth, the President of your country, etc., all
the way to your own father and yourself, and then from you to
God, and so on. In this way you will be doing a work of light
and life which will, at the same time, help your country's leaders.
By linking them to Heaven, you will be doing your part in ob-
taining inspiration for them in the accomplishment of their duties.
Most people throw only criticism and abuse in the direction of
the unfortunate people who bear the burden of government, so
that the added burden of so many negative, harmful thoughts,
leads to their making the wrong decisions. And, of course, it is
the whole population that suffers from their mistakes. If you want
to help your country, you have to make contact with the person
in charge and send him a great deal of light, so that he may always
be well inspired. You cannot help a whole country, the task is
too great. But it is not necessary to aim at helping the whole country : it is enough to help one man, just one. That is much easier
to do, and he, in turn will help everybody else. So much depends
on that one person. If he passes just laws in the areas of public
health, employment, housing and education, the whole population will benefit, simply because one man, at the head of the country, was well inspired !

This is the teaching of Esoteric Science ; the only true, complete and accurate science. And now my rosary looks a little less
ridiculous, doesn't it, when you think of the currents flowing from
the sun to you, and through you, to others, in an endless chain ?
This is just one more method to use in working with the sun. Try
it one day when you have nothing else to do ! Instead of yawn-

ing and being bored, think of this rosary, run its beads through your fingers and then wear it round your neck, and you will see the results ! Wherever you go, you see people who are against something or someone : against their parents, against their husband or wife, against the boss, the mayor, the President, etc., etc. But if human beings realized how important it was to send good thoughts to those who govern them, the situation would improve rapidly in every country.

The Bonfin, 3 August 1967 (morning)

Chapter Six

The Master and the Seven-bead Rosary —
Every Creature Needs to Own
and Protect its Dwelling Place — The Aura

This morning, on the Rock, when I was talking about the seven
beads of the rosary, several of you will have remembered that
I had already talked about that, but that this time there was a
difference. Last time I included your Master, and this time I
replaced him with the mayor ! Yes, you can change people, if
you like, but it is important always to have seven beads. You could
say that, because of the mayor, this morning's rosary was more
'administrative' ! It is not so easy to know just where to put a
Master because there is no social significance attached to his role.
The father of a family, a mayor, President or King, all represent
a social rank and responsibility, whereas a Master represents a
certain level of consciousness.

The word 'master' calls to mind someone who directs, commands, organizes or instructs others. We speak of the master of
the house, a schoolmaster, a master carpenter, etc. And barristers,
musicians, writers or painters are often called 'Maestro' or
'Master'. We even speak of a man having a 'mistress' (sometimes
several of them !), but all that is quite different. The truth is that
a Master is a symbol ; like the sun, he contains, expresses and
gives concrete reality to an immense variety of riches. If, in addition to this, he is entrusted with a specific task on earth, such
as to direct and instruct a handful of men, for instance, this is

72   *The Splendour of Tiphareth*

secondary. A true Master is everywhere, for he participates in God's work, in the work of the sun and of the Regent of the Earth. But, first and foremost, he is master of himself ; this is the primary meaning of the word 'master'.

Sometimes I amuse myself by replacing the word *'maître'* by *'mètre'**. A *'mètre'* enables us to measure distances : length, breadth, depth and thickness. You can carry it about in your pocket and take it out to measure anything you like : without it we might miscalculate badly ! So we need measuring instruments ; but not only instruments with which to measure distance, thickness or length, that is to say, to measure the three dimensions. We also need to measure things in the fourth and fifth dimensions, that is to say, in the psychic and spiritual dimensions. And this is where a *Maître* or Master comes in : a Master is necessary to help us to find our own inner Master, that being who is always within us and with whom we have to identify and unite. It is in becoming one with that inner Master that we become master of ourselves, capable of ruling, enlightening and educating the teeming population of cells and entities that inhabit us. To be a Master is, first and foremost, to possess both self-mastery and absolute criteria of discernment. Very few men in the world fulfil these conditions ; in fact, there is a hierarchy amongst Masters : they do not all reach the same degree of perfection. There are different degrees reaching all the way to the sun, to the Lord Himself, and it is a magnificent thing to be part of this hierarchy of Masters.

He who aspires to be a Master must fulfil three conditions. First he must know the essential truths ; not what men have written, created or taught, but those things which are essential in the eyes of Cosmic Intelligence.

Secondly, he must have the will to dominate, master and control every aspect of himself.

* The French word 'mètre', is used to express both the measurement (approximately 39") and the measuring rod or tape. The pronunciation closely resembles that of the word 'maître', meaning master. (Translator's note)

And finally, his knowledge and self-dominance must be used exclusively to manifest the qualities and virtues of disinterested love. Yes, knowledge and will are simply means which must be put at the service of love and kindness. What a contrast this is to the usual order of things ! The things that most men consider to be ends in themselves, an Initiate considers as means, and vice versa. What is the point of learning ? Is it an end in itself ? No, it is not. And what is the purpose of work ? Why exert oneself and develop one's strength ? Simply in order to manifest love : to allow love to flow throughout the world and bring life and joy to every creature. There is only one end, one goal : love. This is what the sun tells us.

So, to get back to the rosary : if you want to put your Master on it, you may certainly do so, and as he is, after all, greater and far more elevated than a king or a president, you can place him above them, just before the Regent of the Earth. And after the Regent of the Earth comes the sun.

Now, I also want to add a few words to what I told you yesterday about dwellings or houses, so that you may learn to read the Book of Nature. Nature has given each creature its own place. Birds build nests and every animal has its lair, run, burrow or lodge (there are all kinds of words for this), and if another animal tries to take its place, they fight for it. Each one has its own private territory ; even certain species of fish defend their own territory.

Cuckoos are an exception : they do not build a nest of their own, but they are very good at finding other nests in which to lay their eggs !

As a general rule, therefore, Nature has given all creatures the instinctive need to mark out a space for themselves which others are not allowed to enter, because she wanted to be sure that they would all have sufficient peace and quiet to bring their offspring into the world or to create. This is a law. And this is why certain communistic theories can never be put into practice, even by communists themselves. It is a great mistake to try to

abolish all individual property. You will ask, 'But if you belong
to the Universal White Brotherhood, doesn't this mean that you
must be very broad-minded and generous and put the collectivity before yourself ?' Yes, it does indeed : but not just anyhow !
Initiatic Science broadens the notion of communism to include
other dimensions. We are true communists. It is not good to
deprive people of everything they possess, even if you do so in
order to help others, for this way of doing things kills what is
essential in any being : his freedom to create. A bird cannot lay
eggs if it does not have its own nest.

Nature has given every creature the inherent right to certain
private possessions which others may not dispose of as they please.
Take the physical body, for example : no one has the right to
do what he likes with someone else's body ; it is the private property of each person. Each person is the owner, also, of his or
her own heart. Take the example of a young girl : no one has
the right to dispose of her heart, but if she gives it away to a young
man, then she no longer has a heart and he has two ! And as
he is probably clumsy and does not know how to carry two
'watermelons' under one arm at the same time, he drops the girl's
heart and breaks it. Then the girl starts weeping and lamenting,
'He's broken my heart !' 'Well, it's your own fault. You shouldn't
have given it to him.' 'But I love him ; I love him...' 'Yes, you
love him, but you should have given him your tenderness and
devotion, your love, your music, anything except your heart. You
should have kept your heart for yourself.' And you can say the
same for the intellect and the will. Nature has given human beings a physical body, a heart, an intelligence and a will, and they
must keep them for themselves and only give away their fruits ;
that is to say, their thoughts and feelings, their work and activities,
their creations.

Esoteric Science teaches that evil spirits do not have the right
to enter the dwelling of an Initiate. An Initiate can refuse entry
to these spirits ; in fact, he can put up a sign to warn them of
the punishment that they incur by defying the injunction. And

before performing a magic rite or undertaking an important spiritual work, when he needs to invoke higher spirits, an Initiate designates and consecrates a certain area, so as to prevent evil spirits from entering. Then he makes sure that he will be left alone to work in peace by marking the boundary of this area with a circle and inscribing certain sacred names in it. Only higher entities have the right to enter this space ; inferior creatures are obliged to stay outside, and they can rant and rage as much as they like, but if they try to get in they are struck down instantaneously. Why does an Initiate take these precautions ? Because when someone needs to create, he is like a pregnant woman or a mother bird when the time has come to lay her eggs : he needs a nest, a quiet, peaceful retreat. In the invisible world the laws are exactly the same : in the infinite expanse of space, each spirit has a place set aside for its own use. Each spiritual being occupies its own special domain which is marked out and protected by certain vibrations or colours or by a particular quintessence, and no being with conflicting vibrations is allowed to create a disturbance by entering it. Only spirits of a higher order have the right to go wherever they like, because they never disturb anything.

And now we come to the practical application of all this : unknown to human beings, the places in which they live and work are also inhabited by millions and billions of entities who come and go as they please. If you fail to put up a 'No entrance' sign, therefore, and do not consecrate your house, creatures of a lower order will find your doors open and can come in and rob you. And you cannot expect the divine courts of justice to give you redress, because you will only be told, 'It's your own fault : you should have put up a notice to show that it was private property, or at least put a symbolic wire round it.' If your vineyard is not fenced in you need not be surprised if someone comes and steals your grapes ! In Bulgaria we say, 'If the lid is on the can, the cat can't get at the milk.'

In the same way, if your hearts, souls and spirits are wide open and unprotected instead of being consecrated and surrounded by

a wall of light, spirits have a right to enter, to soil and plunder
and rob you of all your treasures. They will not be punished for
it : it is up to the owner to take the necessary precautions. Just
as, in days gone by, towns and castles were protected by moats,
ramparts and drawbridges, so a disciple has to surround himself
with walls, ramparts and fortifications. For a disciple, as for an
Initiate, the best protection against all negative currents and evil
spirits, is their aura. The brighter it is, the purer its colours and
the further it extends, the safer the disciple, for the aura performs
the function of a shell or coat of armour : it protects its owner
from all the harmful currents that surround him. Do you ever
think about this ? No, you leave yourselves wide open to the com-
ings and goings of unwanted visitors* and then you complain that
you have been looted, or that you feel tired, dispirited and depress-
ed. In nature, every creature is on the lookout for marauders :
birds, wild animals and even insects surround themselves with
various obstacles to prevent predators from catching and eating
them. Why does man have to be so unsuspecting and trustful as
to believe that he is in no danger and that his enemies will spare
him ? Millions of beings have sworn to destroy man and wipe
him off the face of the earth, and they are hard at work, day
and night, in an effort to do just that. It is just as well that
mankind has its protectors ! It is only thanks to them that, in
spite of all the suffering and torments inflicted on it, it has not
already been destroyed !

So, what conclusion shall we draw from all this ? The conclusion that you should work at developing your aura. How can
you do this ? When you are watching the sunrise in the morning
and see the glorious aura of colours that surrounds it, say to
yourself, 'I, too, want to be surrounded with all the most gorgeous
colours.' Close your eyes and imagine yourself surrounded by
purple, blue, green, yellow, orange and red light. Spend a long
time bathing in all that light ; picture it shining and radiating out

* See *Complete Works*, vol. 5, chap. 7.

to a great distance ; picture the blessings it brings to all those who are touched by it, to all those with whom you are in contact in one way or another. In this way your aura will be a protection for you and, at the same time, a blessing for others, because you will be able to use it to help all creatures.

Some of you will protest, 'But we haven't got time to do all these different exercises.' Ah, when I hear someone saying, 'I haven't got the time ; I'm too busy...' I tell them, 'Yes, yes. I understand.' 'What do you understand ?' 'I understand that you will have plenty of time in which to be unhappy, to search in all directions for some way out of your misery, to weep and moan. When someone has no time for good, he finds plenty of time for evil !' You are looking at me and thinking how harsh and cruel I am. But I am not, really. I am just telling you how things are in nature : if you have no time for light, you will have plenty for darkness. Yes, my dear brothers and sisters, that is the way of it : it is a mathematical certainty ; an absolute !

The Bonfin, 3 August 1967 (afternoon)

Chapter Seven

The Heliocentric Point of View

I have already told you that when you come up to the Rock to meditate at sunrise, you must not begin to concentrate too abruptly ; you must allow your thoughts to wander, let them drift about and play a little. You have to keep an eye on them, of course, so that they don't get lost, but you can just sit there, quietly relaxed, not in a hurry, gazing at the sun. After a few minutes, you can bring your thoughts back to the subject you have chosen for your meditation, and your mind, which has been allowed to flit from one thing to another and dance and play a little, will be more docile. Then, very gently and gradually, without hurrying, you put such an agreeable, attractive idea before it that it lets itself be tempted and begins to concentrate. If you do this you will find that you can meditate for hours ! You have to learn to be extremely diplomatic with your intellect because it is its nature to be very, very sly and rebellious.

But now let me get to what I want to talk to you about, to-day. You will have noticed that the sun does not appear at exactly the same spot on the horizon each day : at this time of year it is moving towards the south, but if you had been here in April, May and June, you would have seen that it was moving towards the north. So there is an oscillatory movement : from 22 December until 22 June the sun moves in one direction and, from 22 June until the following 22 December, it moves back in the opposite

direction in this very slow swing of the pendulum which takes
months and months to complete. And, we might ask, what is the
sun telling us with this movement which determines the change
of seasons ? In the summer, the sun follows an immense curve
through the heavens from east to west whereas, in winter, it
follows a much shorter, lower curve. The extraordinary
geometrical figures described by the sun in its movements through
the heavens are very significant and eloquent. In winter the sun
does not have time to warm the earth, so everything is cold, con-
gealed and frozen, whereas in spring and summer, it follows a
fuller curve which gives it more time in which to warm and animate
the earth and produce fruit.

In actual fact, as you very well know, this movement of the
sun is only apparent. The sun follows its own trajectory which,
according to astronomers, is taking it in the direction of the con-
stellation of Hercules ; it is not the sun that gravitates round the
earth but the earth that gravitates round the sun on an orbit that
takes it alternately closer or farther from the centre. It is this varia-
tion in the movement of the earth that creates the alternating
seasons. If we rely on appearances, therefore, and see things from
the point of view of the earth, we shall be led to believe that the
sun rises and sinks as it moves in orbit round the earth. This proves
that when human beings are in the habit of seeing things from
the geocentric point of view, the point of view of the earth, they
necessarily have a false view of reality. Their whole philosophy
is false because it is based on the illusion that the sun gravitates
round the earth. Initiates know that it is the earth that gravitates
round the sun, so they look at reality from the opposite point
of view : they take up their positions in the sun and look at
everything from there and, in this way, they see the truth.

You will object, 'But everyone knows that it is the earth that
gravitates round the sun.' Yes, you all know it theoretically, but
in practice you behave as though the sun went round the earth.
This is why I keep repeating : 'As long as you do not try to find
the centre, your own centre which is your own divine dimension,

as long as you do not make it your permanent abode, seeing and doing all things from this centre, you will never discern the truth. You will see everything in a false light.'

If this seems incomprehensible, it is because you do not know that the earth and the sun are to be found, also, in man. The earth is the belly and the sun is the brain, the intelligence. Unfortunately, men have lived on the level of the belly for centuries ; they see everything from the point of view of the belly, that is to say, from the point of view of material life. For them, all the rest is unimportant. And this is why it is such a struggle for anyone who tries to get them to return to that other centre : the head, intelligence or light ; in other words, to get them to adopt the heliocentric point of view ! How can you get men to understand that by drawing closer to the centre of the solar system they are, at the same time, drawing closer to their own centre around which everything else must gravitate. When a man wants to be the centre, as he thinks, of his own life, in point of fact he is gravitating round all kinds of things which are not himself, and this is why he is always tormented and tossed to and fro, unable to grasp the truth.

I mean to use every means, every argument and all the knowledge at my disposal, to get you to see this dazzling truth : that you must work to unite yourselves with the centre of our solar system, the sun, the source of life ; that, on the spiritual level, you must centre yourselves upon the greatest and most powerful Being, the Lord Himself ; that the hub of your own being, the divine spark in you, your own higher Self, must fuse into one with these two supreme centres, for it is only in this way that you will, at last, find yourselves and discover truth. You are still plunged in a world of illusion and torment because you have still not found your centre, you have not started to revolve round your own hub and become one with it. You are still ruled by your desires, your passing whims and appetites ; it is they that still constitute the centre round which you are revolving. This has got to stop ; henceforth it is they that must be made to revolve round

you ; they must obey and be subject to you. If you are obliged
to spend your time running here and there to satisfy their demands,
not only will you never succeed in satisfying them, but you will
lose everything else. It is they that must serve you and work for
you, and you must be the centre, the head, the lord and master
of your own kingdom.

A few moments ago I mentioned the four seasons. There is
great wisdom in knowing how to work in rhythm with the seasons.
A farmer has to know when to plough or plant his seed otherwise he will not have a good harvest. Solomon said, 'To everything
there is a season, a time for every purpose under heaven : A time
to be born, and a time to die... A time to plant, and a time to
pluck what is planted... A time to embrace and a time to refrain
from embracing... A time to break down, and a time to build
up.' And many people who have read Ecclesiastes have never
understood that he was expressing a magic, cabbalistic truth. How
can we determine the time suited for each thing ? The Cabbalah
explains this, and it takes a great deal of learning to know how
to establish the connection with the four elements, the four car-
dinal points of the compass and the four Archangels, season by
season. A truly extraordinary system of correspondences exists
in this respect. I could give you a chart that represents the four
regions of the world and the distribution in these four regions
of all the different elements, crystals, precious stones, entities and
so on, but what would you do with it ? Perhaps I shall give it
to you, one day, but what I want you to understand, today, is
that when you go and watch the sun rise, you must realize that
you have to change your point of view and, instead of living permanently on the outer fringes of your own being, in the world
of appearances, concentrate on finding the source that exists
within you.

What is really important, what matters most at the moment,
is that you change your point of view. Now that you know what
a treasure trove is waiting to be explored, instead of grumbling,
'Oh, Lord, I've got to get up for the sunrise again ! What good

can it do me ? I'm incapable of meditating. My brain has seized up !', you will get up in a different frame of mind in the morning. I want to increase your love of the sun, to strengthen your conviction that it must be the one thing that matters most in your lives. And if I succeed in this, you will all be new beings. I think it might astonish you if I told you about my own attitude towards the sun : even at night I am in communion with him ! And when I am out for a walk, for instance, he is always with me, talking to me and instructing me. In fact, I tell you candidly, I have chosen him to be my instructor and Master. Every day he reveals something new to me ; why shouldn't he do the same for you, too ? It all depends on your own attitude towards him.

If you have been influenced by mechanistic philosophy, and think that the sun is unable to talk to you and help you ; if you think that it has neither intelligence nor life, you are putting an insuperable barrier in your own path and you will never make any progress ; you will never be able really to feel the sun or to talk to him or understand him. Unfortunately, the education human beings have received has left them convinced of only one thing : death. They think that everything except man is dead : man is the only creature endowed with life and intelligence. Well, let me tell you this : a philosophy like that is very destructive and it must be replaced. You have to realize, on the contrary, that everything is alive, that everything we see manifests intelligence, that the sun is a living, intelligent light. And when you have grasped this, he will immediately speak to you. If the sun has already revealed so much to me, it is because I see him exactly as he is, that is, as an extraordinarily exalted spirit of great beauty, power and intelligence — so great, in fact, that everything else pales in comparison ! Try asking him something : he will answer you. You may not be able to decipher his reply immediately, but sooner or later it will show up on the screen of your mind. The sun sends us his answers instantaneously, like a computer, but man is not sufficiently advanced to be able to understand them immediately.

And now, let me interpret yet another page out of the great Book of Living Nature.

If you observe the behaviour of human beings, you will see that they instinctively try to clamber as high as possible up the social ladder, and obtain positions of responsibility and command. On their way up they are obliged to pass a certain number of exams, and it is only when they have proved their worth that they are chosen for the highest posts. Of course, there are countries in which people use violence and deceit to gain power, but I am speaking in general, for civilized countries. If human beings have this desire for high-ranking jobs and positions of responsibility, it is because they know that certain privileges go with them : in exchange for less work, they will have better pay, greater freedom and greater possibilities to impose their own views and change the existing order. Or take the example of competitions — beauty contests for the title of Miss World, for instance : the jury selects the most beautiful girl in the world (actually, that is not true ; for the most beautiful girls don't take part in such contests !), goes through the formality of asking her a few simple questions that anyone could answer, and proclaims her the world's Queen of Beauty. And once she has the title, she receives money, clothes, proposals of marriage and offers of television or film contracts.

In other words, everybody knows that if you can get a title of some kind in this world, you also get the advantages that go with it. Why have they never seen that it is exactly the same in the spiritual world ? Initiates and genuine disciples know that, on the spiritual level, there are other juries, other examiners, who observe how they solve life's problems, so they work very, very hard inwardly, and if they pass their exams, they are given a higher position and wider powers. And the higher they climb and the nearer they get to the top, to perfection, the more diplomas and important positions Heaven gives them until, one day, they are given the fullness of power, and command even the forces of nature — but always and only for good.

This is what happens to those who are enlightened, who know how to read the Book of Nature and how to extrapolate what they read onto other levels and thus decipher the true laws. Instead of trying to compete with their fellow human beings for the position of governor, minister or president, they leave all that to others, and devote their efforts exclusively to the inner dimension. And their ceaseless work and their constant accession to ever greater heights are rewarded with the gift of greater and greater powers, until they become kings, and reign over life itself !

Now that you have embarked on this great adventure of going to watch the sunrise, you must go much further in your reflection and concentration, in your work and all your activity, until you discover the significance of this act on every level. The more you love and understand the sun, the higher you will climb towards the summit of your own being. For the summit is the same point as the centre, seen from another angle. If you want to depict a mountain, you can draw it either as a cone with the point at the top, or as the geometrical projection of the cone : a circle with the central dot which represents the summit. Whether you progress towards the centre of your circle, towards your soul and spirit, or whether you seek to climb upwards towards the sun, towards the summit, it comes to the same thing. To ascend to the highest point or to penetrate to the central core of one's be-

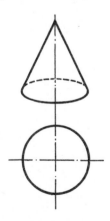

ing, are one and the same undertaking expressed differently, and the benefits to be gained are identical : peace, serenity, power, illumination, authority, lucidity and love. This is the ideal of life !

It is by understanding the sun that you can create your own future : but you must understand ; you will accomplish nothing unless you understand. The sun reveals what is essential, the major principles of life. Go and watch the sunrise every morning for years, and you will become like the sun ; you will have reached a great height, you will have reached the centre, you yourself will be a centre, a centre of strength, power and life !

The Bonfin, 4 August 1967

Chapter Eight

Love as the Sun Loves

Men have lived on this earth for so many millions of years that they have ended by understanding how necessary it is, and how many advantages are to be gained, from collaborating and helping each other. In fact, it is thanks to this human solidarity that culture and civilization advance. In the past, a disaster such as a fire, for example, brought immediate help from all the neighbours : the whole village would turn out to fight the blaze and help the victims, and what love they showed in working all together to rebuild their unfortunate friend's house. All the technical progress of recent years seems to have made people more personal and selfish and less heedful of others than in the past, but the same sense of solidarity can sometimes be seen even now. When there is a special emergency such as an air disaster, an avalanche or a shipwreck, for instance, you will see men rushing to the rescue with helicopters and parachutes, and all kinds of special rescue equipment. So, even though we hear people complaining that men have become more egotistical, they have still not lost all sense of kindness and generosity.

But the love of humans pales by comparison with that of the sun. Even the love of Initiates, who are more devoted and more willing to sacrifice themselves than other men, even their love pales beside the love of the sun. One is told of saints who gave

everything they had to the poor ; of benefactors who bequeath-
ed huge sums of money to build hospitals, orphanages or institutes
of scientific research and, of course, all that is very laudable, but
you can hardly compare them to the sun ! 'But what does the
sun actually do that's so special ?' you will ask. And this shows
that you are exactly like Mullah Nashrudin.* When his pupils
asked him which was more important, the sun or the moon, he
replied, 'Why, the moon of course, for what good is the sun in
the daytime ? It serves no useful purpose. Whereas the moon,
at least, is useful : if it weren't there, how would we see at night ?'

Initiates, who always take the most exalted beings as their
models, have chosen to follow the example of the sun. They have
seen how, during all the millions of years that men have been
on this earth, the sun, which was there long before man, has
poured out such quantities of heat and light that no one, not even
a computer, is capable of evaluating it. The sun is the symbol
of divine love. However great the love of human beings, or even
that of Initiates who teach us to offer the other cheek and to love
and forgive our enemies, it is nothing in comparison with the sun's
love. If you compare your love and generosity to the love and
generosity of other men, you will never find an example sufficiently perfect to stir your divine centres into action. Whereas
if you concentrate on the sun and take it as your model — well,
you will see the results for yourselves !

The sun gives light and life ; it distributes its gifts of life and
warmth to every creature without discrimination, to criminals as
well as to holy and upright men. Why does it do that ? Is it blind ?
Can't it see the crimes that men commit ? Is it nothing more than
a machine without intelligence or discernment, totally indifferent
to the goodness or viciousness, the honesty or dishonesty of men ?
No, the sun sees the faults and crimes of men well enough, better than anyone, in fact ; but he also sees that these are tiny, insignificant details compared to the immensity of his heat and light.

* A popular figure of fun in Turkish folklore. (Translator's note)

All those things that seem to us so monstrous and terrible, are little errors to him, just dirty, petty, destructive little incidents. He washes and mends and repairs the damage, and continues with boundless patience to help human beings until they reach perfection.

So now, perhaps, you will ask, 'But what is the reason for all that generosity ? What is the sun's philosophy ?' Ah, well that is just what we are now going to see : the sun has his own conception of human beings. He recognizes the eternity and immortality of the human soul, and he knows very well that man is still immature, still a hard, sour, unripe fruit. So, as he is very good at getting fruit to ripen on trees, and knows exactly how to pour sugar and perfume into them so that they become juicy and delicious, he wants to help man to ripen too. But he knows that man is going to take much longer to ripen than fruit, and he has decided to be very patient. He knows that even criminals, if he continues to shower them with his warmth, will, one day, be so disgusted with themselves that they will give themselves up to the influence of his beneficial rays. And once they do that, what is to prevent them from becoming lovable, sensitive creatures : poets and musicians and benefactors of the human race !

The sun will never abandon mankind because he knows that if he abandoned them their evolution would be aborted ; there would be no more ripe fruit, no more saints, prophets or divinities on earth. So he continues to give warmth and light to men because he knows all causes and effects, all beginnings and ends and he understands the path of evolution. If he did not, he would be furiously angry with men : he would shut off the flow of gifts and turn off his light, and that would be the end of the human race ! If the sun is still shining, it is because he knows the goal that he is working for and the purpose of creation, and has decided to go on helping human beings to reach maturity with the utmost patience, generosity and love.

The sun is the only being that never gives up. Every other creature gets tired, shuts up shop and drops out of sight : dead and buried ! Not so the sun ! He is always there, triumphant and radiant. He says, 'Come and slake your thirst, take what you need. Have you done something stupid ? I won't hold it against you. Human beings are selfish, vicious and vindictive and if they catch you I can't answer for your safety. But I will never hurt you ; come, drink in my rays... I will give you more...' The disciple who models himself on the sun, therefore, becomes a kinder and better person ; he finds the courage to forget all the difficulties and disappointments inflicted on him by his fellow men, and he never loses patience. Everybody else gives up and ends by turning you out : 'Go away. I don't want to see you any more ! I've done all I can for you and I'm tired, tired, tired. Leave me alone !' But the sun is never tired. I think you understand, now, why I want you to turn to the sun ; it is because he, and he alone, can fill you with noble, divine sentiments.

You have to think of the sun often, therefore ; you have to spend time with him and talk to him. Ask him, 'Dearest Sun, tell me : how did you become what you are ? Please explain it to me because I want to be like you, but I don't even know how to begin. I've read all kinds of books by philosophers and other learned men, but they all have such a peculiar scale of values, so petty and mean ! You are the only one who has the right yardstick ; the yardstick of immensity, abundance, wealth and splendour. Please tell me how you managed it.' And the sun will answer, 'It is thanks to the Elixir of Everlasting Life.' 'And where can I find that Elixir ?' you will ask. And the sun will reply, 'Here, in me, of course !' So, if you want to live with the same life as the sun, you must drink the Elixir of Everlasting Life which never ceases to flow from him into the atmosphere. And I am not feeding you on fables : this is a truth which is truly true.

If you want to begin to understand and decipher the meaning of life, if you want to become free and capable of ever greater and more beautiful undertakings, you must adopt the sun as your model. Try to look at everything through the eyes of the sun, to measure everything with the yardstick of the sun, to feel things as the sun feels them, and you will see how petty, crude, insignificant and mediocre are all those things that you had once thought important. I am introducing you to a world in which the units of measurement are far greater than any you have used before. This does not mean that, from one day to the next, you will be as rich, patient and generous as the sun, nor that you will live for billions of years, like him. No, but if you take him as your model you will get much further. Of course, when I speak of living 'billions of years', I am not talking of your spirit ; for your spirit a billion years is nothing, since it lives eternally. No, I am talking of your physical bodies. The sun lives for billions of years in his physical body because he is pure.

And now, some more questions for the sun : 'Why are you so pure ?' 'Because purity is the basis of everything else, and I am careful to maintain and strengthen it ceaselessly.'* 'And why are you so generous and kind ?' 'Ah, that's because I know that my kindness and generosity will trigger something good in human beings, and that one day they will turn to me with praise and song and music. In fact, it makes me very happy to see that there are already some who turn to me, for that proves that they are intelligent and full of love.'

This is the kind of thing the sun is always telling me, for I never stop questioning him. And when I asked him why he was so brilliant and alive, he said, 'It is because I have so much love. Love makes all my particles move so fast that no instrument is capable of measuring their vibrations.' 'Ah, then I'm going to try and do the same !' I said. 'You won't succeed,' he replied, 'But you're right to try, anyway ! The exercise will do you a lot of good because it will force you to transcend your human limitations.' Then I asked him another question : 'But can a man become so bright and shining that he can light up the night ?' 'Yes,' he replied ; 'He can ; it is possible. But it takes a tremendous amount of work, for matter is very opaque and dense and

* See *Complete Works*, vol. 7.

it vibrates very slowly. However, if man manages to make the particles of his physical body subtler ; if he can get them to vibrate much more rapidly, then he can become a lamp to light up the whole world.'

I have asked the sun many more things besides, but this is not the moment to tell you about them all. Just this one thing : I asked him whether all that strength that he possesses, and all that light that he distributes throughout the world, could be found in a human being ? And he told me that they could, and he even showed me exactly where that energy is stored in the human body and how it emanates from different parts of the bodies of men and women. Yes, an energy which is of the same nature as the energy of the sun.

So, my dear brothers and sisters, think of the sun day and night, because by thinking of him you are in touch with a world of power, purity and light. When you think of the sun you are raising yourself up, you are becoming nobler, more magnanimous, more indulgent and generous. The sun gives, strengthens and vivifies without ceasing, and we must imitate him in this.

Of course, as long as a disciple has too many personal problems to solve, he is not free to be more open and broad-minded and to think of anything but himself ; he is too busy ! But as soon as he has begun to see his way more clearly and solve his own problems, as soon as he is a little freer, he can begin to concern himself with the whole of mankind and become like the sun. In fact, to be responsible for twenty, fifty, a hundred people, would not be enough for him ; he is so free that he feels the need to extend the scope of his love and concern to take in the whole human race. So he pictures humanity as a single person, and pours out on it streams of love from the superabundance in his heart, and bright rays of light of every colour. When a man reaches this level, he experiences indescribable happiness and fulfilment. When he is still preoccupied with himself, his wife and children and friends, he is not capable of such happiness. But a disciple who begins to distribute all his love and light to all human beings as though it were one man, without worrying about how many they are or where they are, resembles the sun. It is in this way that human beings can become suns.

When you have a spare moment, up on the Rock, at sunrise — or anywhere else, for that matter — think to yourself, for example : 'Today I want to fly away on the wings of love ! I want to be more generous and indulgent, and forgive every wrong that has ever been done to me !' And the sun will give you a shining example of how to forgive and forget injuries. Then you will feel so light and happy that you will feel like singing out loud and, remembering how miserable you felt in the past when you kept thinking about the injustices and insults that others had inflicted on you, you will begin to regret not having learned to forgive sooner ! The sun tells you, 'Listen, old man, get rid of all that just as soon as you can ! Do you think I keep harping on all the crimes and wars and massacres that have happened on earth ? Wipe it all from your mind : you will work much better if you stop moaning and groaning about the past. Do as I do : keep on sending your love and light to everybody !'

When you have a problem or a difficulty, talk to the sun about it as though you were talking to a person. 'My dear Sun, what would you do in my place ?' And the sun will smile (As you know, children always draw the sun with a big smile on his face !) and say : 'Oh my ! If I were in your place I would have committed suicide long ago. You'd do much better to put yourself in my place. Why should I climb down into your place ? It's not possible. It is you who have to climb up and put yourself in my place. And once you are in my place you will do thus and so...' and he will give you the solutions you need.

The Bonfin, 6 August 1967

Chapter Nine

A Master Must be Like the Sun
and Remain at the Centre —
Some Prayers to Say at Sunrise

Once again, we have been privileged by the most glorious
sunrise. The sun is with us, as smiling and generous and vivifying as ever. Yes, I must say that we are being very spoiled.

Now, imagine that someone who has an exceptional responsibility in the world, an Initiate or Master, for instance, asks the
sun for advice. 'My dear Sun, so many people love me and want
to have a special relationship with me. Please tell me what you
think about it. What should I do ?' The sun will reply, 'Look
at me and do as I do. The planets all love me very much, too ;
they are always revolving round me, wanting me to hug and pet
them. But I can't let myself be beguiled by any one planet. I have
to stay in the centre. It's not that I don't love them : I do. I love
every one of them even more than they love me. The love of all
the planets put together is nothing compared to the immensity
of my love, because my love contains no self-interest ; it contains
only light, warmth and life. But I owe it to them to stay where
I am. It is for their own good. If I started to pursue one or other
of them there would be a universal cataclysm. I have to stay at
the centre, you see : it is the only way to ensure harmony, life
and happiness throughout the whole universe. And you must do
the same ; there is nothing to stop you from loving every single
human being. There is nothing to prevent you from giving them
light, inspiring them, uplifting them and spurring them on to reach

the heavenly heights, but you must not leave your place at the centre !' 'Yes, but they are always begging me...' 'That just can't be helped', replies the sun ; 'If you were obliged to satisfy everybody's whims and wishes the whole edifice would come tumbling down !'

What I want you to understand from this is that an Initiatic School is like a solar system : the Master is in the centre, like the sun, and that is where he has to stay ; and the planets have to revolve round him (I am sorry to say that there are even some comets, which come close to the sun and then fly off again into space !). I know that this is a particularly difficult question, and many Initiates have failed to resolve it satisfactorily. It is said that even Pythagoras succumbed to the charms of one of his disciples, and it cost him very dearly. The young woman, whose name was Theano, was very beautiful, and when she declared her love for him, Pythagoras made her his wife. It is thought that it was because of this that some other disciples set fire to his school.

A true Master is like the sun : he remains at the centre. He showers an abundance of blessings on his disciples, giving them his own light, strength and warmth as well as his ideas, but he never abandons his position at the centre. Many Masters, who failed to realize that such a decision would lead to disaster, married one of their disciples, with the result that the others abandoned them. A Master who does that is not a true sun. In fact, he is more like a symbol of the moon, for the moon is a symbol of someone who is unstable, sentimental and easily influenced ; it is attracted by the earth. There have already been several moons in our solar system, and some of them fell down to earth ! You may not believe me, but this is all on record in the archives of Initiatic Science.

Initiates who are strongly influenced by their 'lunar' dimension, that is to say, whose emotions and affections are highly developed, are drawn towards human beings and end by succumbing and abandoning their position at the centre. But those who are true suns are guided by their reason and remain inflexible.

This does not mean that they are hard-hearted and cold or egotistical, not at all. Quite the reverse, in fact ; they give all their love, light and strength to their disciples, but they remain where they belong : in the centre. Even the most ravishing beauties, even a princess cannot sway them : they stay where they are ! They say, 'I will give you my light and my affection, but let me stay where I am !'

You can see how the sun sheds light on a question which is not at all clear to a great many men and women. When you begin to think in this way, you will free yourselves from many things that torment and worry you. So this is what the sun teaches us : all for the sun and the sun for all.

And now, let me give you some formulas that you can say to yourselves as you watch the sun rising. Wait until you see the first rays of sunlight and then, very lovingly, say these words.

As the sun rises over the world, so may the Sun of Truth, Freedom, Immortality and Eternity, rise in my spirit !

As the sun rises above the world, so may the Sun of Love and Immensity rise in my soul !

As the sun rises above the world, so may the Sun of Intelligence, Light and Wisdom rise in my intellect !

As the sun rises above the world, so may the Sun of gentleness, kindness, joy, happiness and purity rise in my heart !

As this luminous, radiant sun rises over the world, so may the Sun of strength, power, force, dynamic energy and activity rise in my will !

And as this luminous, radiant, living sun rises over the world, so may the Sun of health, vitality and vigour rise in my body !

Amen. So be it, for the Kingdom of God and His Righteousness !

Amen. So be it, for the Glory of God !

This is a very powerful magical formula.

With all the exercises I have given you, you have enough, now, to fill your whole lives. In this way, all the brothers and sisters will be as radiant, shining and beautiful as the Kerubim and Seraphim, as children of God ; they will walk through life praising the Lord and spreading his Glory throughout the world, so that the Kingdom of God and His Righteousness may be established on this earth as soon as possible. Then life will be filled with gladness and joy, poetry and music ; all men will thrill with delight and live together as brothers. Rivers will flow, flowers will perfume the air, the birds will sing divine melodies. The whole of life will sing the song of the Glory of God. There will be no more wars, no more destruction or distress, no more illness or crime ; for the first time, the earth will be really and truly a Land of the Living.

Why not work for this to come true ? Why spend your days and nights plunged in sadness, darkness and fear, instead of orientating your lives in a spirit of harmony and unity, together with all the members of the Universal White Brotherhood, towards the highest and most beautiful regions of creation ? This is what our Teaching is all about !

May the Angels and Archangels open the floodgates and pour out their generosity onto the children of God, onto all mankind. May there be an abundance of light and understanding, an abundance of joy and happiness so that man may, at last, accomplish the exalted mission for which he is on earth : to reflect and express the Creator and the glorious beauty of Heaven.

Blessed are those who are aware of this !

Blessed are those who are consumed by the sacred fire !

Blessed are those who have made up their minds to be conductors of their Heavenly Father ! Blessed are the meek !

Blessed are those who know peace ! Blessed are those who want to work and make sacrifices !

Blessed, blessed, blessed be the children of the Universal White Brotherhood !

The Bonfin, 12 August 1967

Chapter Ten

Rise Above the Clouds —
The Sephirah Tiphareth

When the sky is pure and cloudless you can see the sun, and when it is full of clouds, they hide the sun. But when you go up in an aeroplane to a thousand metres or more, you find yourself above the clouds, where the sun is always shining and never hidden. That is all very simple and obvious ; childishly simple, you will perhaps think ; but you will soon see how these phenomena can be interpreted.

From the esoteric point of view, clouds correspond to dark, drab, opaque thoughts and feelings which, as they drift through our hearts and minds, cloud the sky and hide the sun from view. The sun is always there, always shining at the core of our being ; a sun that is God Himself, the Source of all light and life. He is always within us, but He is hidden ; we cannot see or feel Him, and we go about in the dark and the cold, shivering and nearly lifeless. Yes, there are certain regions within a man where, almost every day, thick clouds gather and block out the sun, simply because he does not know how to rise to the limpid, sunlit regions above. It is important for man to learn how to rise and remain above the clouds, so as to be independent and free. Otherwise he will be obliged to wait a very long time for his clouds to scatter before he can know joy and warmth and light. The atmospheric conditions within each human being vary according to his thoughts and feelings and his way of life and, in most cases, they are such as to fill his inner sky with heavy black clouds which prevent the rays of the spiritual Sun from reaching him. It is because of this that men suffer constantly from the cold and the darkness of their lives ; they receive none of the countless blessings pouring from the sun because they remain on too low a level.

A true disciple is conscious of this. He knows that the atmosphere is sometimes filled with smoke, dust and thick mists, and sometimes clear and transparent — as it was this morning, for instance : you saw for yourselves how brilliantly the sun shone ! If you knew how to look at it, how to create a bond between yourself and the sun, how to open your doors and windows to it, you would be in a state of ecstasy. Such peaceful, cloudless translucency offers the best possible conditions for looking into yourself and solving many of your problems. It is an opportunity for you to understand that you have been wasting your time and ruining your health, that you have allowed yourselves to be led in the wrong direction and have become selfish and rebellious and ready to pick a quarrel with anyone and everyone. And, little by little, you will come to see how and why you have reached such a pass and how, if you change, if you begin to envisage things differently, to live differently, if you let this divine light have its way with you, everything in life will begin to look quite different ; everything will become wondrously clear and translucent.

Air corresponds to the mental plane, to the intellect, and when our intellect is darkened we must try to find out where this darkness comes from. In nature, clouds are formed by the water vapour rising from the surface of lakes, rivers and oceans. Water represents the astral plane, the heart and feelings, and when evaporation is too heavy, that is to say, when man has allowed himself to be dominated by his sentimentality and emotions, clouds begin to gather within him and block out the sun. What should he do when this happens ? The very first thing he has to understand is that he must purify his inner atmosphere, his sky, his air. Instead of passively accepting the grey sky, he must concentrate so as to break up and scatter the clouds or rise above them, to where the sky is a clear, bright blue. Most human beings never think of moving into a different region ; they are content to wallow in their misery and wait for the conditions themselves to change. Is it any wonder that the clouds remain ; there is no reason why they should not stay there for years and years ! Whereas a disciple tells the clouds, 'It's all the same to me if you're there or not, because I'm going to go up above you !' And up he goes, and no one can stop him ! And once up there, above the clouds, he finds bright sunshine. In other words, once you rise above your trials and tribulations, above all those things that worry you and make you unhappy, you can always find the Lord. He is always there, high up above you, and it is up to you to seek Him out. Don't just sit and wait : do something to find Him and draw closer to Him.

When I was still very young there were certain exercises that I loved to do. One day I was with some friends at the top of Mount Musala and the lakes of Rila and the other peaks were hidden by fog ; it was so thick that we could barely see each other. So, just for fun, I asked my friends, 'Do you want to see the view ? Tell me what you want to see and I'll show it to you.' Well, one of them asked to see the third lake — or perhaps it was the fifth ; I don't remember exactly. I had climbed the Musala so often, that I knew exactly where each lake or peak of the Pirin-Rhodope mountains was, so I stretched out my hand in the direction of the third lake, the fog cleared and the lake appeared. Of course, they all exclaimed in surprise. Then I lowered my hand and, gradually, the lake was once more hidden by fog. Then another of my friends wanted to see the Macedonian mountains. I stretched out my hand in that direction and once again the fog lifted and the mountains appeared. After that the sun came out. My friends were absolutely dumbfounded and, for the first time, they understood how powerful thought can be. This story is absolutely

true ; I know that the invisible world is listening to me and I have
no desire to lie to you.

If it is possible to influence and change external clouds, how
much more easily should we be able to influence our inner clouds !
When you feel that dense clouds created by certain negative
thoughts are beginning to pile up and undermine your faith or
love and hide the glory of God, the splendour of the Teaching,
or even the merits of your instructor from you, then it is time
to concentrate and send the purest rays of light in the direction
of the fog. If you do this you will see that the clouds will gradually
disappear, leaving your sky clearer, purer and brighter, and you
will be overcome with gratitude to Heaven. There : these were
just a few things I wanted to say to you to stimulate you to work
better and better.

It is by means of thought that one rises above the clouds.
Thought is like a rocket or a beam of light. You can aim or focus
it on a given point : the Source of life, the Eternal Sun, your inner centre or the Lord Himself, and within a few minutes it will
pierce the clouds, however thick they may be, and you will find
yourself up above, bathed in crystal-clear light.

Of course, when I speak of the sun I am touching on only
one part of reality, for day is not the whole story : night exists
too. When the sun is no longer there and the night sky is clear,
we can gaze on immensity with its thousands of stars and constellations. We catch a glimpse of the Infinite, of immense wealth
and splendour. Whereas, when the sun appears, space seems to
shrink ; the sun shuts out immensity and allows us to see only
the visible, material world. Where can we find the answer to this
riddle ? On the one hand, the sun gives us a clear, precise vision
of the real world, it brings things to life and we see them clearly
defined. On the other hand, when it is not there, we are able to
see immensity, and immensity is so prodigiously rich that it enables
our souls and spirits to travel and lose themselves in infinity. Does
this mean that the sun does not show us the whole truth ? But

let's leave the question for another time. In the meantime you can think about it.*

The night has sometimes been seen as the symbol of evil, and the day as the symbol of good. And yet it is often at night that Initiates work, meditate and pray and, in the past, it was during the night that they put their disciples through the trials of Initiation. So night is not as bad as all that ! Of course, when we speak of 'darkness', the word implies evil, a lack of intelligence, love and kindness. But night is something else and, in fact, it is perfectly possible for the light of the spirit to shine brightly at night, just as it is possible for darkness to reign in broad daylight : it all depends on one's state of consciousness. Night and day are two different symbols of one reality : divine manifestation. God — or truth, if you prefer — is manifested just as well by night as by day, but the aspect will be different in each case. Many forces need darkness for their work : the unborn child begins to take shape and the seed begins to sprout in darkness.

This means that we also need to know how to work with night. Where would you find more ideal conditions for melting into the immensity of space, than the peace and stillness of a summer night ? Lying on your back in the grass, when everybody else is asleep and the silence of the night is barely troubled by the chirping of the crickets and the croaking of an occasional frog, you can gaze up at that immensity studded with millions of stars and try to understand them, to imagine what they must be like and what entities, what intelligent beings dwell in them. For it is impossible that, amongst all the worlds that have been created, this tiny grain of dust that is the earth should be the only one to be peopled ; peopled by pygmies who spend their days and nights philosophizing, or by theologians who can think of nothing better to do than to argue about how many devils can sit on the point of a pin, or what became of Jesus' prepuce after the circumcision ! What fascinating topics of discussion, to be sure !

* See Chapter 17 of this volume.

Stretch out on your back in the grass, then, and try to pick
out the star you like best, the one with which you seem to feel
a special closeness : look at it, love it, attach yourself to it and
imagine that you are rising towards it, or that it is coming down
to talk to you. Then all your petty little problems, the little dramas
of your life, all the little things you have lost, will seem so insignificant that you will realize that it would be ridiculous to waste
any tears on them. In the face of such solemn, majestic immensity, you will wonder how you could ever have made so much
fuss about so little. There are astronomers who have admitted
that their work has completely changed their outlook on life :
everyday struggles, problems and worries take up far less room
in their lives, and they are constantly amazed to see the importance that human beings attach to small details. If you have the
opportunity, I advise you to try this, and even to sleep under the
stars.

Try to become more and more conscious of the fact that when
you are present at the sunrise in the morning, you have the best
possible conditions for making progress in your spiritual work.
You must stop worrying about all the clouds, all your apprehen-
sions and grudges, all your desires and ambitions, and make
yourself available for a tremendous spiritual task. Those who are
capable of freeing themselves from their clouds are capable of
moving heaven and earth ; they are creators of the new life and
the Lord appreciates them.

So many of you have told me that they continued to be present at the sunrise, but without gaining anything from it, because
they were continually pestered by unruly thoughts which prevented
them from concentrating ! But if you take the exercises I have
given you seriously, you will begin to gain something from the
sunrise. You must use your will-power to master and control all
the anarchical forces within you, to get all your cells to vibrate
in rhythm with your ideal, in a single direction. If you don't do
this you will continue to be weak, threatened by the slightest puff

of wind, constantly vulnerable to attack from sorrow, grief or tribulation. Sometimes one meets people for whom the sun never seems to have risen. If a few chance rays light up their horizons they are delirious with joy, but their joy does not last ; after a moment they are as gloomy as ever. This is because they refuse to change their philosophy.

Taking the Egyptian formula : 'To know, to love, to have power (I often say, 'to dare', but it comes to the same thing) and to keep silence', I interpret it as follows : 'To know' means to know that the sun exists but that clouds exist also, and that we have to disperse them. 'To love' is to love the sun and adhere to it. 'To have power' is to muster all the forces of one's will and dare to launch into this work, to make a gesture, pronounce a formula or do something that signifies an act of the will. 'To know' concerns the mental plane ; 'to love' concerns the astral plane, and 'to have power' concerns the physical plane ; and this means that we have to bring our knowledge and our love down onto the physical plane.

Many spiritual people function only on the level of their thoughts and feelings ; they seem to be incapable of giving them concrete expression, even in words. But without the intervention of the spoken word, thoughts and feelings cannot easily become concrete reality on earth, on the physical plane, because they have no vehicle, no body. In fact, if someone stores up his thoughts and feelings for too long without expressing them or giving them form, they can cause serious psychic disturbance. Sound waves have a very powerful effect on matter, and the formulation of a few appropriate words is enough to set in motion the particles and atoms of matter, so that as soon as thoughts and feelings are manifested verbally, they begin to enter the realm of physical reality. The spoken word is extremely powerful ; it can be compared to the signature on the bottom of a legal document, order or contract : as you know, if an official document bears no signature it is nul and void.

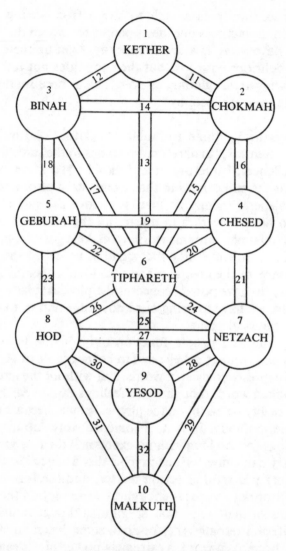

The Sephirotic Tree of Life

I have already spoken to you about the Sephirotic Tree of Life and, in particular, about Yesod, the Sephirah which is nearest to the earth and which is the region of the moon.* It is a mysterious region which contains great riches and also many dangers, for its lower layers are formed by the vapours, emanations and mists rising from the earth and from human beings. If you manage to get through this shadowy region of illusion, aberration and falsehood, through this fearful twilight world of deceit, and reach the higher levels of Yesod, then you will discover purity, transparency, life, clairvoyance and true poetry. Many mediums, clairvoyants and even mystics and, above all, many poets have been caught in the treacherous quicksands of the lower regions of Yesod. They did not have the knowledge that would have enabled them to rise above this zone and reach daylight, and this is why so many of them ended their lives in insanity or alcoholism or committed suicide. They did not know that they should have risen far higher, to Tiphareth, the region of the sun, where all is crystal-clear and luminous.

Tiphareth means beauty or splendour. It is the fifth Sephirah on the Tree of Life, counting from the bottom, and the sixth, counting from the top. It is at the centre of the Tree which represents the universe, just as the sun is at the centre of the solar system. In a human body, the region of the heart and solar plexus corresponds to this Sephirah. The Cabbalah says that the Deity manifests Himself in Tiphareth under the name of Eloha ve Daath, and that the Archangel Michael is in command of the angelic order of Melachim or Kings, which correspond to the 'Virtues' in the Christian tradition. The visible, material dimension of Tiphareth is, as you know, represented by the sun (*Chemesh* in Hebrew).

If you have read the Book of Genesis you will have noticed that the very first creature created by God was light : 'Then God said, "Let there be light" ; and there was light.' Everything begins, therefore, with light. And that light is the Christ, the solar Spirit.

* See *Complete Works,* vol. 7.

For the Spirit of Christ, who manifests Himself as the primeval Glory, the Word, in the Sephirah Chokmah, and of which St John spoke, saying that 'Without Him was made nothing that was made', manifests Himself again, under a different aspect in the sun. The roots of Tiphareth are in Chokmah, region of Videlinata, the Divine Light which is invisible to our eyes. For me and for all Initiates, the Solar Spirit is the Spirit of Christ for, as I have already told you, the sun is far, far more than what we can see. It is a world inhabited by an innumerable population and which has its own rich civilization and culture. But we are still a very long way from understanding what the sun is.

There are several different ways in which we can study the Sephirotic Tree of Life, and one of them consists in dividing it into three pillars or columns : Kether, Tiphareth, Yesod and Malkuth form the central pillar, the Pillar of Equilibrium ; on one side is the Pillar of Mercy formed by Chokmah, Chesed and Netzach, and on the other is the Pillar of Rigour or Severity, formed by Binah, Geburah and Hod. When one descends the Pillar of Equilibrium, from Kether, Tiphareth is the first Sephirah one comes to. In this sense one could say that the sun represents the Spirit of God, rather than the Spirit of Christ. In reality, however, it represents both of them equally, for the Spirit of Christ is identical with the Spirit of God ; they are just two different ways of approaching the one reality. You have to become familiar with all these different notions and learn to juggle with them.

Each morning, when you come up to watch the sunrise, remember that by creating a bond with the sun you are creating a bond between yourself and the Spirit of the Sun, the Christ-Spirit which is an emanation of God Himself. It is not enough to expose yourself physically to the sun : if you want to receive its light, life and power, it is your spirit that must reach out to it, expose itself to its rays, create a close bond with it and work its way into the depths of its heart. This is the only way to enter this other world, a world which will give you knowledge and illumination.

The Bonfin, 15 August 1967

Chapter Eleven

The Spirits of the Seven Lights

It is written in the Book of Zohar :
'Seven lights are there in the Most-High, and therein dwells the Most Ancient of all the Ancients, the Secret of all Secrets, the Hidden of all the Hidden Ones : Ain Soph.'

These seven lights are the seven colours of the spectrum : red, orange, yellow, green, blue, indigo and purple. They are the seven Spirits who stand forever before the Throne of God. The seven colours of the prism, therefore, also have symbolic value. Why do you think that my very first lecture was about the sun and a spring of water ? Because light is like water flowing from a spring, the spring of the sun. Yes, the sun is a spring, a source of light ; the true Source is on high. Light is the water that flows from the sun, the water of life. Light is white and water on earth is transparent, but the symbol is the same.

When you look at the light of the sun through a prism, you discover a world of untold richness and splendour. But how is it that when light, which is one, is passed through a prism, which is three, it becomes seven ? Yes : one, three and seven. This phenomenon has always intrigued me ever since I was a child, and it has always been a delight to me to see the wealth of beauty and purity contained in the light of the sun. It is this that led me to see that man himself, like the prism, is a trinity. In order for the light of the sun to be perfectly diffracted into the seven colours, it is essential that the three facets of the prism be equilateral as well as perfectly transparent. Similarly, a human being must achieve the harmonious, 'equilateral' development of the triangle formed by his mind, heart and will, so that the light of God, the light of the sun, may shine through him and be manifested in all the splendour of the seven colours. Only disciples and Initiates who have worked to develop their intelligence, who have accustomed their hearts to feel and love correctly and who have become strong through constant striving and the determination to overcome all that is negative, only they can diffract white light into seven colours, and their aura grows continually in beauty, purity and size. Those who fail to develop their triangle of mind, heart and will as they should, have only two or three colours in their aura ; all the others are absent. And if, in addition, their triangle is warped and out of proportion, then their intellect becomes malicious, cunning and aggressive, their heart is filled with hatred, spite, sensuality and cruelty and the desire for revenge, and their will is at the service of the forces of desolation and destruction. When this is the case, not only does their aura lose all its shimmering, vivid colours, but it becomes full of all kinds of foul and horrible things.

In Initiatic Science, red light is identified as the Spirit of Life. Red signifies life, and it is perhaps because it is the vehicle of life that blood is red. If you rob a man of his blood you are robbing him of life, and if he is very weak and you give him blood it restores his vigour. This is how the technique of blood transfusion was discovered. What effect does red have on human beings ? The vibrations of this colour create a bond between human beings and the Spirit of Life ; their effect is to stimulate and enhance man's vitality. But there are thousands of different shades of red, and each one of them represents a different force : love, violence, war and anger, sensuality, dynamic energy, drunkenness and so on.

Orange light is identified with the Spirit of Sanctity, the second Spirit. With the help of orange light, therefore, one can create a bond between oneself and sanctity. But here, too, there are innumerable different shades representing different forces : individualism, dignity, even pride ; a certain shade will be beneficial to health, another inspires and strengthens faith. But, above all, orange is associated with health and sanctity.

Golden yellow is the Spirit of Wisdom. Its vibrations encourage men to read, reflect, meditate and seek wisdom, and to be guided by reason and prudence in their actions.

Green light is the Spirit of Eternity and Evolution. Like all the others, green light has innumerable shades ; in fact, if I had some samples with me I could show you how each shade differs in its effects. But the most authentic colours, those that are closest to the divine essence, are those we see in the prism. It is these that you should use in your spiritual work ; other shades may represent many other virtues, but the essential virtues are those represented by the spectrum. As I have said, for years and years I have been in the habit of contemplating these colours and working with them : it is a form of nourishment for me. I often turn the crystal of my stick to the sun and look at the seven colours ; I contemplate them, rejoice in them and nourish myself on them, then I give thanks to Heaven and go on with my work.

Green, therefore, is the colour of growth and development and also of wealth. It is related to hope and it helps human beings to move forward on the path of evolution. One day, soon, I will tell you how the vibrations of each colour correspond to one of our organs and facilitate certain functions.

Blue light is identified with the Spirit of Truth. Blue is associated with religion, peace and music ; it helps to develop musical sensibility, pacifies the nervous system and heals the lungs. It also has a beneficial influence on the eyes, which are the symbol of truth.

Indigo light is the Spirit of Strength, the Spirit of Royalty. It has approximately the same properties as blue.

And now we come to purple. Purple is the Spirit of Divine Omnipotence and Spiritual Love ; it is the Spirit of Sacrifice. Purple is a very powerful colour and a protection for man. It is an extremely subtle, mystical colour which makes it easier for the astral body to leave the physical body and visit other worlds. It also helps man to understand the love of God. It is not at all beneficial, on the other hand, to plant life.

When I was a boy of fifteen or sixteen, I worked a great deal with colours. Not only did I picture them in my mind and meditate on them, but I daubed different colours onto the windows of my room to see what effect they would have on me. I would meditate in the room filled with the coloured light filtering through the painted glass and observe the effects of each colour. Then I would wash off the first colour and begin all over again with the next one. I hardly need to tell you that my parents and the neighbours feared for my sanity ! But I was quite unperturbed and went on with my experiments. When my room was filled with purple light I would soar away into other worlds and, one day, I invited some friends in to see what effect it would have on them, and all they did was to go to sleep ! And my plants wilted and died : the purple light killed them ! But I must say that I have a great fondness for purple !

When the red of a person's aura is not clear and pure, it means that he has given way to anger, drunkenness or sensuality. For each one of these vices, the shade of red is different, and clairvoyants can distinguish them quite easily. From time immemorial red has always been associated with blood and war. It is a beautiful colour, but only if it is very pure, such that, when mixed with white, it produces a clear, luminous pink.

Pink also denotes love : the white in it contributes an element of purity and harmony ; it has a pacifying influence. In the absence of violence and egoism love becomes wiser and more tender. This is why pink is seen as the symbol of tenderness, of delicate sentiments. I advise those of you who have excessive vitality to cultivate a special bond with white or to associate with people who have a lot of white in their make-up, that is to say, who are pure and honest. In this way there will be a certain blending, your red will become pink and you will no longer be harried and tormented by the excessive energies of red within you. Pink also has a beneficial influence on man's intelligence. To say that someone wears 'rose-coloured spectacles' means that he is an optimist ; he looks on the bright side of life, his mind is not encumbered by worry or sombre, negative ideas ; he is a happy person.

The same general remarks can be made for the other colours : certain shades of blue in a person's aura reveal that he has lost his faith, that he is no longer firmly rooted in peace and truth. If the yellow is dull or discoloured, it means that the person is not faithful to the dictates of his reason or that he is incapable of deep thought and understanding ; you cannot rely on his intellectual capacities. But I do not want to prolong these explanations, for I have other things to talk to you about today. It is enough if you remember that the seven Spirits who stand forever in the presence of the Everlasting Lord, are the Spirit of Life, red ; the Spirit of Holiness, orange ; the Spirit of Wisdom, yellow ; the Spirit of Eternity, green ; the Spirit of Truth, blue ; the Spirit of Strength, indigo ; and the Spirit of Sacrifice, purple.

If you want to obtain any one colour, you can always do so by combining two others. Purple and orange, for instance, will combine to give you red ; red and yellow produce orange ; orange and green make yellow, and so on. Each colour is the offspring of two other colours which are like its father and mother ; but if you do not know which colours to mix you will not get good results. Why not ? Because the oppositions and affinities that exist between colours, exist also between the planets that correspond to these colours.

Red corresponds to Mars, and Mars is impetuous, violent and destructive. He is the representative *par excellence* of the masculine principle, but only on one plane, for the Sun (although the Sun is not, strictly speaking, a planet) and Jupiter are also masculine, but on a higher plane. Green corresponds to Venus, and people in whom red is the dominant colour, are attracted to those in which green predominates because they set each other off to their mutual advantage, and this is excellent. But if they form a union and blend with each other they will give birth to a monster ! They can talk to each other, go for walks together, look at each other and, in this way, exalt each other's good qualities, but they must not unite, because the mixture of red and green produces a horrible dirty colour. Similarly, orange and blue must never be mixed, but when you put them side by side each one becomes more vibrant and expressive ; each enhances the virtues of the other. You have a good example of this here (the Master points to the stained glass symbols behind him) : the blue sets off the orange and vice versa ; the blue seems bluer and the orange more orange. And similarly, for the red and green in the other window. Blue corresponds to the planet Jupiter and orange to the Sun, both of which are positive or masculine, and this is why they should not marry each other.

And now, take the example of yellow and purple which should never be mixed either. Yellow corresponds to Mercury and, according to the Cabbalah, purple corresponds to the Moon. However, we usually associate white with the Moon and, in that case, we can attribute purple to Neptune, for Neptune is the exact equivalent of the Moon but on a higher plane. Mercury also has its equivalent on a higher plane, and this is Uranus. You will have a better grasp of these correspondences and relationships if you look at the positions of the planets on the Sephirotic Tree of Life (Cf p. 124).

Mercury (Hod) is in opposition to Uranus (Chokmah). On another axis, Venus (Netzach) is in opposition to Saturn (Binah). On the central pillar, the Moon (Yesod) is in opposition to Neptune (Kether). And on the horizontal level, Mars (Geburah), on the Pillar of Severity, is in opposition to Jupiter (Chesed), on the Pillar of Mercy. One day I will explain all these relationships to you, and you will see how Venus and Saturn represent almost the same reality manifested in two different regions. It is possible that this contradicts all that you have learned previously, but you will see how, on the column of love, the love of Venus becomes the intelligence of Saturn, and how, on the other column, the practical intelligence of Mercury, the intelligence of reasoning, speech and commerce, becomes the wisdom of Uranus when it is transposed onto the higher plane.

You will not find much about these correspondences in books, but I thank Heaven that many of them have been revealed to me. It is not by chance that the Sephiroth are where they are on the Tree of Life : they are in significant geometrical relation to each other. But all this is very remote from your everyday concerns ; you have no need to study these abstract, philosophical questions. Today, simply remember what I have said about the different colours so that you can make effective use of them in order to advance your evolution. Work with a different colour every day. You can begin with red, the colour nearest to the earth, for instance, and progress from red to orange, yellow, green and so on, up the scale. Or you can start with purple and work downwards, whichever seems preferable or most in keeping with your usual way of doing things.

Red is the colour that is nearest to the earth, that is why the floor of our Meeting Hall* is red whereas the upper parts of the building are blue. The sky is blue and the earth red. The Hebrew name for the first man was *Adam*, the place where he lived was called *Eden*, the word for 'earth' is *Adamah*, and 'red' is *adom*. The Hebrew words for 'man', 'earth', 'red' and 'Eden', therefore, all have the same root. This is why the Cabbalah refers to Adam as 'the red man'. But the old Adam must die and make way for the new, the Christ. And blue is the colour that symbolizes the Christ. And wasn't this precisely the work of alchemists : the transformation of red into blue ? This means that all that is still crude, violent and brutish in man must be refined, transformed

* At the Bonfin, in Fréjus, France.

and sublimated. Red and blue are the two opposite poles, and if you want to move from one to the other, you can ask the alchemists how to do it, and they will tell you that you must learn to work with acid and alkali. If you know how to work with these two principles, the masculine and the feminine, you can change red into blue and vice versa by adding a few drops of acid or alkali. So, you see, chemistry can throw light on certain religious precepts, but religious people don't know this — and nor do chemists, for that matter ! To a scientist, these are purely material phenomena ; it would never occur to him to interpret them. Science limits itself to the observation of facts and never looks for meaning or an underlying reason for their existence. But I am not like that : I enjoy interpreting them for you.

So we are the Red Adam and we must give way and make room for the Christ. This transformation is possible : indeed it is the goal and purpose of religion. The old man, Adam, dominated by his own passions (red), must be replaced by the Christ, the new man (blue), who dwells in truth, peace and harmony. Blessed are those who understand ! Blessed are those who follow the light !

And now let me conclude by quoting those words from the Zohar again, for I love them dearly and often repeat them to myself :

'Seven lights are there in the Most-High, and therein dwells the Most Ancient of all the Ancients, the Secret of all Secrets, the Hidden of all the Hidden Ones : Ain Soph.'

Aren't those magnificent words ? Repeat them to yourselves often, and let there be Light ! Henceforth may you all work at light, with light and for the light !

The Bonfin, 17 August 1967

Chapter Twelve

The Prism, Symbol of Man

Yesterday I talked to you about sunlight and the effect of a prism which diffracts the white light of the sun into the seven colours of the spectrum. I told you that these seven colours represented the qualities and virtues of the seven Spirits who stand before the Throne of God, and today I want to add a few words about this, for I did not tell you everything.

I remember that I was still very young when I first experimented with the prism and that, at the time, it made a great impression on me, but it was only later that I understood the richness of this symbol. For example, the seven colours, the three facets of the prism and light, add up to eleven. Naturally, you will object that I am adding up a collection of heterogeneous elements, but Initiates have their own kind of arithmetic and you will have to get accustomed to it. What does eleven represent ? In the Cabbalah, eleven represents the ten Sephiroth traditionally referred to, plus the hidden Sephirah Daath, which is rarely mentioned. Daath is knowledge, the archives of the universe, the Akasha Chronica.

As I have already said, the three-sided prism which decomposes light into seven colours, is a symbol of man and his three faculties : mind, heart and will. Man is a trinity, a reflection of the Divine Trinity. And if the human trinity is to radiate the seven colours in perfect harmony, it must form a transparent, equilateral triangle with the apex pointing downwards. Only if these three conditions are met will the white light passing through it radiate upwards, in a beam of seven colours. A person who wants to radiate the seven rays, symbols of the seven virtues, has to work inwardly to develop the three sides of his prism equally and harmoniously. He does not have to worry about the light : that is always there, ready and waiting to pass through him and do its work ; it is he who is not ready, who is still impure and insufficiently developed. And, like light, God, too, is always ready to enter into a human being and manifest Himself in all the splendour of His seven colours, that is, to bestow all the virtues and powers on him : it is man who is drab and lacklustre, lopsided or ill, so that God can only manifest Himself very imperfectly through him.

The first thing to do, therefore, is to restore one's inner balance. If, for example, you have always given priority to the development of your mental faculties, you must now find the conditions you need to help you develop your heart by coming to live a fraternal life in the Brotherhood rather than shutting yourself away in your own little cubby-hole, and start working and doing various exercises to strengthen your will. Once a man's triangle of heart, mind and will is developed equally, the light that enters him automatically splits up into the seven colours.

And now let's have a look at how the different functions of our physical body reproduce the phenomenon of the prism. When you eat, for example, your food represents light and your stomach represents the prism and it, too, must be in good condition in order to digest your food and distribute the seven forces (or colours) throughout your body. It sends the red rays to the muscles, orange to the circulatory system, yellow to the nervous system, green to the digestive system, blue to the respiratory system, indigo to the skeleton and, finally, purple to the glands and chakras.

Incidentally, I forgot to say, yesterday, that indigo is the colour of Saturn. Ordinarily Saturn is considered to be black, because it is seen as a malefic planet ; but this is incorrect. Saturn is the planet of stability, which is why Indigo, which corresponds to the skeletal structure, is Saturn's colour, for the bones are the hardest, most stable parts of the body. Saturn is the planet which corresponds to the Sephirah Binah. Do you remember the formula I gave you one day : 'I am stable, son of the stable one, conceived and engendered in the territory of stability' ? He who has achieved the stability of Saturn is entitled to apply this formula to himself.

But let's go on. Just as with food, the air we breathe also represents the light of the sun and, like the stomach, the nostrils and lungs represent the prism. When the newly purified, oxygenated blood leaves the heart, it carries the seven rays of strength to the body. And the same phenomenon can be seen in the sense of sight and hearing : images and sounds are perceived by the eyes and ears as though by prisms which decompose and transmit them in the form of sense impressions. Everything, in fact, that enters man, everything that he perceives or absorbs, can be compared to the white light entering a prism which decomposes and radiates it in the form of seven colours. The same process can be seen in all these different areas.

Let's look, now, at the pattern of distribution : when the stomach distributes energy, it sends four parts to the belly and sexual organs, two parts to the lungs and heart and only one part to the brain. The reason for this becomes clearer if we call to mind that, in another instance, we saw that our physical body could be divided into three : the head, the thorax and the belly. The head corresponds to the divine world, the world of intelligence ; the heart and lungs to the astral world, and the stomach and other digestive organs to the physical world. This is the traditional division used by esoterics. The stomach, therefore, which has the task of absorbing food and distributing it to the rest of the body, keeps four parts for itself, sends two parts to the heart and lungs and only one to the brain. The lungs, on the other hand, send two parts of the air they breathe to the stomach, two to the brain and keep three for themselves and the heart. And, finally, when the brain receives energy from the sun, it keeps four parts for itself, sends two to the heart and lungs and only one to the stomach. It is the nervous system which receives nearly all of the spiritual elements which, as we know, produce very little waste, and the stomach receives much less ; whereas almost all the energy generated by food and drink goes to the muscles and the belly : very little of it goes to the brain.

Now, let me say just a little more about colours. Red is related to life, increased vitality and even war, for the need for land and food is one of the principal reasons why men fight each other in the hope of getting more for themselves. Orange is related to health and medicine as well as to research in all areas related to healing. Yellow is related to science, observation, reflection and analysis. Green is the colour of agriculture and, broadly speaking, of the economy, for economics and finance stem from agriculture which is at the origin of every civilization ; those who know how to work with green can become very rich. Blue is related to the religious, ethical and moral dimension ; indigo to metaphysics and abstractions, the quest for the first causes, and purple is the expression of the highest spiritual world. 'What about art ?' you will ask : 'Which colour corresponds to art ?' All the colours correspond to art, for art belongs to every region : all actions, all creation are the domain of art. There is no one domain which is purely artistic ; art is everywhere.

So, there you have a little more information about colours. But the most important thing for you is to understand that you must work on yourselves so as to become as pure as crystal and reach a harmonious development of your prism composed of head, heart and stomach. When you achieve this, the light in which we are all immersed will enter and pass through you, emerging in the form of seven beautiful, glittering colours.

Look at these two triangles* : one is pointing up and the other down. Some of you already know that these equilateral triangles symbolize man and woman who have attained a balanced perfection of heart, mind and will. The blue triangle which symbolizes man points down, because man represents the Cosmic Spirit which comes down to earth to vivify and spiritualize human beings and give them a share in His energy. This is the triangle of involution. The red triangle, on the other hand, symbolizes woman and points upwards, because woman represents matter which reaches upwards to unite with its beloved, the spirit ; and this is evolution. Each one goes half-way, and when the two meet and embrace and become one, they are both totally fulfilled. This fusion of spirit and matter is symbolized by the Seal of Solomon, the six-pointed star or hexagram, a very rich symbol in which an immense science lies concealed.

Between the two stained-glass triangles in the wall behind me is a pentagram, and this figure represents perfected man who possesses the five virtues and in whom the two principles have fused into one. The number Six represents the animal, whereas Five represents man who has freed himself from his animal nature, symbolized by the tail. But what are the five virtues of perfected man ? I have already mentioned them, but let me tell you again : they are kindness, justice, love, wisdom and truth. The five virtues correspond to five parts of the human body. Kindness corresponds to the legs, because man uses his legs to take him to wherever he can do good. Justice corresponds to the hands, because the hands are used to make a just distribution. Love is related to the mouth, because a man can use his mouth to pacify and utter words of consolation and healing. Wisdom corresponds to the ears, because a man uses his ears to understand and penetrate divine wisdom. And, finally, truth corresponds to the eyes, because it is with the eyes that one gazes on truth. The five

---

* In the lecture hall at the Bonfin, there are three large stained-glassed windows in the east wall, in the shape of a pentagram and two triangles.

virtues are also symbolized by the five fingers of our hands. Five, therefore, is the number of him who is perfect. And if we have placed these symbols here, it is because I want you to reflect on them and, through the two principles of emissivity and receptivity — the two principles of involution and evolution represented by the two triangles — become a pentagram, a perfect being like Jesus. It was not a question of chance that Jesus was given this name (*Yeheshuah*) which incorporates the five letters, י Yod, ה He, ש Schin, ו Vau, ה He, for Jesus is the perfect man.

But let's get back to the subject of the prism. We have seen that everything is distributed in human beings in keeping with the numbers One, Three and Seven. When a man and woman unite to create a child, for instance, we can see the same law in operation : that which the man gives to the woman is One, the light ; the woman represents the Three, the prism, and she produces the seven forces : a complete human being. And if the woman is unevenly developed, instead of producing a perfect spectrum of colours, that is to say, a human being with a full range of faculties and qualities, she will produce a crippled, handicapped child. This depends on the mother, but not only on the mother ; it also depends on the father, for what is provided by the father is not always as pure and luminous as sunlight. The only thing we can be sure of is that he gives light of a kind, and that this light, whether it be pure and bright or dull and dim, enters the prism of the mother — which may be more or less distorted — from which it emerges in the shape of a child, who will, consequently, be more or less perfectly formed. Whatever the final outcome, the correspondences are absolute.

All that I have told you about the two triangles and the pentagram can be found in esoteric literature. But nowhere else will you find any reference to the correspondences between a human being and a prism. And now, let me reveal something else, equally extraordinary, that you will never find in a book. An Initiate possesses the two triangles, the masculine and feminine principles, within himself : in his own person he represents the marriage of spirit and matter. When he is filled with kindness, love and compassion and all his attention is focused on man's well-being, he represents the triangle of the spirit with its apex pointing down towards mankind. At this moment he receives light from God and, although he is concentrating all his activity in a downwards direction, towards human beings, that light emerges from him in the form of a beam of seven colours rising upwards, towards Heaven, and the Angels and Archangels and even God Himself marvel at it. And yet this man, this Initiate, was thinking only of human beings.

As for the other principle, symbolized by the triangle of matter, the triangle of woman, which points upwards, it is in intimate contact with the centre of the earth, and the centre of the earth also projects light, but a dark, infernal light which can have a disastrous effect on someone who is not vigilant, intelligent and pure. As I have just said, therefore, when an Initiate loves mankind with total disinterestedness and prays with all his strength and all his soul that the whole of mankind may live in joy, abundance, peace and plenitude, a beam of seven colours streams from him. And, at this moment, something extremely important takes place : the Initiate receives these dark forces from Hell and purifies and transforms them and uses them for his work. There is no evil that a great Initiate cannot transform into light and joy. The influence of the subterranean world can disturb a human being and cause him to fall only if he is not firmly anchored in light, if he has not developed his intelligence and will.

Hermes Trismegistus said, 'That which is below is like to that which is above, and that which is above is like to that which is below'. If man receives forces and energy from above, therefore, it follows that he must also receive them from below. Obviously, the forces and energies received from above are of a different nature to those received from below, but the laws involved are identical. Hermes Trismegistus did not say that that which was below was of the same matter, the same nature, even less of the same splendour, as that which was above. By the use of the term 'like', Hermes Trismegistus meant that the same correspondences and relationships and the same laws prevailed both above and below ; but the matter of the two worlds is different : below, it is dark and opaque, whereas above, it is subtle and luminous.

We could, for instance, use the expressions 'above' and 'below', to refer respectively to the brain and the stomach, for here again, the same laws prevail. The brain digests thoughts just as the stomach digests food, and yet they are not exactly alike. And on a still lower level, the sexual organ also resembles the brain : not by its nature or the matter of which it is made, but by its function, which is creation. Hermes Trismegistus did not say that Hell, which is 'below', was as beautiful as that which was 'above', in Heaven, but that the processes of fusion, penetration and creation which existed on high, existed also below, although their splendour, immensity and power were in no way comparable. It would never do for you to start thinking that Hell is exactly the same as Heaven !

In human beings, therefore, there is also an 'above' and a 'below', and if we apply Hermes Trismegistus' formula to a man and woman in the act of creating a child, we see that that which is below (the woman) is like to that which is above (the man) ; for woman is fashioned like man except that everything is reversed : that which is full in the one is empty in the other, like a glove turned inside out. They are identical, therefore. In addition, he is above and she is below, their positions are reversed. I shall say no more about this at the moment, but I could give you many details — you would be amazed ! Think about it. I have still not revealed all that lies hidden in these words of Hermes Trismegistus, because Heaven has forbidden me to do so, but when it was revealed to me I was dumbfounded. A lot of people repeat the phrase without ever having understood it. That which is below is like to that which is above, and that which is above is like to that which is below because there is a web of relationships and magic processes that you cannot even begin to imagine.

The brain, lungs and stomach each distribute seven forces throughout the different systems of the human organism ; $3 \times 7 = 21$ and if you add man himself to this, you get 22. The twenty-two keys or Trump cards of the Tarot. Or, if you don't want to add man as a separate item, because he can be said to be included in the twenty-one forces, you could replace him with the light that produces all these forces. The Tarot has this same organization into groups of seven : seven energies which correspond to the stomach, seven to the lungs and seven to the brain. The sun is also included ; it is the nineteenth card. So, in this experiment with sunlight and a prism, we find the twenty-two cards of the Tarot plus the eleven Sephiroth. To sum up, then : we have seven Tarot cards for the head, seven for the lungs and heart, seven for the stomach and belly ; add to this the sun, and we get a total of twenty-two.

Where does the word 'Tarot' come from ? If we switch the syllables and vowels, we get the word Rota, which means wheel, or Thora, which is the Jewish Law, and many esoterics, not least amongst them the French cabbalist William Postel, have given much study to these three words, Tarot, Rota and Thora. But why are the Egyptian Initiatic cards called Tarot ? Rota is the wheel that both Ezekiel and St John saw in their visions, a wheel whose rim was studded with eyes, and this is the Sephirah Chokmah. The Thora is the Jewish religious Law and Moses gave it this name because his father-in-law was called Yothorah (Jethro). Yothorah was a priest of Midian and a great Initiate, and Moses lived with him and studied under him for forty years, and when he had passed his final ordeals with success, Yothorah gave him his daughter Zipporah in marriage. Zipporah, Sephirah... it is almost the same name. When he had completed his Initiation, Moses left his father-in-law's house and set out on his mission to free the Jews from the Egyptian yoke.

I am not going to reveal everything to you, for you have to

meditate and discover certain truths for yourselves ; if you make
a sincere effort, perhaps some friends from above will come and
help you. You must try to get them to come, for without them
nothing will ever be revealed to you. But one can only attract
the luminous spirits of the invisible world with purity, love and
harmony ; if there is the slightest trace of inner disharmony they
go away. I have often had occasion to ascertain the truth of this.
In the Yosemite Park in the United States, for instance, there are
some magnificent trees 4,000 years old, but they are no longer
inhabited : their devas have left this glorious region because of
all the noise and agitation brought in by the tourists. Normally,
every tree has its own living creature, but the gigantic trees in
this park are no longer vibrant and expressive, for they are no
longer inhabited.

But let's get back, once again, to the prism. The whole of life,
the vast multitude of affinities and correspondences which constitutes life, is represented in this image of white light diffracted
by the prism into seven rays of different colours. And now let
me say this : make it your guiding rule to seek light. Imagine that
you are a prism and that you are so successful at adopting just
the right position, that white light floods into you and radiates
from you in all directions in the form of seven glorious colours.
If you knew how important light was you would not always
give it the last place in your preoccupations. Perhaps you
remember that, in another lecture, I told you that when you found
the light it would manifest its presence within you in many extraordinary ways, the first of which is to renew your zest for
everything. Whatever your occupation may be, whether you are
eating or drinking, walking or reading, you begin to realize that
everything has a very special, exquisite flavour. And if you lose
your light again, you will lose this new sense of taste, for to lose
the light is to lose everything. If the salt loses its flavour it is good
for nothing but to be thrown out and trampled underfoot by men.
If you lose your light you will be ground to powder by events,

for you will have neglected the one thing most apt to make you strong and invulnerable. You see ? You have been taught everything except the one thing that is essential. To have a skill or profession, to earn a lot of money, to climb up the social ladder, these are the things that really matter to most people. No one ever talks about how to find the light ! Oh, of course, there are a few mystics who seek the light, but people jeer at them or pity them ; they are so ridiculous, poor creatures !

I have often wondered why human beings turned their backs on what is essential and chased enthusiastically after all those things which can only lead to disappointment, illness and grief. And to think that this is what they call civilization ! You only have to see what most people understand by intelligence ; they think it means to be shrewd and cunning : for them, a good 'confidence man' is the epitome of intelligence ! No, this is not true intelligence ! True intelligence is light, and light never cheats others or tries to take advantage of them. On the contrary, its one idea is to give to others and to light their path. The essential property of light is to make things visible ; it lights up our path so that we can see the snares and dangers, but also the blessings. It is light that enables us to find truth. Everything that exists ; earth, water, oil, a tree, a bird, everything has its own particular properties, but only light has the property of enabling us to see, of lighting up our path. You switch on your torch and, all of a sudden, you can see the gulf yawning at your feet. 'Heavens above !' you exclaim ; 'Only two more steps and I'd have been over the edge !' As I say, everything has its own specific properties and qualities. Light will not give you either food or money, of course, but it may well show you where treasure has been hidden, and then you can go and dig it up and become very rich ! Whereas, without light, even if you have a lot of money, it will only be stolen, for when someone is stupid there are always others ready to relieve him of his wealth.

This is all very simple, obvious and elementary. The property of light is to enable us to see what exists all round us and to

take measurements in one direction or another ; for when it is
daylight we can take our bearings and judge distances. And if
you feel like running, that is all right, too, for light is far more
rapid than you are and will always be ahead of you. Why is it
more rapid ? Because it understood long ago that it was not good
to overburden oneself and take on all kinds of stupid and un-
necessary commitments that only hold one back. But the other
reason is that light has so much love that it is in a hurry to go
to the help of human beings : its love spurs it on to move with
tremendous speed so as to be useful at once. Others are always
so burdened and weighed down by all kinds of cares and concerns, that the person they go to help is usually dead by the time
they get there : a man is dying, and a hundred years later his friend
arrives to save him ! That is how rapid human beings are. Light
is more intelligent than anything or anyone, because it has chosen
to remain free ; it refuses to let itself be weighed down, and this
is why all those who wish to resemble the light refuse to assume
heavy loads or to be caught in the snares of matter by putting
down roots.

It is light that bestows powers, it is light that bestows wealth
(not money, wealth) and it is also light that bestows the only true
kind of pleasure : when you possess light you find pleasure in
absolutely everything. Even a glass of water can seem like the
Elixir of Everlasting Life ; your thirst is quenched as though the
water were coursing through your veins. The sensation is beyond
description !

Blessed are those who have enthroned light in their heads and
souls, in their hearts and spirits ! When I speak of light, of course,
I am not speaking only of physical light ; anyone can have physical
light : you only have to switch on a lamp. What I am talking about
is the spiritual light which, once it has entered into the depths
of a person's being, brings him illumination. But illumination
is the final degree of Initiation, when every cell of the Initiate's
body is so totally immersed in and impregnated by light that it
begins to shine out through his head. Spiritual light, inner light,

this is the whole wealth of Initiates. With this light they can obtain everything.

Perhaps some of you would like to ask : 'But how can one obtain this inner light ?' What a question ! Don't you know how primitive peoples obtained fire ? They would rub two pieces of wood together until the friction produced heat, and they would go on rubbing until, eventually, a tiny flame, light, appeared ! It has to be done in three stages, therefore : movement (the will), heat (love) and finally light (intelligence, thought). So, in order to reach that light you must decide to act, to get your will working, until heat, that is to say, love, begins to take possession of you and, eventually, turns into light. This is how you can obtain light : meditate and pray and do spiritual exercises until you have learned to love them and they become indispensable to you and, in the long run, light will appear. Or, if you like, you can follow the reverse movement : you can transform light into heat and heat into movement. The knowledge of certain things can kindle love in you, and your love can lead you to act. Each element can be transformed and become successively one of the others. Look how easy it all is ! And yet people can spend years wondering how to obtain light, how to live a spiritual life, and never succeeding in spite of it being so clear and simple !

The Bonfin, 18 August 1967

Chapter Thirteen

A New Heaven and a New Earth — Spiritual Grafting

I think that all of you, when you come up here and watch the sun rising for the very first time, have the same experience : you are unable really to feel it as a vibrant, living being. It is too far away, too foreign to you. You gaze at it but without feeling anything ; it has not become part of you, or rather, you have not yet become part of it. But if you persevere, if you continue to contemplate the sun every morning in spite of that sense of distance, the day will come when you feel the closeness of its living presence so strongly that you will be incapable of detaching yourself from it. Moments like that are very important and very precious, and they can repeat themselves year after year.

It could be, also, that you managed to establish a close relationship with the sun last year : it opened its doors to you and gave you so much. And now, this year, the contact seems to be broken. Why ? Because you have let several months go by without thinking of it. You have grown further and further from the sun, getting yourself wrapped up in other concerns, forging bonds with other people and frequenting other regions, so that you have been influenced by other vibrations. This is why the sun seems so distant and you are having trouble renewing the contact. But once it is renewed, what a delight : the sensation is beyond description !

At any event, you must be ready, in the beginning, to go

through a very difficult phase, a period in which you feel as though
you were wandering in an arid wilderness, until the sun opens
its treasure-house and floods you with light, intelligence and vitality. Many of you have told me how difficult it was for them, in
the beginning, to make this personal contact with the sun, but
that now they had no words with which to express their joy. It
is as though their whole being was coming back to life, and
understanding and feeling were waking in them for the first time.
So it is worth coming up here every morning, even if there are
days when you are drowsy and numb and your brain seems to
seize up. Be patient and persevere, and you will see what happens : the experience of feeling the sun alive and vibrant within
you, even if it only happened once, would be sufficient reward
for all your trouble.

The sun is the symbol of the very highest ideal, and only those
who cherish a high ideal can hope to renew their contact with
it. Only those who have decided to work for light, love and justice,
who want to attain perfection and become stronger and more intelligent, will feel this bond with the sun. If your ideal is very
down-to-earth and has nothing to do with the Principle of Life,
with the Creator and Source of life, you will simply be bored and
go to sleep. The sun will not speak to you in any way because
the vibrations of your being are not synchronized with those of
the sun.

Actually, this is exactly what happens when someone listens
to my lectures : his reactions are determined by his ideal. If his
ideal is limited to making money, having a good time and the
pursuit of pleasure, in other words, to the crudest and most down-
to-earth things in life, then even if I talk about the most sublime
truths and the greatest laws, nothing awakens a response in his
heart or soul. But if, on the contrary, someone is seeking to elevate
and perfect himself, you will see how he vibrates, how deeply he
is touched and how he concentrates all his attention on these
truths. For that was what he was looking for : he has found the
nourishment he needed.

Yes, some people vibrate in response to the sun, to the life of the sun, and others go to sleep : the sun means nothing to them. If they only knew ! When the sun gets up in the morning, it is not only animals and plants and a few human beings who are there, but all the luminous spirits of nature are there to rejoice and draw strength from it. The whole of creation, all creatures draw strength from the sun. Each creature, according to its degree of evolution, harvests the particles it needs : plants take what they need to produce colourful, scented flowers ; trees take what they need to produce fruit. As for man, although he is not actually built like a tree, he has a great many points in common with a tree, and he, too, must produce fruit. Without the sun, man's fruits would always be hard and unripe. Just as a tree needs sunshine in order to bear delicious fruit, so man needs to expose himself to the light of the sun in order to stop being so vicious, cruel and selfish and learn to produce luscious fruit. In each case the law is the same : one has to expose oneself to the light of the sun.

Today, I want to tell you about yet another aspect of the sun which you can use in your spiritual work.

In the Apocalypse, St John says, 'And I saw a new heaven and a new earth, for the first heaven and the first earth had passed away.' Does this mean that the first heaven and the first earth had become obsolete and worn out ? At a stretch you might think that the earth could get old for it is, after all, made of materials which are not always of the very highest quality and, with time, it could get a bit shabby. But heaven is supposed to be made of absolutely pure, luminous, eternal materials which never tarnish or rust, so how could it get old ? Also, since Genesis tells us that when the Lord created heaven and earth, He looked at them and 'saw that they were good', how could He now find that the earth He had created was not so good after all, and that He was going to have to make another one ? This does not say much for the perfection of God ! Besides, where could we put all the inhabitants while the renovations are going on ? They would probably be furious and start sending petitions, and that would mean still more problems for the Lord ! Obviously, all that is utter nonsense, so we shall have to interpret things differently.

Heaven and earth represent a unit, they are not two separate entities, and this is true in man himself : heaven is the head and earth the belly. Heaven, therefore, is the spiritual part of man and the earth is his manifestations. In the language of Initiates, the language of eternal symbols, a 'new heaven' means new ideas, a new perception and understanding, a new philosophy ; and a 'new earth' means a new behaviour, a new way of doing things ; in other words, a new way of thinking and a new way of living. Our heads are in heaven and our feet are on earth. The feet walk in the direction indicated by the head ; they go where the head leads them, into terrain that it, the head, has already explored. In other words, man's behaviour, the things he does and the way he does them, will change in line with the changed head, that is to say, the new philosophy.

But is this new heaven that God is busy creating really new ? No, not really : it has been there for all eternity, but to human beings, it will be new. It has always been there but they have never seen it, so when they discover it all of a sudden, it will seem new. A new heaven and a new earth ! In point of fact we don't even know what the word 'new' means. Look at any river : the Seine, the Danube or the Thames ; the name remains the same but the water is always new. And the sun, also, is always new, for its emanations and radiations are always different. What is new is life, the content ; once one rises high enough to know the content, life itself, then one sees that everything is new. 'A new heaven and a new earth', therefore, means that human beings will go to greater heights where they will discover that which has always existed but which they have never known. The situation with the sun is exactly the same : the sun has always been there but man has never understood it. As long as our hearts have not learned to rejoice in the sun, as long as we do not contemplate it and yearn to resemble it, it means that we have still not discovered it, that we are still in the outdated, worm-eaten, mouldy heaven of the past.

The new earth will be a new way of behaving, of doing things ; new ways of eating, breathing and using our eyes, and this new earth is nearer every day. But everything has to begin with the new heaven, that is to say, with the sun : start by seeing how luminous it is and how warm, vivifying, beautiful and pure, how noble, powerful and generous, and how it represents all glory and every quality and virtue. Such is the new heaven which will soon dawn for man ! And it is the sun that is going to open our eyes to this heaven which has always existed and in which dwell the Initiates, great Masters and Prophets who have left this earth, as well as the Angels, Archangels and Divinities. This is the heavenly dwelling that Jesus called 'My father's house', and many, many beings inhabit it. It is certainly not this heaven that will ever need to be changed, improved or renovated in any way, for it renews itself constantly ; it is never the same. And, similarly, the sun is never the same either, for all that energy, light, warmth and life that flows through it is always new and different.

And now you will be wondering whether you can dwell in this heaven. Why, yes, of course. Today and every day you can be a part of it : every time you entertain pure thoughts and feelings, every time you decide to work for a high ideal, you are already in the new heaven, and the new heaven inevitably brings the new earth with it. For he who embraces a sublime philosophy is obliged to change his behaviour and his way of doing things. All the methods that you are learning here with regard to nutrition, breathing, words and gestures : all this is the new earth.

Yes, and this new earth is going to oblige you to adopt a new attitude towards creation as a whole. Last winter, at Videlinata, I touched on this question. I remember I said, 'Do you want me to show you just a tiny particle of the new earth ? Very well : when I leave my chalet in the morning to go to the lecture hall,

I look at the sun and the mountains, the lake, the forest and the sparkling snow and I speak to them, just as I speak to all the luminous creatures of nature. I raise my hand to them in greeting and tell them how beautiful they are.' There are not very many human beings who make this kind of gesture because, in their view, everything is dead and nature is empty : so why try to speak to it ? Yes, but people like that are still living on the old earth, they never make the slightest gesture of friendship towards creation. If they only knew what forces a little gesture like that can trigger and set in motion ! The man who dwells on the new earth feels protected and cherished by the whole of creation, because he knows that it is alive and conscious ; he recognizes it and greets it as a friend. Yes, but you have to change your whole attitude and dwell in the new heaven before you can make even this simple gesture.

As a matter of fact, even the planet earth, this little speck of dust which took billions and billions of years to reach its present state of development, even the earth changes and transforms itself. The earth's etheric body is never the same. It is in constant contact with the sun and the stars from which it constantly receives new elements and, one day, thanks to all its hard work, it will become transparent, crystalline and translucent and will shine as brightly as the sun. At the moment the earth is still unripe, but the heat of the sun is making it ripen, and one day it will be a delicious, ripe fruit, just like the sun. For the father of the earth is the sun, and children always end by resembling their parents. At the moment, the earth is like a rather drab little girl, but one day she will be as brilliant as her father, the sun. When this day comes, human beings will be living on other planets, they will have left the earth to the animals, and then it will be the turn of animals to be educated, instructed and cared for. Yes, animals will become much more intelligent, more beautiful and expressive ; in fact, some of them will play the piano, write books and give interminable speeches !

A new light is dawning, my dear brothers and sisters, and

everything will be alive, clear, luminous and harmonious. There will be no more quarrels, revolutions or wars on the new earth. There will be such harmony and unity amongst men that they will be as one great family, and brotherliness and peace will reign throughout the world. But I have already told you about the raging tempests and disasters man is going to have to experience before all this can come about ; and these events are coming nearer ! But after the torment, peace will be restored and those who are alive then will ascertain the truth of my words. For the moment, put all the new information you have received to good use in striving to attain perfection.

So, there you have a few words of explanation about the new heaven and the new earth. It is time, now, to enter that new heaven, that is to say, to adopt the new philosophy and put it into practice. And it is this, the putting into practice, that constitutes the new earth. But, as you see, all this has to be understood symbolically, otherwise none of it makes sense. The same thing is true for the prophecies in the Gospels : Jesus said, 'In those days, after that tribulation, the sun will be darkened, and the moon will not give its light... the stars of heaven will fall', and there are Christians who take it all quite literally and who are waiting for the sun to grow dark and the stars to start falling on our heads. But it seems to me that our poor little planet is so tiny that nothing could possibly fall onto it. A single star is thousands of times bigger than the earth : what a business it would be if they all started to fall on us at once ! I suppose someone will blow a whistle and then they'll fall, all together, just to please the ignoramuses of this world ! No, the stars are going to stay just where they are. They don't even know of the existence of the speck of dust that calls itself earth, with its population of microbes so busy discussing religion and philosophy : whatever would make them want to fall on it ? No, the stars are not going to fall from the heavens. But, symbolically, a great many 'stars' are going to fall : those who shine with earthly glory, those who have been put on a pedestal without having deserved it. When the new heaven and new earth are established they will be toppled from their perches and banished.

The sun that is going to be darkened is the human philosophy which claims to enlighten mankind. In those days it will be darkened, that is to say it will no longer be capable of solving the new problems that arise. The sun which has guided human beings for so long is going to lose its light. As for the moon, it represents religious beliefs and they, too, will lose their brightness, for they are too vague and nebulous : they will be seen to be inadequate. Yes, in his prophecy Jesus spoke of the sun, moon and stars, but he was not talking about those we see in the heavens. The fact that all the so-called prophets and prophetesses have always been mistaken in their calculations and predictions makes this very obvious.

I have often had letters from prophetesses, foretelling the day on which the sun would be darkened and everything would come to an end, but such predictions only made me smile because, naturally, I knew that they were not true. And then, when the fatal day had come and gone and nothing had happened, I would have more letters from the prophetess, telling me that she had made a mistake, but that she had calculated the whole thing all over again, and this time she knew the exact date. And I ? I just went on smiling. It does not cost anything to smile after all ! And, once again, the new day came and went and, once again, a new series of letters arrived ! How is it possible that Christians have never got any further. Some of them are still waiting for Christ to appear, riding on a cloud : they have been waiting for 2,000 years and he still has not come ! What is holding him up ? Well, they can go on waiting — in fact I suggest they adopt the Tino Rossi song, '*J'attendrai*', as their theme-song ! But the trouble is that they are so busy waiting that they still have not begun to work ! And when He does come, I suppose they will parade through the streets singing, 'Arise, awake ! The Lord has come !' And then what a feasting, with turkeys and chickens and lambs slaughtered to celebrate the coming of Christ ! You only have to see how Christians celebrate Christmas, the New Year and Easter by slaughtering hundreds of innocent animals to fill their own stomachs ! Well I am not waiting for the coming of Christ because he has already come. Yes, he has come, he is coming and he will come. For the wise, the Initiates, he has already come, for disciples he is coming and for all the others who have not even begun to understand, he will come, but no one knows when.

Now, I want to talk to you about spiritual grafting. But before I do so, let me remind you of what I have already explained about stereotypes or imprints. I told you that when you read a piece of music, for example, for the first time, or tried to memorize a text, you should not try to run through it quickly. Everything leaves its imprint on the matter of your brain, just as type prints a letter on a piece of paper, and you must be extremely attentive so that the first stereotype may be faultless. If you make a mistake from haste or inattention, that same mistake will crop up again every time in exactly the same place.

And now, if we transpose this onto another plane, and look at how human beings go about life, we see that they are not good psychologists : they rush at situations and other people with a total lack of attention, delicacy or precision, with the result that they make all kinds of blunders which they go on repeating for the rest of their lives. Later, of course, they attempt to remedy their mistakes, but without success : they repeat the same clumsy errors, the same failings and vices for the rest of their days. And finally, when they see the futility of their efforts to do better and repair their errors, they give way to disappointment and despair, some, even, to the point of suicide. Why do they fail so miserably ? Because they are ignorant, they know nothing of how man is constructed or of the relations between his feelings, thoughts and actions and, owing to this ignorance, they are unable to straighten out their lives.

The stereotypes in our brains are etheric and, therefore, invisible, and you will, perhaps, understand this better if I illustrate it with an example. What is a seed ? A seed is a stereotype. You cannot see the lines of force traced on it, but if you sow it and water it and allow the sun to warm it, you will soon see, first a shoot and then a stem, pushing up out of the ground. All the necessary instructions have been written into the seed from the start, by a very intelligent hand ; how could one explain its perfect proportions and the beauty of the mature plant if it did not contain a secret blueprint to define the lines of force and channel the energies at work in the growing seed ? Similarly, if certain human beings are continually impelled to commit a particular type of crime, it is because they have inner stereotypes which are like lines of force constantly urging them to do so. At some moment in the past — we cannot know exactly when ; perhaps in this life or in a previous incarnation — they entertained a thought or feeling or committed an act which etched itself into the etheric matter of the brain. And once this etching exists, that original act or thought or feeling goes on repeating itself, for nature is faithful and true. If you start putting your hand into other people's pockets, you will soon find that the habit has become stronger than you ; you will not be able to stop your little 'voyages of exploration' ! This is what they call kleptomania ! Ah, yes : all the vices go by scientific names, nowadays ! This reminds me of the man who went to see his doctor. He said, 'Listen, Doctor, I feel terrible ; tell me what's wrong with me. But for goodness' sake, no Greek or Latin ; tell me in plain language so that I can understand.' So, after he had examined him, the doctor said, 'Well, it's nothing complicated : you're a glutton and a drunkard ; that's all !' 'For God's sake, Doctor', said the patient ; 'I can't tell my wife that. Give me a Greek or Latin word I can repeat to her !'

Everybody wants to experience as many sensations as possible, to see, hear, taste and touch everything. It is the fashion of the day. They have to try everything, all the pleasures, passions and follies, just once. Yes, that is what they say : 'Just once !' and then they get accustomed to it, the stereotype is there and they are incapable of undoing the damage. And yet there is a science that you should know, for it would enable you not only to remedy your faults and passions and inferior tendencies, but even to benefit from them. This is the science of grafting.

As you know, grafting is something that man has learned to do in order to improve the quality of fruit. For instance, you can graft a slip from a cultivated pear tree which gives sweet, succulent fruit, onto the stock of a wild pear tree which is very sturdy and vigorous, but which produces only hard, inedible fruit. The cutting will benefit from the vigour of the wild stock and produce delicious, juicy pears. Human beings have become pastmasters in techniques of this kind, but when it comes to the psychic or spiritual domain they are not nearly so capable or ingenious. One sees so many distinguished people : scientists, well-known writers and artists, philosophers and statesmen, all in the grip of some vice or passion and incapable of freeing themselves from it. So many artists of talent — of genius even — drank, took drugs or ruined themselves at the gaming tables or with women ! There is no point in telling you their names, but they have all gone to the grave with their weaknesses still intact. If they had only known the rules of spiritual grafts they could have grafted all kinds of qualities and virtues onto their weaknesses.

Now, how is this done ? Suppose, for instance, that you have a very loving nature, but that your love is very sensual. You can look on it as a great strength, use it as you would a tall, vigorous tree and harness its energies to nourish and strengthen a cutting from another kind of love, a love that is pure, noble and disinterested. The sap produced by your lower nature will rise and circulate through the new branches, that is, through the new stereotypes, the new circuits etched into your brain, and produce magnificent fruit, the fruit of a prodigious love which will enrapture and inspire you in ways you never thought possible.

Or perhaps it is your overweening vanity which absorbs all your energies : there, too, you can graft a quality onto it. Instead of always trying to be great and glorious in the eyes of the world, in the eyes of gossips and gawking idiots, you must set to work to seek the glory of Heavenly things, a divine, unalterable glory which will never fade.

If you have a violent temper it is more than likely that, in a fit of rage, you have already destroyed more than one friendship and spoiled your chances of future promotion. Well, instead of letting the blind force of your anger explode like a thunderbolt, you can do a graft and transform and sublimate it. If you do this you will be tireless in the battle against all your weaknesses and evil tendencies ; you will become a valiant servant of God, an invincible soldier of Christ. Instead of creating havoc and laying waste all around you, your Martian energies can be used to build something positive. All you have to do is to find a cutting to graft onto them.

You may say, 'I have read about such and such a hero, saint or prophet who lived in the past, and I find his life tremendously inspiring. I have great admiration for him. Do you think he could provide me with a graft ?' It is quite possible. The only trouble is that, as someone like that existed a long time ago, you cannot be in close touch with him and talk to him as you could with a living being. In fact, even if you choose a human being who is still alive — a friend, a renowned philosopher or artist, for instance — and whom you admire greatly, the graft would still be somewhat imperfect, because everybody has some weakness or defect. No one is absolutely strong, luminous, powerful, warm and generous. Ah, but there is someone who is infinitely more intelligent, more loving, more powerful and more generous than anyone you could ever find on earth, and who has a storehouse full of cuttings which are ideal for the grafts you need : and that being is the sun ! He is the one you have to go to for your cuttings.

From now on, when you are in front of the rising sun, speak to him and ask him for the grafts you need : 'Oh, Sun, my friend, there are so many things I'd love to understand, but my intelligence is so limited. But you who are all light, you who give light to the whole world, I know how generous you are : please give me a few little cuttings from your immense intelligence !'

And he will, you know ! He'll give them to you free of charge, and you can graft them into your brain. In fact, if you are not sure how to set about it, he will even send you an expert to help you ! Then you can ask him for other cuttings : kindness, beauty or wisdom, for example. You can ask him for all the cuttings you need ; he has them all. But don't ask for them all at the same time, you would not be able to graft them all at once and some of them would wilt and die from lack of attention. Ask for them one by one.

Several of you are wondering if I'm making fun of you : and the answer is, 'No, absolutely not !' I am perfectly serious about this. I have used these methods myself, for years, and I can assure you that they are very effective. In fact there are many other things I have not told you about grafting, but what you don't learn from me you will learn directly from the sun. Everything I know has been revealed to me by the sun. You may be astonished to hear that the sun can reveal things to human beings, but it is true, nevertheless !

Of course, it is possible to use cuttings from a great Master, because he represents the sun. But still, you cannot really compare a Master with the sun ! True, a human being can resemble the sun to the extent to which he spreads warmth, light and life to those who approach him. But the sun gives light, warmth and nourishment to the entire world ; every living thing which grows and reaches maturity, every creature that lives and moves on this earth does so thanks to the sun. An Initiate can do some good to mankind but he can never have such power as this : no mortal can be compared to the sun.

I want to be sure that you understand exactly what I am saying : only the sun's rays are capable of replacing all that is impure, worn out or obscure within you, and they can only do so if you learn how to receive them. If you welcome them with your whole heart, they will begin their work of replacing the 'old man' in you, so that you will be wholly regenerated, renewed and resuscitated ; your thoughts, feelings and acts will all be different.

Only the sun's rays are capable of working this transformation within you, nothing else. Unfortunately, human beings, who experience all kinds of enjoyable sensations when they are eating and drinking, smoking or kissing each other, feel nothing when they are in the presence of the sun. And this is because they are on too low a vibratory level : the lowest levels of reality make a great impression on them, whereas they are impervious to sunlight. But when a disciple begins to advance and evolve, he becomes more sensitive to the sun's rays and they give him revelations and raptures and truly heavenly sensations.

And this, too, is something new : psychology has not yet discovered that it is we who determine whether or not the effects produced within our hearts and souls by the sun's rays will be powerful enough to regenerate and resuscitate us. And, in view of this, of course, we have to prepare ourselves, for otherwise the sun will always be a stranger to us. One has to prepare for days, even months, in advance, so as to be perfectly calm, free and lucid and capable of tuning in to the power and the divine purity of the sun's rays.

I have studied the nature of the sun's rays and I find that they are like so many little wagons filled with food : they contain all we shall ever need for our food and drink and understanding, all that we shall ever need to become active, happy and intelligent. But human beings are so ignorant and inattentive that they let them slip by, and then start calling for help and complaining that they are hungry and thirsty ! And yet everything they need is within hand's reach in the rays of sunlight. And if you only knew who sends us these little wagons ! There are many beings in the sun who are far, far superior to us, and they look down and smile at us (if they had not got such perfect manners, they might even laugh a little at our expense), and I have heard them saying, 'Oh, look at all those dear little children on the Rock. They may not seem to be anything out of the ordinary at the moment, but one day they will be divinities.' Yes, their hope, faith and love are truly extraordinary ! They are the only ones who are really convinced that we shall end by being divinities. Here, on earth, nobody believes it ; but they believe it ! I have also heard them saying, 'Isn't that nice to see so many of them, there : they are there because of us. Of course, they are still a bit drowsy ; they don't know that we are smiling at them and holding out all kinds of gifts to them ; they are unaware of us. They are immersed in memories of the past : what they have eaten and drunk, how they fought with So-and-so, how they kissed and made love. What can we do to attract their attention ? But there is always hope. True, they're nothing to write home about for the moment, but when they grow up they're going to be divinities.' And these beings are happy because of their hope. Don't you believe me ? Well, go and find out for yourselves ? They are the only ones who are quite confident that, one day, we shall be true children of God.

There : that is what I wanted to tell you. But, remember, you must prepare yourselves ; you are never sufficiently prepared. How often have I already told you : 'Get ready in advance for the sunrise ; go to bed the night before with the thought that it is the Lord Himself that you will gaze on tomorrow in the sun.' But do you do this ? Do you ever prepare yourselves ? No, and that is why the years go by and, in spite of all the hours you have spent looking at the sun, you have still understood and discovered nothing ! You should have discovered the meaning of life, years ago, from looking at the sun ; for he and he alone can open your eyes to the meaning of life. Have you any idea what it is that enables me continually to advance and make progress ? It is the fact that, every morning, I realize more acutely that I have still not really any idea of the greatness of the sun. Each day, I say to myself, 'Well, yesterday I thought I knew the sun and now, today, I see that I had not really understood anything at all. But at last I'm beginning to understand.' And the following day I find myself saying exactly the same thing, whereas you always think you know everything. Your reaction is always to say, 'I know, I know. That's old stuff !' Yes, each day I realize that I have still not understood the immensity, the splendour of the sun. When one begins to think that there is nothing left to discover, that one knows it all, one begins to stagnate and become mummified, and all hope of progress comes to an end. You must never do that ; you must continually tell yourselves : 'Today, for the first time, I'm beginning to see the sun ; today I'm going to begin to understand', and this will help you to advance steadily, little by little, every day. You see ? Yet another new and marvellously effective method.

The Bonfin, August 23, 1967

The Sun Has the Solution
to the Problem of Love — Telesma

What a sunrise ! Wasn't it absolutely extraordinary ? It was even more glorious, more extraordinary, than all the others ! Really and truly, today we have seen heavenly glory and purity, heavenly splendour. It is beyond the power of words to express ! The only thing I feel like saying, all day long, is 'Thank you, thank you, thank you.'

The sun, as I have already told you, can solve all our problems ; in particular, it can solve the one problem which torments everybody : the problem of love and sexuality. People look for solutions to this problem from every quarter. They go to biologists, doctors and psychoanalysts. They study the experiments attempted in Holland, Denmark and the United States, but the poor things find only contradictory answers to their questions. And I ? Well, I am telling you that the solution to all the problems arising from sexuality can be found in the sun. Yes, the sun alone can give you the secret, and it is a particularly important secret in our day, when people reject all the old moral traditions and have to find inspiration within themselves.

Are you curious to know what the secret of the sun is ? I wonder what you have done in the past to earn this privilege ! No, my dear brothers and sisters, it is something too precious ;

I cannot reveal it to you, but if you seek for it sincerely you will find it for yourselves. It is the most important revelation man can receive from the sun, and you must ask him for it. Just so long as you refuse to consider the sun as an intelligent being, he will give you nothing. He will teach you nothing. Henceforth, when you come up to the sunrise, ask him with all your heart and soul to reveal his secret to you, and then wait. He will make you feel the answer. For, of course, the sun does not talk as we do ; he speaks through silence ; he sends waves and particles and we have to decipher them. Once you have learned to listen to what the sun is saying and to interpret his words, you will be amazed to find that he is, in all truth, capable of solving every problem, even the toughest and most inextricable. But before you can experience this, you have to stop regarding the sun as something lifeless and purely mechanical ; you have to believe that he is a living being, the most powerful and intelligent of beings ; that he is endowed with a higher, sublime, divine consciousness, that he possesses eternal wisdom and absolute power. In this way you can actually make contact with him, your vibrations will be more and more attuned to his, a relationship of genuine communication will begin to exist between you, and you will begin to receive inner revelations. New conceptions and the light of a new understanding will develop within you without your even being aware that it is the sun that has put them there.

As I have already told you, the most perfect yoga that I have ever found is Surya-yoga, for it is the yoga of immensity, the yoga of fulfilment and abundance, the yoga of eternity and absolute splendour. You can practise the other yogas if you wish, but you risk wasting many years with nothing to show for them. Whereas here, even if you sleep, you can still get some benefit from the sun, he will still give you a few particles. He can see that you had very wonderful and praiseworthy intentions in coming up here, so even if you have gone to sleep along the way, it is not too shameful. The sun is indulgent and merciful ; he says, 'He's only a child, so even if he's fallen asleep, let's give him something.

After all, he meant well ; his intention was divine.' Whereas with
the other kinds of yoga, Hatha-yoga, for example, which is so
popular in the West today, if you get tired or go to sleep during
your exercises, no one will come and hold you up or help you :
you are left to your own devices. You have to do your breathing
exercises and get yourself into all sorts of postures, with your head
on the ground and your legs in the air, and if you cannot do them
or do them incorrectly, even if you work at it for years, you will
get nothing out of it... unless, of course, you actually do yourself
harm ! Whereas Surya-yoga is, as you see, a very beneficial form
of yoga. In fact, there is nothing to prevent you, afterwards, from
doing all the other kinds of yoga that we have talked about :
Surya-yoga will probably help you to do them much better.

When you are preparing to go out hiking for the day, or to
go on a journey, you see to it that you are properly equipped :
you take a packet of sandwiches and even, possibly, a bottle of
something to bolster your courage from time to time, on the way !
Well, that is exactly what you are doing here : before leaving for
the day, you come up here. For the sunrise is a special kind of
shop where you can find the sandwiches and water (or rakia or
sake, if you prefer) you need to keep you going for the rest of
the day ; then you set off on your expedition, knowing that your
knapsack is full of all those good things you received at the sunrise
in the morning. Yes, the sunrise is a spring of clear water, a shop
full of delicious foods of every kind. If you don't want to draw
on the supplies it offers, your sack will remain empty, and when
you go off on a long journey, that is to say, when you go twenty
yards or so lower down to visit your beloved and talk to her and
contemplate her... well, it is a pity, but you will be so empty and
tired and inexpressive that you will be unable to give her anything.
You must come up to the sunrise so as to be better able to look
at her and talk to her, so as to be better able to lead your beloved
Heavenwards.

But let's leave all that ; I can hear myself giving you all these
arguments and they strike me as so miserable, so inadequate, that

I don't want to continue. When the sun is so luminous and radiant, so full of love, I become speechless. I feel so happy, so
deeply enraptured, but when I try to express some of that in words,
I cannot find them, they have all flown away in the direction of
the sun, and I have to fly after them and try to get them back.
Even words are so enchanted by the sun that they leave us and
there is no getting them back !

And now, how are you feeling ? I must say I have the privilege
of being in the best position in relation to the sun for it is behind
me, and one receives more energy through one's back. Yes, you
should expose your back to the sun from time to time because
the roots of the chakras lie along the spinal column, and when
you have your back to the sun they absorb the solar energies which
can set them in motion.

I think this must be the most feeble lecture I have ever given
you ! Although in fact, for me, it is one of the most substantial,
for I have been speaking to you with all my soul, all my heart
and all my spirit. Ah, but I can hear you saying : 'What about
that secret about love that you were talking about earlier ? Aren't
you going to tell us ?' If I reveal this secret to you it will scan-
dalize many Christian consciences. That is why I do not dare to
talk about it. Human beings have their own ideas about things,
and they never seem to think that God might see things differently.
It was God, after all, who created the sun, and the sun is a model
for us ; a model through which God teaches us how to love and
how to understand love in a way that helps us to be healthy and
well balanced. But I have very little confidence in Christians, I
am afraid they are going to be the last ones to understand this
great mystery of cosmic, divine love.

Thousands of years ago, many Buddhists, Hindus, Tibetans,
Sufis and Cabbalists understood exactly what had to be
understood, with the result that they now benefit from untold
strength, beauty, intelligence and clairvoyance. If Christians had

understood the Gospels, they would have realized that Jesus knew the secret I am talking about. Yes, he knew it, but he revealed it only to his disciples ; others were not ready to understand it.

So, I advise you to ask the sun to reveal his secret about love to you. I cannot risk explaining it to you because some of you are not yet instructed or enlightened, or not sufficiently sure of their directions, and it would be dangerous to reveal things to them that would be so far beyond their powers of comprehension : either they would lose their heads or they would turn on me and rend me. You know what Jesus said : 'Cast not your pearls before swine, lest they trample them under their feet, and turn and tear you in pieces.'

The greatest of all Initiates, the father of Initiatic Science, not only in Egypt but in the whole world, Hermes Trismegistus, whose name signifies 'three times greatest', says in the Emerald Tablet : 'This thing is the strength of all strengths for it overcomes every subtle thing and penetrates every solid substance.' This 'strength of all strengths' he calls Telesma, saying also 'Its father is the Sun, its mother the Moon. The Wind carried it in its womb, the Earth is its nurse.' And in yet another passage, he says, 'Thus you will possess the glory of the brightness of the whole world, and all obscurity will fly from you.' These few words are enough to indicate the importance of our sunrises. It means that, for the disciple who has understood that light is all-powerful, everything negative, all illness and torment will disappear and a solar strength will emanate from him which all men will be obliged to acknowledge.

You will say, 'Yes, but all that hasn't happened yet !' No, of course it has not happened yet, and it will not happen until you have understood why you have to come and contemplate the sunrise every morning. It is your degree of consciousness, the way you look at things that will make it happen.

Hermes Trismegistus penetrated the depths of nature's mysteries, and his Emerald Tablet is a summary of the whole body of ancient Wisdom, but even the alchemists failed to understand him. When Hermes Trismegistus spoke of sun, moon, air and earth he was really talking about the four elements, whereas alchemists used the same words to express something quite different. And yet it is all quite clear and simple. It is the four elements that produce that 'strength of all strengths' which he calls Telesma. All the magi and magicians, occultists or sorcerers who make talismans, attempt to imbue objects with the force of Telesma (hence the name, talisman), but they do not always know where it comes from nor how to capture and direct it. And yet Hermes Trismegistus said it quite clearly : 'Its father is the Sun' ; it must be sought, therefore, in the sun. 'Its mother is the Moon' ; the lower aspect of the moon represents the world of illusion, delirium and madness, whereas its higher aspect symbolizes the world of purity of the divine life. It is this higher aspect of the moon that is the mother of Telesma. The sun, therefore, the father, produces this force, and the wind, that is to say, air, carries it to the womb of its mother, the moon, who begins her work on it. But this force, which Hermes Trismegistus speaks of as though it were a child, needs to be nourished, and it is the earth that nourishes it.

Hermes Trismegistus said it quite clearly, therefore : there is a force that comes from the sun. And as the sun is going to be more and more important in the future, you must hurry up and understand it and acquire a new consciousness toward it, so that you will be ready and prepared to receive the fragrance and strength flowing from it. Behind the light of the sun are many other forces, and Telesma is a force so potent that, as the Emerald Tablet puts it, 'it overcomes every subtle thing and penetrates every solid substance'. But, for this force to be truly effective on the physical plane, it must be 'fixed', it must become earth ; 'it descends to Earth, and unites in itself the force from things superior and things inferior' says Hermes Trismegistus. In its original state, this force is fire ; and the fire must become earth. Fire is volatile and earth is fixed. And here we find the two terms, 'volatile' and 'fixed' which alchemists used so widely. In other words, this very subtle force has to crystallize and condense and become solid matter ; only on this condition can it be all-powerful, not otherwise. This is what Hermes Trismegistus implies, but he veils the truth so well that you could read the Emerald Tablet hundreds of times and still not see it.

This is what the sun revealed to me. 'What ?' you will say ; 'Can the sun really reveal things like that ?' Indeed he can ; after all, he is the source of all things, so he is well able to reveal all the mysteries. Obviously, this work of bringing the force of Telesma down and condensing it in our own cells until it becomes a tangible, material reality, is a gigantic task which demands a very long time, years and even centuries, and a great deal of hard work. You can also see this idea expressed in the interlaced triangles which form the Seal of Solomon.

The lower triangle which points upwards is a symbol of matter which must rise to a higher plane and grow increasingly subtle until it virtually disappears into infinity. Whereas the higher triangle, which points downwards, is a symbol of the spirit which descends into the matter of the physical body until, eventually, it substitutes its own matter for the denser, physical matter of the body. In reality both triangles continue to exist, but under another form : the apex of the first touches the heavens, and that of the second touches the depths of the subconscious. And the combination of the two together produce perfection and fulfilment.

Those who are capable of understanding will understand me. Everything I say to you converges on just one idea : matter must be spiritualized and the spirit must be materialized. The betrothed bride speeds upwards to greet her beloved as he descends from the heavenly regions, and they embrace and become one somewhere in space. When the spirit descends into the deepest reaches of a human being, all his native crudity and passion disappears, making way for the magnanimity, nobility, intelligence, light, beauty, love, purity and sweetness of the spirit.

The whole of a disciple's work is summed up in this. Whatever you undertake, whatever may be your profession, whatever books you read, whatever exercises or experiments you do, they must all contribute to the attainment of this one goal : the spiritualization of matter and the materialization of the spirit. In summing this up in these few words I am practising Nature's way of doing things : condensing and developing. Nature condenses a whole tree in a single seed. But if you plant that seed, it will develop to such an extent that a whole lifetime would not be enough to analyze all that it produces ! And this new tree, in turn, with all its fruit and flowers, can be condensed and summed up, once again, in a single seed.

The Initiates, who imitate Nature, have managed to condense the whole of their great knowledge into the Tarot, for instance. But if you want to understand it, you have to become familiar with their methods. The cards of the Tarot are like seeds : they have to be planted, watered and cared for and, if you do this, great trees, animals, living beings and worlds will grow out of them ! When you see this you will realize that those who created the Tarot were highly skilled in the art of symbols. For a symbol is nothing more than a complex body of laws, truths and concepts all summarized and presented in the simplest of geometrical figures : a triangle, a circle, a square, a cross or a cone. And, incidentally, children show themselves to be true Initiates when they draw a man with two or three simple lines. If you cannot understand what I am saying it is because you are not Initiates. A child who draws a man like that is summarizing the man, but you have to understand !

The Bonfin, August 30, 1967

Chapter Fifteen

The Sun is in the Image and Likeness of God — 'In Spirit and in Truth'

A few days ago I was talking to a brother, and in the course of our conversation we came to the subject of the Blessed Trinity. The brother was a Christian and, as is the case for most Christians, the question was not at all clear for him. But what can be done about it ? How can one lead men to the light if they persist in not wanting to study Initiatic Science, the only science capable of giving us clear, precise, coherent ideas. In fact, you could say that the difference between an ordinary thinker and an Initiate is that the Initiate has a framework in his head, a structured pattern which enables him to see the world as a great edifice in which each individual element has its place, whereas in the head of non-Initiates all the disparate elements are scattered and disconnected. In these conditions how can they possibly have an accurate idea of the cosmos with all the entities and forces at work in it ?

Unfortunately, this is how schools and families continue to educate their children. No one has ever introduced them to the idea of the unity of creation, of the connecting links which bind the world of the spirit to the worlds of the soul and of the physical body. Even those who believe in the spirit have no clear idea of what Hermes Trismegistus meant when he said, 'For this reason I am called Hermes Trismegistus, because I possess the wisdom of the three worlds.' Hermes Trismegistus did not name the three worlds, but by these words he was saying that he knew the framework that held the universe together, that he had seen how the different regions were interconnected and how the spirits go up and down from one region to another. This is exactly what is expressed in the Bible, in the tale of Jacob's ladder. This great ladder which reached all the way to Heaven and on which Jacob saw 'the angels of God ascending and descending', is simply the image of the hierarchy which exists in the universe and which includes all beings, from the lowliest creature all the way up to God Himself. People have no inkling even that this hierarchy exists, and even religious people have a very vague notion of it, for no one has ever taught them about it.

In the Old and New Testaments there are a few indications which can be taken as clues and pointers left by the Initiates, Apostles and Prophets, and it is up to us to use these materials to reconstruct the edifice. Take the case of the Archangels, for example : the Christian religion mentions only four : Uriel, Gabriel, Raphael and Michael ; that is all. No mention of any others. But then one wonders, 'Isn't that a bit niggardly ? Is it possible that there are only four archangels for a universe so immense we do not even know where it ends ?' But the Cabbalah gives us the whole picture, for there have been people, in the past, who travelled great distances to contemplate this hierarchy and who have left us a record of their findings. So we know that there is a hierarchy of angels under the command not only of those four archangels but of others as well. But you know all that : I have already talked to you about the Sephirotic Tree of Life a long time ago, so you already know how to work with it.

So, as I was saying, I was discussing the Blessed Trinity with this brother, and I asked him to tell me what the Father, Son and Holy Spirit represented for him. Of course, he gave me the answer that all religious people give : God is the Father, and He is Omnipotence ; Christ is the Son, and He is Love, and the Holy Spirit is the Consoler. 'You are very near to the truth,' I told him ; 'But it is not clear. Let me try to help you to understand by showing you what happens in life, in nature. I do this because if I begin by giving you my own opinion you will think that there is no reason why it should be any more valid than yours, and no one will know who is right. If we want to find out the truth about something we have to turn to an authority on the matter, to someone or something eternal and unchanging, that never makes a mistake. This is why we have to ask Nature herself what she thinks about it.' This idea was quite a surprise for the brother ; it had never occurred to him that we have to verify our ideas and opinions by referring to the highest authority : Nature.

And I went on : 'But, first let's see what the Scriptures say ; we'll consult Nature later. We read in the Book of Genesis, "Then God said, 'Let Us make man in Our image, according to Our likeness'." And a little further on, it says, "So God created man in His own image ; in the image of God He created him." Why did Moses use the word "image" twice in this second passage, and leave out the word "likeness" ? This was a way of indicating that God's intention was to create man according to His likeness, but that He did not do so ; He created him only in His image. But what does it mean when we speak of the "image and likeness of God" ? Are we supposed to think that God has a nose, eyes, a mouth, a stomach and a pair of legs ? Or does "image" mean something quite different ? And what does "likeness" mean ? Take a seed : does it look like a tree ? It does not, and yet it is in the image of its parent tree ; it contains this image within it. And when you plant it, it begins to grow and to be "like" the tree.

'Image and likeness are two different things : the likeness is the perfect development of the image. If you plant an acorn it will begin to grow into an oak tree. In other words the acorn eventually becomes "like" its father, the oak, whereas it began by being in its image. But we should not conclude from this that if God created us in His image, it means that He has eyes and ears and hair like ours ; these details are totally unimportant. What is important is that in each one of us there is a being who thinks, feels and acts ; it is that being that is in the image of God, for God also thinks, feels and acts. Yes, but since man does not possess the omnipotence, omniscience or infinite love of God, he does not think, feel or act exactly as God does, so he is only in His image ; not in His likeness. Besides, the fact that man committed a fault back there, in Paradise, makes it obvious that he was not in God's likeness. When he has grown up and become fully mature he will be like Him ; but for the moment, man is just a tiny seed.

'The same phenomenon can be seen in a child. When a child is very young he is still only in the image of his father or mother : he does not yet have their intelligence, strength or love ; he is not interested in the good of others, he is only concerned with himself and his own wants, and he eats and drinks and cries and screams to get what he wants. But as he grows up, he begins to be like his father, and learns to reflect and work and think of others and make sacrifices for them.

'But a disciple's ideal is more exalted than that of resembling his earthly parents. In the past it was the tradition for a son to follow in his father's footsteps : if the father was a cooper, a smith, a carpenter or a gangster, his son took up the same trade. There is nothing wrong in that, of course, but it is not particularly glorious ! Our ideal is to come, one day, to resemble our Heavenly Father or, to be accurate, the Blessed Trinity, since Father, Son and Holy Spirit are inseparable. But how ? What means can we use to attain this likeness ? The Initiates searched the whole of creation for a model, and they found none more perfect or ideal than the sun.

'Let's look at the sun's role in nature. The sun is light, heat and life. If we take light to represent intelligence, heat to represent love and life to represent power and the will, we see that the sun is not only in the image of God, it is also in His likeness, because it is not limited and restricted as man is ; on the contrary, it is so rich in light, heat and life that it is capable of illuminating, heating and vivifying the planets. So, if you want to understand the Trinity you have to question the sun. The Father is He who creates, He is the Source of the life which manifests itself in the form of light, heat, movement, etc. ; you can think of the Son, Christ, as heat or love, and the Holy Spirit as Light, for it is He who brings revelation and gives the power to prophesy and foresee the future and to speak in tongues.

'You can also reverse this, if you prefer, and see the Holy Spirit as Love and Christ as Light, for Jesus said, "I am the light of the world." The only absolute in this — and this is important to understand — is that the Father represents life with its twofold manifestation : light and warmth. Can you see, now, how Nature can be our teacher ? In Nature, everything is perfectly clear and precise ; it is impossible not to be convinced.' During all this time, the brother was listening to me and agreeing with what I was saying, but he was astonished to see that we had new methods, here, which enabled us to question Nature herself about the deepest mysteries of religion.

Then I added, 'Don't you find it surprising that men appreciate and admire the works of the sun, but forget all about the sun itself ? It is he who has given us all the things we find in nature. Even gold, which men lust after so tirelessly and for which they are ready to resort to crime ; yes, even gold is the gift of the sun. And yet they turn their backs on the creator and are only interested in what he has created and which is not really him !'

There is something seriously warped in the way human beings understand things ; they forget the Prime Cause and go chasing after the husks, the slag, the dregs of creation. As long as men refuse to change their philosophy, as long as they forsake the essential for the sake of the accidental, the centre for the periphery, they are bound to come to grief. They must start by restoring the sun, the cause of everything, to his rightful place and then the rest will fall into place, first of all in their own minds and, secondly, in society, and everything will run more smoothly. Perhaps you are wondering, 'How can our attitude towards the sun have such great effects ? Surely it's an unimportant detail ?'

Yes, it seems like a mere detail, but with time, this reversal of values has led to extremely serious consequences in every area of life.

Then I questioned the brother about how he attempted to find God : 'What do you do ? Where do you look for Him ?' 'God is everywhere' he replied ; 'We can find Him in a river, a fruit, a mountain... everywhere.' 'You're quite right, of course', I agreed ; 'He is in everything ; you can find Him everywhere. But do you know the best and quickest way to find Him ?' Well, that baffled him : he did not know what to say. And it is not surprising : most people have very hazy notions about this ; even those who practise a religion. It is perfectly true, of course, that God is everywhere ; He is in the air, in water, in the hearts of men, in a child's eyes... But to say that God is everywhere is too vague, and it makes it more difficult to find Him quickly and effectively.

When you want to buy some cheese or a new pair of shoes, you know where to go ; and no one tries to buy spectacles in a hat shop ! But when it comes to finding God, in all His power, splendour, light and love, you look for Him where He is not. You will object, 'But surely, God is in church ? And in the host at Communion ? Can't we find Him there ?' Yes, of course you can find Him in a church, but what church or temple can compare to nature ? And what host can compare to the sun ? You can eat wagon-loads of hosts and still be just as vicious, jealous, sensual, stupid and sickly as ever. Whereas if you communicate every day with that immense host, the sun, you will be obliged to transform yourselves. Because nowhere does God manifest Himself with such power, light and heat as in the sun.

Since God has given us intelligence and the capacity to reason logically, we must use these gifts to reach Him. Which one of you would contradict me if, by using my reason, I arrived at the conclusion that all of man's works were worthless compared to those of the Lord ? You cannot deny that even the hosts used in your churches are made of materials supplied by the sun. And no one ever thinks of thanking the sun for them ! We take everything he produces, wheat and grapes, and never say thank you. In fact, it never occurs to us that, without the sun, we would not have a single host nor a drop of wine. Why have men been so misled ? Why have they been led to believe that the sun was unimportant and that they could find God in bread and wine ? What was the point in concealing the truth from them ? They certainly have not been helped by this, for they have been receiving the bread and wine in communion for 2,000 years now, and they are still as evil and as blind as ever. What progress has been made ?

How can anyone fail to realize that the generosity, the immensity and the eternity of God find their highest and most perfect expression in the sun ? Henceforth, my dear brothers and sisters, that is where you must go to find the Trinity : to the sun. Not to abstractions and theories, for it is not a good educational method to start with abstract, theoretical explanations. Sound pedagogical methods tell us to begin by showing children something concrete, something they can touch and see, before introducing them gradually to abstract notions. This is the method that should have been used in religion : instead of turning the Deity and the Blessed Trinity into abstractions which nobody, or almost nobody, understands, we should have begun with the concrete dimension, and led men to the sun, leaving it to those who were capable of doing so to go behind and beyond the sun, and seek the Spirit, God, the Absolute. You will say that churches, statues, candles and even the host are all concrete. Yes, they are concrete enough, but they are so limited and cold ; they are not alive. Whereas when you look at the sun you can see and feel the light, warmth and life radiating from him. Why do men prefer to pray to an abstract, intangible God in cold, dark churches ? Let them start by turning to the sun and seeking warmth, light and life in him and filling their hearts with gratitude to God ; later, if their mental faculties are up to it, they can seek an abstract God.

The day will come, in fact, when churches and temples will

no longer be useful, for human beings will go to another temple, the immense Temple of living Nature in which the celebrant is the sun and the votive lights the stars. I prophesy to you that this is what is going to happen one day. For the moment, men are not ready for this ; their outlook is still too restricted. Besides, there is nothing wrong in having churches and temples, on the contrary, it is excellent, and they are still necessary ; I have never suggested that they should be destroyed. Even a house can be a temple. But when men are ready to grasp the truth, they will stop going to man-made temples. They will worship in the great Temple built by the hand of God Himself : the universe. And then they will understand that man himself is a temple of God, and that he must progressively cleanse, purify and sanctify himself so as to be a perfect sanctuary. When this day comes every man will be always and everywhere in a temple where he can pray to the Lord, for he will be in his own temple and, at the same time, in the great Temple of the universe. This is what you see symbolized in the stained glass window behind me ; the small pentagram at the centre of the larger one : the microcosm in the macrocosm.

Through his own intelligence, purity, strength and light, man will one day be a living temple.

Today, on the pretext that you are travelling, for instance, you say, 'I can't get to church, so I can't pray ; God wouldn't hear my prayers !' What a good excuse ! But the argument is faulty ; you must be like a snail and carry your temple with you wherever you go. But none of this means that you should despise all the beautiful temples and churches that men have built with such fervour and devotion. I know how much love went into the building of the great cathedrals of the Middle Ages, for instance, and wherever my travels have taken me, to Italy, Spain, England, Greece, India or the United States, I have always visited their temples, churches and mosques, because each one, in its own special way, bears witness to the tremendous devotion to God that moved the men who built them, and this is what I admire. But I am obliged to say these things to you in order to broaden your concepts and help you to grow in your understanding of the truth. It is an excellent thing to go and pray in a temple, but why allow your own temple to decay and be defiled and desecrated by the wild animals prowling through it at will and devouring each other. If you allow this state of affairs to continue, you can be regular church-goers for years without showing any signs of improvement ! Wouldn't it be better to purify your own inner temple and make it fit for the Lord to come and dwell in it ? Why let everybody else build temples, and neglect or defile your own ?

It says in the Scriptures : 'You are the temple of the living God.' What are you waiting for, then ? Are you so accustomed to going to temples built of wood or stone which are not alive, that you take no care of your inner temple ? Of course it is true that, thanks to all the saints and faithful who have prayed in them, these temples have something living in them, but they cannot be compared to a human body that has become so pure and holy that it is a veritable temple. God hears you and grants your prayers when you pray from within your own temple, and if, at the same time, you feel yourself to be in the great Temple of the universe, then you become a whole, fulfilled being. This is what is expressed, as I have said, by the symbol of the small pentagram within the large pentagram. The large pentagram is Christ, the Cosmic Being of light, and man exists within Him. This is the notion you have to try to understand : the little temple within the great temple ; the microcosm within the macrocosm.

And now, just to be sure that I am not misleading you, let's look in the Gospels to see if it does not say that man will, one day, adore God without churches or statues or candles. Remember what Jesus said to the woman at the well who asked him if one should worship on the mountain of Samaria or in Jerusalem : 'Woman, believe me, the hour is coming when you will worship the Father neither on this mountain, nor in Jerusalem... but in spirit and truth.' Of course, we do not hear too many commentaries on these words from Christians. They prefer to ignore them, because if they took them seriously it would mean that they would have to discard or change too many things in their religion. But, having no vested interests in this area, I can interpret Jesus' words : 'In spirit and truth' means that we shall no longer adore God in material, external forms, nor with lies. But what are the temples and churches of religion and their statues ? Are they not material forms in which the faithful hear all kinds of lies ? For example, 2,000 years after the event, you are still asked to venerate a piece of the cross on which Jesus died. A whole forest of these splinters has already disappeared, but you are still shown one that was part of the True Cross ! This is a lie : and it is not the only lie you will find in the Church ; there are others which are far more serious. Jesus knew that it would be like this for some time to come, but he also knew that the day would come when men would adore God in spirit and in truth.

Look at the sun : there is no falsehood in him. He makes no promises that he fails to keep. He says, 'Come to me and I will give you light, warmth and life.' And he is not content with words ; he really does give us light, warmth and heat. We are in the temple of God every morning and the Spirit of truth is there, before our eyes, totally pure, luminous and disinterested ! Wherever else you go there is always someone who is not totally disinterested : you are always being asked to contribute, and the noise of the coins dropping into the collection plate makes prayer impossible. The fact that the noise might disturb people who are praying and meditating does not bother them in the least : the sound of money is music to their ears ! It is all very inglorious !

I cannot say I have much faith in the power of charms, holy pictures or medals to heal or save mankind. If anyone wants to give me one, I ask, 'Is it capable of making grapes and wheat grow and of providing food for the whole world ? No ? Then it's too weak for my purpose ; let me go and find the most powerful one of all.' I am like St Christopher. I presume you know the story of St Christopher ?

Christopher was very big and strong and his ambition was to put himself at the service of the most powerful man in the world. He made inquiries and was told of a powerful king in a distant country, so he set out, requested an audience with the king and was accepted into his service. Then, one day, Christopher was riding in the royal bodyguard when he saw that the king appeared to be very frightened and went out of his way to avoid a particular path which was said to be haunted by the Devil. 'Oho', thought Christopher ; 'If the king is frightened of this person called the Devil, that must mean that he is not the most powerful man in the world.' So he left the king's service and set off to put himself in the service of the Devil, since it was he who was the most powerful. His quest lasted a very long time, and then, one night, he met a troop of horsemen, all dressed in black and riding black horses. Their leader asked him, 'Who are you looking for ?' 'I'm looking for the Devil', said Christopher. 'I am the Devil', answered the horseman : 'What do you want with me ?' 'I want to serve you.' 'Very well ; come with us', said the Devil, and Christopher followed him and served him for a long time until, one day, he noticed that the horsemen always avoided a place where there were some crosses. He asked why they never went that way, and was told about a man called Jesus who had died, long before, on a cross. So, once again, Christopher set out in search of a master who must be even stronger and more powerful than the Devil, since the Devil himself feared him ! He searched and searched, but in vain. And then, in order to earn his living while he went on looking for Jesus, he set up as a ferryman on the banks of a big river. He was so strong and broad shouldered, that he used to carry people over the river, with only a strong staff to help him.

One night he was in his little cabin by the river when a terrific storm broke out, with torrential rain and thunder and lightning. It made so much noise that Christopher could not sleep and, all of a sudden, he heard a slight sound, as though a child were crying. He went out, looked everywhere in the dark, and finally found a little boy. 'What are you doing here, child ?' exclaimed Christopher. 'I want to get to the other side of the river, but I'm too little', replied the child.' 'Don't cry, I'll take you over' said Christopher ; and hoisting the little boy up onto his shoulders, he set off to wade through the river. It had rained so heavily that Christopher staggered in the rushing water and was nearly swept off his feet, while he felt the child on his back becoming heavier and heavier, until he thought he would not be able to go on. Then, on the verge of collapse, he said, 'Child, why are you so heavy ? You are as heavy as the earth itself !' 'Oh', replied the boy ; 'I weigh more than the earth. I am Jesus whom you have been looking for. Henceforth you shall be called Christophoros, the bearer of Christ.' And Christopher was happy !

And that is what I did, too : I looked for the strongest and most powerful being, and I found the sun. Can you tell me of anyone more powerful than the sun ?

So you see, men know where to go to find all the things they need, but they do not know where to go to find God. And yet He is there, in the sun ! All the rest is fake ! Apparently some people are afraid that we might think that the sun is God ! But they really need not worry, there is no danger. God is utterly ineffable, beyond our powers of conception ; there is no question of thinking that the sun is God. The sun is simply a gateway opening onto the Deity. The sun is God's servant ; one of His best and most faithful servants. The others are often tired and discouraged and then they give up ; they do a few little things to help human beings and then, after a while, they disappear. Whereas the sun is always there, always tireless, generous, faithful and true. So many have tried and failed ; so many have gone back on their word, cheated and betrayed ; only the sun is always there. This is something human beings don't think about. They are always running after creatures who are frail and vulnerable, who are not what they seem, never after the only one who invariably manifests himself as he is, the only one who is faithful and true. How absurd human beings are ! I do not feel I can trust them any more. How can one trust someone who turns his back on the sun ?

You will ask, 'But if you don't trust human beings any more, what is going to happen ?' Ah, I have complete confidence in the divine dimension of man ; don't worry. But I cannot trust his purely human dimension, for I know in advance that it will make him go back on his word, fall by the wayside and betray me. The stuff human beings are made of cannot take much wear and tear, it melts like wax and tarnishes like lead ; I know what to expect in this respect. But I also know that there is a divine side to each man, and this I can and do trust, for I know that it will never betray my trust. You have never thought of this, either, have you ? People are too ignorant, they do not know what they can rely on, so they trust what is human and distrust what is divine. They distrust the divine and keep well away from it because they lack discernment, and this is why they are always being deceived and disappointed and are constantly unhappy.

There is something in man, as in everything on this earth, that is destined to lose its light, weaken and die ; but there is also something which, like the sun, is unchanging, eternal and divine. When you are capable of discerning and identifying each human manifestation you will find that every area of your life improves, for you will enter the world of cosmic, eternal truths ; you become the little temple, within the great one ; the microcosm within the macrocosm. There you have yet another interpretation of the symbolism of the pentagram ; but it is a great deal more profound than you have ever thought possible : what I have revealed so far is only a fragment of all the wealth it contains !

Try to understand what I am saying. I am not blaspheming. I am not tearing down all that the great beings of the past have built, I am simply taking you further, much further in truth and the spirit. The moment has already come to adore God in spirit and truth, that is to say with greater breadth, even greater immensity and light ; and in this, only the sun can be the model we need.

Men have abandoned the sun because he is so inaccessible, so perfect that they did not believe it was possible to work with such a model and become like him. This is why they have adopted models which are far easier to imitate : other human beings, or animals ! 'Even animals ?' you will say. Oh, yes. Very much so ! Look at all the people who are just like tigers, or crocodiles, horses, monkeys, bears, snakes and even rabbits ! 'But they're not conscious of it' you will say. True ! But whether it is conscious or unconscious is another matter ; the fact is that they have taken these animals as their models. Some of them are like scared rabbits. Others have an astonishing resemblance to pigs : you can even hear them grunting, exactly like pigs ! Others pounce on their food like beasts of prey, glancing frequently to left and right in case an enemy tries to sneak up and steal it from them. They growl and bark, roar and bellow. Really, human beings are quite amazing ! They refuse to take the sun as their model because his perfection is too distant and too difficult to attain. But is man doomed to be an animal crawling in the dust of the earth for ever ? It is time that he raised his eyes to the immensity above and looked at the sun.

Justice requires that we be honest and noble ; that is to say, that we recognize the truth about ourselves and our situation, and that we correct ourselves and change our attitude ; that we begin to address our gratitude and thanksgiving to him who has earned it. But people are not honest and noble ; they are ungrateful, unjust and dishonest. They use coal, oil, wood, etc., every single day, without ever thinking that these things are products of the sun ; that they are gifts of the sun. Everything produced by industry, even the clothes on our backs, are products of the sun. The whole of our economy is based on the products of the sun, but the sun itself gets forgotten, and that is an injustice ! As long as man goes on being so unjust he will not be wholly successful.

Restore the sun to his rightful place as the cause of everything, the centre of everything, as model and ideal, and you will see that your life will begin to take on an entirely new orientation. I have seen this happen to so many — not to speak of my own case ! So now, instead of criticizing or making fun of what I say, you had better begin to study and verify things for yourselves. Some of you will say, 'I have tried, I really have, but I've never seen any of the things you talk about.' And what I say to that is : 'Yes, perhaps, but the question is *how* you tried and *what* you understood.' The results you achieve will be good or bad depending on how you understand these things. And, as you have not yet reached a correct understanding of the sun, you are not in a position to criticize me. I can only advise you to continue until you manage to think of the sun as a centre, a source of life, a fulcrum, a model and even an instructor. But you will never achieve this either, because you refuse to admit that the sun is the most intelligent of all creatures.

How often I have asked the sun a question ! And he always gives me the clearest, most limpid and luminous answers. You know, he is up there, looking down at all the creatures on earth ; he knows what they are like, he sees all the dirty tricks they get up to and the crimes they commit, and it never even occurs to them that he is watching. No one suspects that the sun can see what we are doing ; they think : 'Oh, he can't see from up there. He doesn't know anything !' But, in point of fact, he knows everything ! He has been there for millions of years and he knows human nature better than anyone. He knows the history of all the different peoples of the earth : Assyrians, Egyptians, Babylonians and Chaldeans and, long before them, the Atlanteans and Lemurians. He can tell you what these monsters of the past were like, because he watched them and saw how they behaved ; and he also knows how humanity is going to evolve in the future.

To conclude, I want to say just this one thing more : as long as human beings continue to think that the sun is not a conscious, intelligent being, as long as they maintain that all the manifestations of the sun and all that flows from it, are the effects of purely mechanical laws, their lives will not show any improvement. It is a question of magic ! Do you want your life to be luminous, sublime and full of beauty ? Then, look on the sun as the most intelligent, the most powerful and the most generous being that exists, as a divine being. These are the most sublime truths but no one ever talks about them or thinks of publishing them, and that is a great pity. The declarations of John Smith and Mary Brown will be recorded and repeated for generations ; but who were they and what did they ever do to earn such renown ? They were nothing out of the ordinary, and yet statues have been raised in their honour. But for the sun ? Nothing !

Oh, of course, lovers think of the sun. They sigh, 'Darling ; you are my sunshine !' or 'Your eyes are as bright as the sun.' Ah yes : you have to be in love — or perhaps a little tipsy — to have eyes that shine like the sun ! Why yes, when people have a little drink together, their eyes start shining. But they don't shine like the sun ! This is important, my dear brothers and sisters ; you must understand that there are different kinds of light, and that some eyes shine like those of a snake ! You must be capable of seeing what kind of light is shining in someone's eyes. Otherwise, watch out, for you may get eaten !

The Bonfin, 4 September 1967

Chapter Sixteen

Christ and the Solar Religion

Today, I want to insist, once again, on the importance of preparing oneself the day before in order to be present at sunrise next morning, with a clear, attentive, active mind. Try not to waste your energy during the day, and not to go to bed too late or in a troubled, anxious state of mind, otherwise you will find your reservoirs empty next morning, and you will sleep instead of doing this work, the most useful work anyone can do, not only for oneself, but for society and the whole of humanity, even for the whole universe. For we are part of the cosmos and we cannot envisage our existence as something separate. If you listen to me, if you respect certain rules and come up here in the morning with your mind centred exclusively on this all-important work, on which depends your future, your happiness, your health and equilibrium, then you will receive the wealth that flows continually from the divine source, the sun.

Health, inner balance, spiritual enrichment depend on such little things as these : vigilance, awareness, attention to what you are doing. But you probably cannot quite see how this can be so : how can health, happiness and inner balance depend on your attention and vigilance ? The connection is quite simple. When you want to get to know certain regions or entities in the universe, you must learn to attune your vibrations to theirs, and this means that you have to discover their exact wavelength. When a man succeeds in vibrating on the same wavelength as another being or object, that is to say, when his vibrations are synchronized with theirs, when he identifies with them, when he fuses into one with them (these are only different ways of expressing the same idea), then he can be said to 'know' them. Knowing is a question of adjusting one's vibrations to those of another, of getting onto the same level, of becoming one with the being or object one wants to know. And when the Bible says that 'Adam knew Eve, his wife,' it means that they were tuned to the same wavelength.

You cannot know someone by embracing them only on the physical plane ; you also have to vibrate, think and feel as they do. And the same is true if you want to know God, the invisible world, the Angels and the great Masters : your vibrations must be synchronized with theirs. You cannot say, 'I have seen and touched, therefore I know !' If only it were so easy ! Do we know the earth simply because we have touched it ? Far from it ! The earth is a great mystery and we are going to have to study it in detail, in the future, so as to know and understand all the processes going on in its laboratories and workshops, and the entities who work there. Only the great Initiates have any idea of what the earth is, because they penetrate mentally into the depths of the earth, to study it. Can you say that you know water, just because you drink it ? And air : do you know air because you inhale it into your lungs and feel the caress of the wind on your face ? And fire ? And sunlight ? It would not be true to say you know them, even though you can see and feel them. In order, really and truly, to know the sun, you must come up here and watch it rise and contemplate it with a clear, limpid, keenly attentive mind. The attention you give it must be carefully developed in advance, for it must be of such high quality that it enables you to synchronize your vibrations with those of the sun and of the light, warmth and life flowing from it. By learning to vibrate with greater and greater intensity, that is, more and more impersonally and universally, one begins to know the sun, and in this knowing, in this contact with the sun, one comes to understand the meaning of life.

There, that was just a brief reminder of the need to prepare yourselves for the sunrise the evening before. Without this preparation you would find yourselves concentrating on all the things that worry or sadden you, or on your own murky plots and plans for the future : there would be absolutely no point in your being here. You would get a little light and warmth from it, nothing more. You would certainly never get to know the sun as God's servant, as a sublime intelligence, the transmitter of the divine will, the inexhaustible reservoir of riches capable of nourishing all your cells. You would know it as nothing more than an incandescent ball that warms the earth and causes fruit, flowers, trees and vegetables to grow... and that is really nothing compared to what you are destined to know.

When Jesus said, 'No one comes to the Father except through me' it was Christ who was speaking through his words, and he meant that no one could go to the Father except through the Spirit of Christ who manifests Himself in the sun. Perhaps you think that this is an arbitrary interpretation, but it is not. I can show you how to put each truth exactly where it belongs. We receive them all mixed up and apparently disconnected, but an Initiate knows how to tie them all together and find where each one belongs in the great Book of Living Nature.

I have already shown you that, for us, here on earth, the sun, with the life, warmth and light that it showers on us so abundantly, is the most perfect image we could have of the Blessed Trinity. The life flowing through the sun is the Father. Its light and heat can be seen equally well as the Son or the Holy Spirit, but, from the Initiatic point of view, the Holy Spirit is seen primarily as heat or love, whereas the Son, Christ, represents light or wisdom. The Holy Spirit is a feminine principle. It is said that mankind first experienced the era of the Father, the era of strength, will, power and severity ; next came the era of the Son, with light and intelligence ; and now it is the era of the Holy Spirit, the era of love.

The light streaming from the sun, therefore, that light which transforms so many things in the universe and showers so many blessings on every creature, that light whose true nature is still a mystery to man, that light is Christ, the Christ-Spirit. The light of the sun is a living spirit, and it is through this light that the Spirit of Christ is still with us, still active, still ceaselessly at work amongst us. If this were not so, what meaning could there be in his words, 'I am the light of the world', or 'My Father and I are one' ? They are one in the sun, for it is in the sun that light and life are one. And Christ also said, 'I am the resurrection and the life.' Who raises beings from the dead ? Who gives life ? Christ, the Spirit of Christ, who dwells in the sun.

Christians always think of Christ as being in some specific place, in Palestine, for example, where Jesus lived. But if He is truly the resurrection and the life, He cannot be living in Palestine ; He is living in the sun. Of course, He is everywhere in nature ; but for us, in a very special way, He is in the sun. This is why, if you get into the habit of looking at the sun in the morning and thinking that it is Christ who is there before your eyes, if you make contact with Him and love Him, your whole being will thrill and vibrate in unison with that Cosmic Light, condensed and made manifest in and through the sun.

Certainly, Christ is far, far greater than the sun ; He is the Son of God, the second Person of the Blessed Trinity, and He does not manifest Himself exclusively in our sun. There are in-numerable other suns in the immensity of the cosmos, far bigger and brighter than ours. This is why, when I speak of Christ, you must realize that I am not speaking of Jesus but of the Cosmic Principle which has neither beginning nor end. Jesus was a man who lived in Palestine 2,000 years ago ; a being of such purity and nobility, so highly evolved that, in his thirtieth year, he receiv-ed the Holy Spirit and, at the same time, the Spirit of Christ. This is why he was called Jesus Christ. But Christ can be born in the heart and soul of all human beings. It was He who manifested Himself in Orpheus, Moses, Zoroaster, Buddha and all the great Initiates of every country and every age. There was only one Jesus, but there are, there can be, thousands of Christs. Jesus will always be a unique being ; he is the head of the Christian religion, just as Buddha is the head of Buddhism or Muhammad the head of Muhamaddanism. But Christ is the head of the whole of humanity and, indeed, of the whole universe. He is not the head of one religion, but of all religions ; it was from Him that they received their inspiration. When the Lord Gautama attained enlightenment he was given the title of Buddha, and all who reach this 'buddhic' state (we would say this 'christic' state), are called Buddhas. So Gautama was not the only one ; there have been many others. The name 'Buddha' or 'Christ' is not the proper name of any particular person ; it is the name of a principle, of a state of consciousness. It is important that you understand this correctly. Christians have never been taught these distinctions, and the result is that they confuse many different notions. With the exception of those who have received the light of Initiatic Science — and they are exceedingly rare — most Christians carry a chaotic jumble of truths and half-truths in their heads.

I have no taste for living in a state of illusion ; in fact, I am the first to demolish illusions, starting with my own. There is no room in my head for an idea that has not been carefully weighed up and checked in advance and, above all, measured against the yardstick of the Intelligence of Nature. I am just like everybody else, you know : I, too, have a great many ideas that come and go in my head, but the difference is that I refuse to take them at face value. I grab them by the scruff of the neck and tell them : 'Come with me. We'll go and see if you are trustworthy ; if you are truthful and honest or not.' And I drag them before the Intelligence of Nature and make them show me proof of what they say. And then I start looking : I take my time and make a thorough search in the stars, the seas and oceans, in flowers, insects and human beings. And if I do not find confirmation of what they are trying to tell me, if I do not see it written anywhere in nature, then I drive them out of my head. Why should I pass on their nonsense to you ? But this is not the method most human beings use. Whatever idea comes into their sick, overheated brain is cherished and nourished as though it were the most sensational discovery ever made. They never, never cross-examine it before the tribunal of Nature's Intelligence to see what it has to say in its own defence ; they are not used to this method. Well, let them get used to it, just as I have ! I never tell you anything which has not been confirmed and endorsed by the Intelligence of Nature. One must possess the most reliable criteria.

Someone who has never been in an Initiatic school has no criteria to judge by. He is ready to swallow anything, and this is very dangerous ; very dangerous indeed ! For there is nothing to prevent the lower entities of the invisible world (all kinds of entities are mentioned in Initiatic books) from leading him, gently and insidiously, into error until, one day, he is completely lost. People accept every idea that comes into their heads, and this is a great mistake. If they could count on their antennae being infallible, if they were utterly pure and perfectly harmonized and synchronized with the sublime regions on high, it would be a different matter. But they are not : the fine tuning on their inner receiver sets is still too rudimentary, so that whatever they receive is always distorted. They behave as though they were perfect, but they are not ; they are very far from perfect, and they should be careful to reexamine all their ideas and all their sensations and impulses. They should examine the origin and nature of every single notion that enters their heads before letting it urge them in a particular direction. If they did this regularly, they would find that nine out of every ten ideas and impulses come from a very low level ; only very, very few come from a higher celestial region. But someone who has no criteria or frame of reference has no way of knowing where his ideas come from, so he rushes to satisfy their demands. There you have the explanation for all your misfortunes : a lack of discernment.

It is time, now, to venture beyond the limits imposed by those who are afraid to go any further, who think that it is forbidden to transcend themselves and broaden their conceptions. They have drawn a circle in chalk or black ink round themselves and everybody else, proclaiming : 'This is the limit. No one can go beyond this line.' And you are all caught in the spell and go on repeating : 'It's true, it's true ; there's a wall there. This is the limit.' But when you come here you are released from that spell ; you are allowed to step over all the imaginary boundaries and venture as far as you like, very, very far into immensity and total freedom.

All the religions that have ever been established on earth have been based on narrow conceptions of race, nation or caste, or on principles which were less than universal. But the time is near when ancient traditions will crumble and disappear ; the coming of the age of Aquarius makes it inevitable. Mankind must have done with all the racial and sectarian aspects of religion. Even Christianity is sectarian. The only truly universal religion is the solar religion ; and the day of its coming is approaching rapidly. As long as they refuse to accept it, human beings will remain limited and fenced in by their old attitudes, always worrying about marking out boundaries and defending themselves from attack, always struggling to conquer others. It is the everlasting cycle of revenge and war, and it is high time such out-dated ways were abandoned ! There was a time when they were justified, even unavoidable, and in those days Heaven encouraged and protected religions based on national interests. But if they were valid in the past they are no longer valid today.

It is time, now, to break out of these narrow, restrictive conceptions and show real greatness of soul ; it is time to learn to be like the sun and love the entire world ! Look at the sun : does it discriminate on the grounds of race, nationality or religion ? Absolutely not ! It bestows its warmth on all men : black, yellow or white, Jews, Buddhists, Christians, Muhammadans and even atheists. You must stop wishing that one religion or one race would dominate the world and impose its own ideas on everyone. We must all move forward, together, towards the one universal

religion of love in which there is no distinction of race or colour.
You must realize that some of the things found in Sacred Scrip-
ture were not intended to prevail for ever.

Besides, the Lord is like the sun : differences of race or religion
mean nothing to Him. All He is interested in is men's virtues and
qualities ; He doesn't give a hoot for the fact that they are Jews,
Catholics or Protestants ! I assure you this is true, He told me
so Himself when we met in a *bistrot*, one day. Don't be shock-
ed ! Didn't you know that there are some very select *bistrots* on
high which serve nectar and ambrosia ? Of course, they are not
open to the general public, but those who are admitted can drink
the Elixir of Everlasting Life and meet Heavenly Entities. In fact,
I must confess that it was not actually the Lord Himself that I
talked to, but one of His representatives, for the Lord has never
yet done anyone the honour of coming down to have a drink with
him !

In any case, as I say, the Lord does not look at the labels or
titles people give themselves. Even if you ask to be admitted to
Heaven on the grounds that you are a member of the august
Universal White Brotherhood, it is more than likely that they'll
say : 'That's all very well, but you are still quarrelsome and vindictive, you still cheat and slander others ; you are not yet a
member of the Universal White Brotherhood, so it's no good
pretending you are ! Out you go !' This is how things are on high.
It is useless to flaunt your membership card, your medals, even
your robes or your crosses, for these are all external insignia and
the only insignia recognized by Heaven are those that are within.
External insignia are for the benefit of human beings, not for
Heaven. They can be very beautiful and even necessary, and I
have nothing against them ; even magi and Initiates have
sometimes accepted to wear them, but one must also possess them
inwardly. Rich silks and velvet, royal purple and jewelled crosses
may be very majestic, but if you have nothing but rags to wear
inwardly, it is simply grotesque to cover your rags with sumptuous outer garments.

If the Inquisition still existed, I know that I would have been burnt at the stake several times already. But now it is my turn to burn them all, and that is exactly what I am going to do : burn them with the fire of the sun. Will they be burnt to death ? No, on the contrary ; they will be raised from the dead ! For there are two different kinds of burning : if you say that you are aflame with love, for instance, it does not mean that you are about to die ; it only means that love has made a poet of you ! Yes, there are different kinds of fire, and I have my own special method for burning people !

Trust me, my dear brothers and sisters ; I will lead you to such heights that, before long, you will love the sun with all your heart and soul, as the most sublime manifestation of God that exists. And then, when you come down after the sunrise in the morning, you will feel the presence of a little sun within you all day long, singing and shining so brightly that it lights up your whole life, even at night.

The Bonfin, 15 September 1967

Chapter Seventeen

Day and Night —
Consciousness and the Subconscious

I

For the last three months we have had marvellously clear, transparent skies at sunrise until today, and today the sky was full of clouds, a veil was drawn over the sun and we were not allowed to see it.

Bad weather generally puts people in a bad mood : they mope and moan and wonder why there have to be clouds and rain and wind and snow. They would like the weather to be idyllic every day ! Well, so would I, but as I understand things a bit differently, I don't let it upset me : I accept the weather as it comes. And now I want to say a few words that will help you to understand and share my way of reasoning and of drawing analogies from these things.

All these phenomena : fine weather, rain and fog, and so on, represent the life of nature, for nature has its own life which manifests itself in different ways, and summer and winter and all the different weather patterns that go with them are a language which we must learn to decipher. Day follows night ; activity follows periods of rest ; waking alternates with sleeping : on every level we find this same pattern of alternation. What does the weather correspond to on a cloudy day like this ? To night. Night and day... What does day represent ? Activity. And night ? Rest. But, at the same time, there is work going on at night, while we are asleep. Not in our conscious minds, of course, but on another level : on the level of the subconscious.

Day, therefore, corresponds to consciousness and night to the subconscious. Day is wakefulness and night is sleep ; day is activity and night is passivity. Or, if you prefer, you can say that day is a time for spending (for all activity implies some form of expenditure) whereas night is a time for recuperation and restoration. One cannot go on spending for too long if there is no compensatory period of recuperation, if one does not take the time to renew and restore one's strength and resources. And the first step in renewing and restoring one's energies is to cleanse oneself, and this is precisely what takes place at night : the subconscious activity that goes on at night is related to various other processes and, first and foremost, to that of cleansing. All the harmful, toxic elements, which tend to clog and hamper the respiratory, circulatory and excretory systems, are eliminated, so that the fluids of the body can flow freely once again.

The work that goes on inside us while we are asleep at night, therefore, is extremely important, but it remains on the level of the subconscious. A man is not consciously aware of what is going on, and when he wakes up in the morning, he never even thinks of giving thanks for being up and about, wide awake and conscious once again. If he only knew the work that went on inside him during the night !

For a man simply to be conscious, awake and mentally active, involves a very considerable expenditure of materials and energy. You have no idea of the fantastic amount of energy the brain uses up in keeping you awake and conscious. And if the forces and materials required are exhausted, a few minutes sleep during the day will often be enough to set you up and make you feel full of energy again. Work is going on ceaselessly, therefore, by night and by day, activity or rest, consciousness or subconsciousness.

But night and day can be found in one form or another everywhere, in every domain. What are spring and summer, for instance ? They are day. And autumn and winter are night, the period during which nature sleeps and recuperates so as to be ready to produce its fruits, once again, when spring and summer come round. This is why the work going on in plants and trees moves up or down, from one level to another, according to the seasons. In autumn and winter the roots are active, whereas the trunk and branches are resting, and leaves, flowers or fruit fall to the ground. This is the period that corresponds to the work of the subconscious. In spring and summer activity begins to move upwards again, to the level which corresponds to consciousness, and at the end of the summer the downwards movement starts again, and so on, in an endless cycle.

Where else can we find this alternation ? Everywhere, in every domain. Within the span of each month there is the alternation of day and night : a day which lasts a fortnight as the moon waxes, and a night which also lasts a fortnight, as it wanes. When the moon is waxing the centre of human activity moves upwards to the brain, and we can afford to spend more energy and be more active and productive. When the moon is on the wane, our centre of activity moves down again to the stomach and sexual organs ; the power and activity of the brain is diminished while that of the sensual, subconscious level increases and we find ourselves inclined to eat and sleep more. You see ? Two weeks of day and two weeks of night. And even in each twenty-four hour day — in fact within each hour, also — there can be the alternation of day and night.

Day, therefore, stands for wakefulness, activity and spending, but if there were no night there could be no day. What is the time of gestation, for instance ? It is night-time. A child spends nine months in the night of its mother's womb : it is not conscious, it sees nothing and nor can anyone see it. Only its mother can occasionally feel faint signs of life. Human life begins with a night of nine months followed by a day that can last for ninety years ! And the long day of life is marked by the alternating rhythm of other days and nights — but you have to understand all this symbolically.

Genesis says, 'The evening and the morning were the first day... The evening and the morning were the second day...' We can understand 'evening' as night and 'morning' as day and we ask, then, 'Why did the Lord begin with night ?' It was not a question of chance : it was because there can be no day before there has been a night. Night prepares the day. Day prepares nothing, it is open-handed, a spendthrift ; all manifestation is prepared by night. Before the sun, moon and stars appeared in the sky there was a time of preparation in darkness, in the obscurity of night. This is what Esoteric Science teaches us : night is a preparation for day. Take the example of coal : it is completely black, but its blackness is a prelude to the brightness of the flame springing from it. Darkness comes first, therefore, and from darkness springs light ; within the womb of darkness, the brightness of day is prepared and made possible.

Darkness represents unorganized, formless matter, the obscure activity of the subconscious which precedes the emergence of light, understanding or comprehension in the conscious mind. But it is not enough to know this in theory : we have to learn to put these notions to practical use. This is why, when the sky is overcast and we cannot see the sun, we should seize the opportunity to work on the level of our subconscious. On other days, the bright sunshine and favourable electromagnetic currents perhaps helped you to work on the conscious or even the super-conscious level, but conditions are different today and you cannot work on the same level. So you must take a different approach, otherwise you will get a headache or go to sleep ! Since a dull, overcast day corresponds to night, your work should be on the level of your subconscious, not in the brain ; put a stop to your mental activity and move down into the solar plexus.

Let's just look at these two organs, the brain and the solar plexus, for a moment.* The solar plexus is the seat of the subconscious, whereas consciousness resides in the brain. The sub-

*See *Complete Works*, vol. 6, chap. 9.

conscious is closely linked to the whole cosmos, to immensity ; it represents the collective aspect of our being. When we work on this level, therefore, we are tuning in to life, immersing ourselves in the ocean of universal life ; the solar plexus is our point of contact with the life of the universe, the channel through which we renew and strengthen our bonds with it, through which we vibrate in rhythm with immensity. When you want to be a conscious, free, isolated individual again, you have to move back to the level of the brain, for the property of the brain is to accentuate individuality, whereas the solar plexus restores us to the collectivity. The work of the solar plexus is a night work.

During the day you see yourself as an individual being, distinct and apart from others. You eat and drink, fight, argue and make plans as a separate, isolated individual, and much of man's unhappiness stems from this. When you are asleep, on the other hand, your individual life is submerged in the collective, universal life ; you become one with immensity. This is the work of nature : turn and turn about, nature accentuates the individual or the collective aspect of our being. In sleep we melt into the ocean of universal life which nourishes us and renews our strength ; we are like fish swimming in the ocean from which they draw their sustenance. Human beings emerge from and then plunge back into this ocean and this is what we call day and night, consciousness and the subconscious, waking and sleep.

There ! With this you have some clear, accurate notions which should be useful to you and help you to understand all the mysteries of nature. You can see, now, that when a disciple understands and knows how to use whatever comes his way, he can do useful work even when conditions are unfavourable. Whereas others, who get everything all mixed up and don't know what their difficult conditions correspond to, simply waste them.

Perhaps you are surprised by my statement that darkness comes before light. Alchemists understood this ; when they spoke of 'light emerging from darkness' they were referring implicitly to light as the fruit of that immense work that takes place in darkness. Bees, too, work in darkness because they have a light all their own. It is possible to work in darkness, for in reality there is no such thing as darkness : the night is lit by a dazzling light but, as it is astral light, we cannot see it. The darkness of some is light to others ; darkness and light coexist at the same time.

You might say that darkness is the mother of light, for a child emerges from its mother's womb, not the other way round. Light has never given birth to darkness ; on the contrary it drives away darkness, but darkness gives birth to light. How this can be is a mystery : the mystery of movement. Without movement there can be no light. There must first be friction, abrasion and movement which produce heat. The first result of movement is heat and as the heat increases it produces a flame, and a flame is light. If you transpose this on to the human level you can say that the will produces movement ; movement produces heat, that is to say, love, and as love increases and intensifies it is obliged to flame up in the form of light, intelligence and wisdom.

The initial movement comes from the will, and the will is obscurity and darkness. Within darkness there is movement, the activity of the will, but we cannot see it ; when this activity produces heat, we still cannot see anything but we begin to feel the heat, and it is only when the heat becomes more intense that we see the light. And this is exactly what happened in the process of creation. Genesis says, 'And the Spirit of God was hovering over the face of the waters'. The waters represent matter and the Spirit of God 'hovering over the face of the waters' means that the Spirit of God caused a movement, that this movement produced heat, and that heat produced light : 'Let there be light !' God created the world by means of the will (movement), love (heat) and wisdom (light). And man is capable of creating in the same way, for there is movement in the form of life in his solar plexus ; there is heat in the form of love in his heart, and there is light in the form of intelligence in his brain.

If you study the Divine Triad of the Hindus, Brahma, Visnu and Siva, you see that the Risis of India, who penetrated into the depths of creation, placed Brahma in the region of the solar plexus, Visnu in the heart and Siva in the brain. Nowadays, however, Hindus do not attach much importance to Brahma ; very few Indian temples are dedicated to Brahma, the Creator ; those dedicated to Visnu, the Preserver, are more numerous, but the majority are dedicated to Siva, the Destroyer. I will explain to you why Hinduism places Siva in the mind and why they say that the mind is the destroyer of reality, but it will have to wait for another day.

When a baby is still in the womb, it is nourished through the umbilical cord which connects it to its mother. The solar plexus was the starting point from which human beings developed and the last organ to appear was the brain. But in daily life man has to follow the reverse movement : he must begin by using his mind to observe and study things, and only when he understands them can he move down to the level of the heart, that is to say to the level of emotion and desire and, finally, to the level of physical work and the achievement of physical results. Wisdom, therefore, comes first, and is followed by love and, finally, by the will which produces concrete realization. It is possible to follow the reverse movement, but only if one is perfect : one must be like God Himself in order to act without thinking, and in this case everything one does will be perfectly magnificent and marvellous and always beneficial. But in general it is preferable to think before one acts. What happens to those who do the reverse ? They want to do what God does without being like Him, so they begin by acting : they go into partnership with others, sign contracts or get married ; then the time comes to suffer from the consequences of their acts : their heart weeps and wails and deplores the situation, and, finally, the mind comes into play to reflect and draw conclusions from what they have done. But, by then, it is a bit late ! You see, they act first, suffer second and think last ; exactly the reverse of what they should do : think first, feel second and act last. You see how clear and simple it is ? As I said, it is possible to do as God does and act first, but only if one is as

perfect as God, for then everything one undertakes is done according to the rules and one is in no danger of going astray. But
as long as you are still imperfect, you must not act until you have
thought ; in this way you will never need to regret your actions.

You might well ask, 'But didn't God think about it before
He created the world ?' Yes, indeed He did. He conceived the
creation of the world in His head before giving the plans to the
workmen who built it. It was He who drew up the plans for the
house, and the workers, masons and carpenters — that is to say,
the Archangels and their armies of Angels — set to work on the
construction. It was they who actually gave it its physical form.
God created the world and the others gave it form. Yes, He
thought about it before creating it ; He put His mind to it, and
when He saw that it was good He put His heart into it too, saying : 'Let it be'. And then, little by little, particle by particle, the
others built up the whole edifice exactly as God had designed it.
Well, actually, some ancient traditions say that the workers made
a few mistakes, and it is true ; they did. I have no desire to criticize
them, but still, they did let a few errors creep in here and there
during the construction, because each worker interpreted the
original plans in his own way ! But that is another story and it
would take far too long to explain it to you. So, like the Church,
the world had only one Creator and many 'formers'. Isn't that
true ? The Church has had quantities of formers : one creator
and many reformers !

And now the sun is coming out !

The Bonfin, 28 September 1967 (morning)

II

Yesterday morning we could not see the sun because of the clouds, and I talked to you about how to use such circumstances in your spiritual work. That led me to explain how life unfolds on two levels, the conscious and the subconscious : I spoke to you about day and night, light and darkness, and the fact that activity in nature is not centred in one spot, but that there is a phenomenon of polarization, a to and fro, which can be seen, for instance, in trees, in which the centre of activity moves back and forth between the roots and the branches and leaves. I also talked about waking and sleeping. I told you that waking is an activity that involves outlay or expenditure, whereas sleep implies recuperation and renewal, and I said that human beings have to sink into the unconscious world of sleep and immerse themselves in the ocean of universal life in order to draw strength from it and replenish their supplies of energy, and then come back to the surface and emerge from that ocean to spend and work, wide awake and conscious once again. We saw that these two processes complement each other so perfectly that if one or the other were missing, life would cease.

There is a world of light, therefore, in which everything can be seen quite distinctly : forms, colours, dimensions, distances and dangers, and a world of darkness where all these realities fade and are replaced by other realities. A child, for example, spends a long night of nine months in its mother's womb, taking shape and preparing itself to emerge into the world, and then it spends the rest of its life repeating this pattern of alternation : sometimes waking and emerging from night, sometimes sleeping and slipping back into night. But if Moses wrote, in the first pages of Genesis : 'The evening and the morning were the first day', it was because, from the Esoteric viewpoint, evening, or night, precedes and prepares day, that is to say, manifestation.

Manifestation is day ; and preparation, construction, the formative process that takes place in darkness and chaos is night. Night precedes day and the most important things take place in the dark. This being so, we might wonder why the Initiates, in their moral philosophy, have always associated night with the principle of evil and day with the principle of good. Why is darkness always seen as a symbol of Hell and evil, whereas light is the symbol of Heaven and good ? The truth is that they are simply one form or aspect of these things, as we shall see later.

Obviously, to say that night is related to sleep and day to waking, is to oversimplify things. Many animals go out at night to hunt for food, and criminals, burglars and murderers commit their crimes in the dark. Performing artists also give their recitals or performances at night. Similarly, when I said that human beings have greater strength and energy during the fortnight in which the moon is waxing because the centre of activity moves up towards the brain, and that during the waning moon they become more sensual and lazy because the centre of activity moves down towards the stomach and sexual organs, I was also speaking very generally, for there are exceptions here, too. But the exceptions mean something. I have known women, for instance, who looked completely washed out and lifeless during the day, but as evening approached their eyes began to sparkle and they became pretty, vivacious and expressive. Why ? Because there was something of the nocturnal animal in their make-up !

In the Psalms it says, 'Give thanks to Him who made great lights. The sun to rule by day, the moon and stars to rule by night.' I will explain to you, one day, what the solar and lunar principles are, and show you that those who have sometimes spoken so harshly about the moon, the feminine principle, did so because they did not fully understand this principle or its true role.

When the sun rises, the objects in the limited area in space lit by its rays become visible to you : you can look at them and learn from them, see where you are going and what you are doing, take measurements, make calculations and investigate reality. And when the sun sets, and shapes and colours fade and objects are no longer clearly visible, you begin to glimpse the immensity, the vastness of boundless space and the thousands of stars in the sky. It is so vast that one's head reels at the grandeur of it ; the soul takes flight and soars away, losing itself and fusing with other beings in that immensity. One's state of consciousness changes, a sense of peace and serenity rises to the surface, for in the face of such immensity, such majesty, many little problems fade into oblivion and one loses oneself in the universal, collective torrent of life. Should we belittle the importance of our sun, simply because there are a great many other suns in the universe ? No. But we have to study Nature's language and understand the role of the sun. The role of the sun is to individualize us : it gives us light so that we can study and work and do all the things we need to do to advance in our evolution. If the sun were not there this would be impossible, for we would lose our way in the immensity of the universe. The sun has an indispensable role to play, therefore, if man is to become individualized and fully conscious.

The sun, moon and stars are all represented within us. The sun is in our minds in the form of light, and in our feelings in the form of love. In our physical bodies it is represented by the heart, the centre and fountainhead from which flows the blood that nourishes our organs, just as the sun nourishes the planets. But the veritable centre of our life is the solar plexus. Why was this plexus given the name of the sun ? Because this is where life originates. The Russians call this part of the body *jivot*, and *jivot* in Bulgarian means 'life'. For the Russians, *jivot* includes the whole region of the belly, stomach and solar plexus, and the Gospels tell us that when a man is pure he becomes a temple of the living God and 'from his heart will flow rivers of living water'. It is from here, from the solar plexus, that living waters flow, and it is from here, through the umbilical cord, that a child receives life from its mother.

If we take the sun as the symbol of the intellect, it is because the intellect is the faculty that throws light on reality and enables us to see and understand. Without the light of the intellect we would be blind and in danger of falling into the pit. The intellect, therefore, represents the sun in the form of understanding, comprehension, clarity and wisdom. This is why the Master Peter Deunov gave us this formula : 'To have a heart as pure as crystal, a mind as luminous as the sun, a soul as vast as the universe, a spirit as powerful as God and one with God !' Our intellect is our sun, but for the moment it is a sun which does not always give us perfect light.

What is the role of the intellect ? Like the sun, the intellect has the power to individualize us, to set each one of us off from the collectivity, from cosmic immensity, so that we may become conscious and capable of learning. It is a very useful faculty, therefore, but at the same time it cuts us off from the ultimate reality which is cosmic immensity. This is why Hinduism sees the intellect as 'the destroyer' of reality. Yes, it is true that the intellect destroys reality in that it conceals it from us, just as the sun allows us to see only one tiny portion of the earth and prevents us from seeing the immensity of space and all the other stars.

The egotistical, egocentric, materialistic intellect that manifests itself today in the work of so many thinkers, philosophers and scholars is the assassin of reality. This is what prevents men from seeing, and the more they rely on it, the more they demand of it, the less capable they become of feeling or believing in cosmic immensity, the more completely they cut themselves off from this greater reality, and become individualistic, personal and destructive. Is this state of affairs going to last for ever ? No, for the development of the intellect is only one phase in the Lord's plan for humanity. Obviously, God knew that if man developed his intellect it would cut him off from the whole, prevent him from perceiving immensity and end by making him sceptical, atheistic, materialistic and positivistic. But He also knew that this state of affairs would not last.

The task of the intellect is to enable man to explore the concrete, material, physical world, and that is what he is doing at the moment. And he is doing it with violence, selfishness and cruelty. But this is only temporary. It is a necessary and inevitable phase, and if it exists it means that the Cosmic Spirit foresaw it. At this stage, man is still studying the purely mechanical, lifeless aspects of nature which constitute only the visible, outer husk. His lower intellect is absorbed in the external, condensed, frozen aspect of reality, but this lower dimension of the intellect is linked to the higher intellect, the causal body.

You probably remember the diagram representing man's seven bodies : physical, etheric, astral, mental, Causal, Buddhic and Atmic. At the centre of the figure are the lower mental body (that which Theosophists call the *manas*) and the Causal or higher mental body which are linked to each other, and this explains why the activity of the lower intellect will eventually stir the higher mental body into wakefulness. Man needs an intellect to enable him to develop as an individual and master the material world. If he worked only in the collective, universal dimension, he would be incapable of doing what has to be done in the material dimension. This is the danger that constantly threatens mystics if they do not know how to work on both levels and devote themselves only to the nebulous, lunar world. Of course, in this way, they experience an occasional joy and even ecstasy, but their earthly tasks and even their own physical bodies deteriorate. In order to develop harmoniously it is essential to learn to work on both levels.

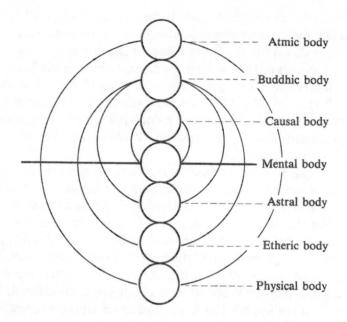

Although the sun prevents us from seeing the rest of creation, that does not mean that it is not there ; on the contrary : it is very real. Astronomers tell us that there are many other suns, much bigger and more powerful than ours. But even if the light of our sun prevents us from seeing this immensity you must not hold it against him. It is a necessary, indispensable phenomenon which corresponds to the work of the intellect. In the distant past, men's intellects were not very highly developed, but their sensitivity was greater and they saw far more with the inner eye. They were in constant touch with the world of spirits, and astral projection came naturally to them, but they did not have a very lively awareness of physical reality. They functioned primarily on the psychic and astral planes, moving easily from the visible to the invisible world in which they communicated with the spirits of the dead. Eventually the Intelligence of Nature decided that it was time for human beings to develop their mental capacities

and now the brain is so highly developed that intuition, clairvoyance and mysticism have been pushed into the background.
There are a few, of course, who still believe in and maintain contact with the invisible, subtle realms of creation, but most people are completely out of touch because they function almost exclusively with their intellect. Chemistry, mathematics and the
biological and physical sciences are the fruit of the work of man's
intellect.

But there are people, nowadays, who feel a certain dissatisfac-
tion with the discoveries of orthodox science, and they are beginning to explore such things as clairvoyance, telepathy and mediumship. This is an indication that, once the intellect has reached the
limits of its development, it will spark a reaction from the higher
intellect to which it is linked, and we shall see a phenomenon
similar to that of a multi-stage spacecraft : when the fuel in the
first stage has been burnt, it ignites the reactors in the second
stage before dropping away ; when the second stage has exhausted
its fuel, it sparks the reactors in the third stage, and so on.

This phenomenon, in fact, holds true for man as a whole :
man is a rocket launched by his Creator towards an unknown
destination. There is no need to worry when your first stage has
used up all its fuel ; the others are still intact, and you can go
on living if you ignite the rockets in the second and in each suc-
cessive stage. But as most people fail to ignite the rockets in their
higher stages, they die before they have burned all their fuel, and
their ascent is aborted. It is not that they have no more energy ;
it is simply that they fail to pass on the flame from one stage to
the next. A lot of people die while a great many of their cells and
organs are still alive ; they had not used up all their reserves and
could have gone on living, but they died. And nowadays certain
organs can be taken from a dead body and put into someone else
to allow them go on living.

But let's get back to our main topic. The essential lesson of
this alternating rhythm of day and night is that man must live
in both worlds : he must develop his mental capacities and have

a clear vision of the physical world in all its details, but he must
not live exclusively on this plane, otherwise he will never be a
whole being. He will lack the immensity of the soul and the heart.
A wise man knows that he must retain a vital link with the collectivity of souls in the universe while, at the same time, working
in the physical world. He lives in both worlds, the divine and the
physical, and in this way he enjoys the wealth of both. To my
way of thinking, a materialist is not very intelligent : he has not
seen all there is to see because he has relied exclusively on his
intellect and, as the intellect is the assassin of reality, the essence
of reality escapes him. The intellect prevents man from seeing
this essence, the prime cause, the living core, the source of all
that is. Intellectuals centre all their attention on objective, material
things ; they have no conception of what exists on a subjective
level : life itself and all the forces and currents, fluids, emanations and quintessences of the universe, all the Heavenly Entities,
the Planetary Spirits and the whole Hierarchy of Angels. They
sense none of this : their intellect has killed reality.

But you must not misunderstand me : I am not belittling the
importance of the sun. Our sun is connected to that other Sun
and is, therefore, the means by which we are in touch with the
Intelligence that dwells in the other Sun. Our sun — our intellect
— is linked to the Sun of the Causal plane which is universal
Wisdom, absolute Knowledge. Our sun, therefore, is a stage, a
gateway, a stepping stone. So don't say, 'Oh, but if the sun conceals reality, I'm not going to have anything to do with it any
more !' The sun does not conceal reality ; it only conceals it from
those who are incapable of going beyond it.

If daylight shows up the importance of details and all the little things that exist on earth, night shows us how unimportant
they really are ! Do you have problems ? Are you worried about
something ? Contemplate the stars in the night sky and you will
feel that everything negative gradually fades and disappears and
you become nobler and more generous, compassionate and merciful ; you will even begin to laugh at injuries and insults. When

a man manages to detach himself from the petty reality of earth and launch out into immensity, he becomes a great and noble being and melts into the Cosmic Spirit. But he must not disappear completely ; he still has to live on earth, he still has work to do here, so, with a little sigh, perhaps, he must come back from his wanderings in the cosmos and resume his appointed task in this world. And if you do not have time to gaze at the stars, you can at least put yourself in the hands of God before going to sleep and ask Him to show you the immensity of Creation : 'Lord God, allow me to know, understand and gaze on all the other splendours of Your Creation'. In this way you will travel great distances at night, instead of perpetually stagnating on earth.

Man was not built to be permanently earthbound ; he was built to journey to other planets and stars, for no obstacle can get in the way of the soul. Our physical bodies are too dense, of course ; they cannot take flight and soar away into space, but the soul has no such limitations : no obstacles, screens or barriers can get in its way. However, if the soul is to be free to travel, its bonds with the body must not be too powerful. If it is held to the physical body by strong appetites, desires and lusts, it will remain a prisoner ; it will be unable to fly away and taste higher joys. And this brings us back, once more, to the moral teaching of the Initiates. The Initiates did not invent morality, they discovered it in the Universe.

Now, suppose that you want to see the sun rise, but there are too many clouds and you don't seem to be able to meditate : what should you do ? Well, since the conditions are not conducive to conscious mental activity, you would do better to work on the subconscious level. Let yourself float away on a cosmic ocean of love and bliss. Entrust yourself wholly to God, saying, 'Lord God, let me be carried away in this ocean of light, I place all my trust in you.' And then, keeping just a tiny flame alight in your mind so that nothing evil can slip in, you let yourself go, and drift away on an ocean of beatific joy. This is the kind of work you can do on a cloudy day : just let yourself be cradled in peace, thinking of nothing — but without falling asleep, of course — and simply glancing into yourself from time to time to see what is going on.

The Sacred Books tell us that he who manages to suspend thought, experiences beatitude and immortality. But it is precisely this that is so difficult, in fact it is the most difficult thing of all : to attain perfect inner silence while remaining alert at the same time ; to arrest thought, to remain awake and simply to feel, withont thinking. It is a state in which feeling and understanding seem to become one. We don't know how or by what means we understand ; we only know that it is not by means of the brain. The brain is not our only means of understanding. Scientists have not yet discovered this, but I assure you that it is so : the brain that we know is not the only organ that has been specially prepared to understand ; there are others. A comparison of the solar plexus and the brain shows that they are both made of the same kinds of tissue, grey and white, but that the relative positions of the two kinds of tissue are reversed. The grey matter of the brain

is on the surface and the white inside, whereas in the solar plexus it is just the reverse. And it is the grey matter that enables man to understand while the white enables him to feel. The grey matter of the brain, therefore, being on the outside, disposes us to understand the outer aspects of reality, whereas that of the solar plexus disposes us to grasp the inner, more profound spiritual dimension. This is one of the most important lessons of Initiatic Science.

And now I feel very tempted to reveal more of the hidden meaning of these symbols, the two triangles and the pentagram, which are always there, before your eyes but which you still cannot fully interpret.* Many years ago, already, when I first talked to you about the Sephirotic Tree of Life which is usually shown as having ten Sephiroth, I mentioned that there was an eleventh, hidden, mysterious Sephirah which is very rarely discussed and which the Cabbalah calls Daath. The word *daath* in Hebrew means knowledge, and this Sephirah lies on the central Pillar, between Tiphareth, the Sun, and Kether. Every Cabbalist knows that the Sephirotic Tree consists of three Pillars : the central pillar, the Pillar of Equilibrium, which is flanked on one side by the Pillar of Mercy and on the other by the Pillar of Severity. Someone who works with the Sephiroth of the Pillar of Equilibrium develops his consciousness and his super-consciousness, and the other two Pillars represent the forces or powers at his disposal : the masculine powers of the Pillar of Severity and the feminine powers of the Pillar of Mercy.

On the Pillar of Mercy, counting from the top downwards, we find Chokmah, Chesed and Netzach ; on the Pillar of Severity are Binah, Geburah and Hod, and on the Pillar of Equilibrium are Kether, Daath, Tiphareth, Yesod and Malkuth. This group of five Sephiroth correspond to the five points of the pentagram which represent the five virtues man must acquire in order to become the Pillar of Equilibrium : kindness, justice, love, wisdom

* See note of page 143.

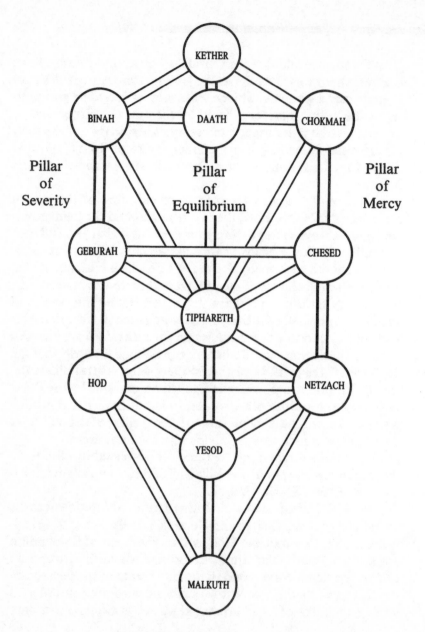

The Sephirotic Tree of Life

and truth. And the two lateral pillars, each of which has three Sephiroth, correspond to the two triangles which combine to form the Seal of Solomon. The three symbolic figures that you see in the wall in front of you, therefore, with the pentagram in the centre, flanked on either side by a triangle, are a schematic representation of the Sephirotic Tree of Life. You must learn to work principally with the central pillar, the Pillar of Equilibrium, on which lie the five Sephiroth, Kether, Daath, Tiphareth, Yesod and Malkuth.

And now I want to show you that much of the knowledge of the Initiates still exists in human culture in the form of symbols, popular sayings, myths and legends which men continue to use in everyday life, without really grasping the profound truth they contain. You have probably read esoteric books which spoke of the Philosophers' Stone, the Elixir of Everlasting Life, the Universal Panacea, the Magic Mirror or the Caduceus of Hermes, but can you tell me where to place them on the pentagram. Think ! Try and find the answer ! You will see how much the pentagram could teach you if you understood it.

When you have succeeded in acquiring the virtues of the pentagram you will be immortal, you will be able to transform metals into gold, cure every illness, see and understand all secrets and hidden truths and work miracles. But so far, you don't even know what the Philosophers' Stone, the Elixir of Everlasting Life and the Universal Panacea are, nor where to find them in yourself. And did you know that you also possess the Magic Mirror ? Yes, but you don't know where it is and you cannot see anything in it for it is dirty and mildewed and covered in dust. And where is your Caduceus of Hermes with which you should be working miracles ? Try and find the answers to these questions for yourselves ; I cannot tell you everything in one lecture. I have given you a few indications, and if you work as you should you will discover the depths of our Teaching.

And now I would like to draw a conclusion from what I have
been saying. Light and darkness are two divine principles. There
is nothing intrinsically evil in the night, any more than in the day.
Evil exists only in men's minds because there are things they don't
understand, but in nature there is no such thing as evil. Darkness
does the work for which it was created ; light does the same, and
light is born of darkness ; it is darkness that gives birth to light.
Remember what I told you about that, yesterday.

Are you less anxious to go and see the sun rise, now that you
know that it prevents us from seeing the immensity of the
cosmos ? No, I can see that you are not. Besides, isn't there always
something of this in life ? If you have a great admiration for your
teacher, guide or Master, everything else pales in comparison and
you have eyes only for what he shows you. There will always be
greater, more powerful lights to outshine lesser ones, and pro-
gressing from light to light we shall end by finding God Himself !
You must accept the fact of this law. Knowing it, I have always
been extremely careful not to lead my friends astray. Unlike most
spiritual teachers, occultists or religious leaders, I have never said
that there was no one above me. Most Masters try to prevent their
disciples from going to others more perfect than they ; John the
Baptist was the only one who did not have that weakness. Speaking of Jesus, he said, 'It is he who, coming after me, is preferred
before me, whose sandal strap I am not worthy to loose'. He had
his own disciples, but one day, as he saw Jesus coming towards
him he said, 'Behold ! The Lamb of God', and his disciples left
him and followed Jesus. Yes, St John the Baptist was an extraordinary being !

The Bonfin, 29 September 1967 (morning)

III

When I got home this morning I went over everything I had said to you earlier and, as usual, I found several gaps. For example, I did not talk about the moon at all, and yet the moon has a very important role in man's psychic life which most people know nothing about. As a rule they underestimate the influence of the moon, in fact it has acquired rather a bad name, as we can see from a word such as 'lunatic' or the expression 'to be in the moon'. But the fact is that everybody is affected by the moon to some extent, and some unduly so, but they don't know or recognize this. But, let's leave the moon alone for today...

This morning I said that the light from the sun eclipsed that of the stars and prevented us from seeing more than a few details on earth. How is it possible for the sun to eclipse the whole universe in this way ? It is possible because the sun is so bright and luminous. If you yourself become extremely luminous, warm and powerful, all those round you will pale by comparison. Actually, this does not mean that you hide the universe ; it means that you represent the universe and prevent others from groping about and losing themselves in the dark. You proclaim : 'Here I am. Look at me !' and by your light and warmth you represent all the other suns.

By analogy, therefore, our sun reveals the entire universe to us. But man's intellect is so limited that it prevents him from seeing and feeling the presence of the divine world, because it never goes below the surface of things. But this intellect which, for the time being, has pushed the divine world into the shadows, is capable of rising to far greater heights. The day will come when it will attain the higher levels of intelligence to which it is linked, the pure, sublime intelligence of first causes. When this day comes, men will know not only the objective, concrete, material world, but also the invisible, subtle, divine world of the spirit. We must never try to do away with the intellect for, of all the faculties that God has given us, it is the intellect that enables us to seek and find Him. If we did not have this intelligence, however limited and mediocre it may be, we would never discover anything at all. God gave man his intellect, therefore, so that he could find Him and yet, at the moment, it is his intellect which prevents man from seeing truth. But this will not always be so. In the future it will be different.

Although, at the moment, the human intellect has the regrettable capacity for hiding and obscuring everything else, a sincere philosopher or thinker who really wants to find truth can do so. This is why I say that the very same intellect which turns men into materialists, sceptics and atheists, can also, if they are guided and informed by Initiates, lead them to discover the highest truths. Even the most ordinary people, if they knew how to reason correctly, would be able to prove the existence of God for themselves. As I once said, if a murder has been committed or burglars have been to your house and ransacked everything, the police come and look for fingerprints and other clues. Why ? Because they are convinced, absolutely convinced, that behind every crime, indeed every act, there is necessarily an author. How is it, then, that human beings do not follow this same line of argument in respect to the universe ? If they did, they would be bound to arrive at the conclusion that the universe with its unutterably complex and harmonious laws, the stars and constellations, the trees and mountains, and even our own brains must also have their author. Oh, no ! Everything in our everyday experience has an author, but not the natural world ! What a disastrous piece of reasoning !

And yet, human intelligence, limited though it may be, has already discovered a great deal — it can even send men to the moon — and it is capable of understanding the great mysteries of life. The only problem is that it needs someone to point it in the right direction, and that is what we do here in the divine School of the Universal White Brotherhood. If you have no one to guide and instruct you, you will never discover the truths which are indispensable in life.

We must not underestimate the intellect. I often talk about the way in which it manifests itself today, and the fact that we must recognize its limitations, but I have no intention of maligning or belittling the immense role that it plays in our lives, for it is thanks to the intellect, after all, that man can come to know his God and Creator. But human beings really should be more logical : if they acknowledge that every crime committed on earth has its author and then deny that the universe also has one, it is patently absurd. Human beings are so incredibly gullible for some things and, for others, they are equally incredulous and sceptical. They believe neither in a Creator nor in a Cosmic Intelligence nor in the existence of a divine world ; they believe neither in justice nor in mercy, and yet they believe that they will reap great rewards without ever planting or sowing a single seed. When you know about reincarnation and the laws of cause and effect, you know that it is no good just waiting and hoping ; that you have to prepare the ground if you want to get what you ask for, and that if you had worked harder in the past you would already have everything you wanted in this life.

So, you see, human beings don't believe in Divine Intelligence, but they believe in the absurd and in blind chance. Some materialists even believe that atoms combine by pure chance in such a way as to form minds endowed with intelligence ! But just ask a farmer if it is chance that reigns in nature ! He will tell you that figs don't grow on grapevines, nor plums on thistles. And if he

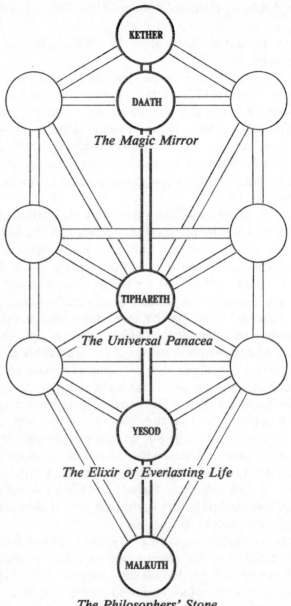

The Central Pillar

knows that much, he will also know that intelligence produces intelligence and the absurd produces the absurd. How can scientists possibly believe that witless, chaotic chance could create a world that is so intelligently organized ? Really, it seems incredible !

But let's get back to what I was saying this morning about the pentagram. I told you that you could place five different symbols on the five points. The first of these is the Philosophers' Stone by means of which metals can be transmuted into gold : this corresponds to the physical plane, that is, the Sephirah Malkuth. The second symbol is the Elixir of Everlasting Life, and this corresponds to the pure life, Yesod, the second Sephirah. The third is the Universal Panacea which corresponds to Tiphareth, the Sun, the light which cures all ills. The fourth is the Magic Mirror which enables us to see and know all things, and this is the Sephirah Daath which contains all knowledge and the archives of the universe. Many magicians prepare magic mirrors with spells and incantations, but what do they see in them ? All the horrors and crimes of the world, all the elementals and demons who haunt human beings. The true Magic Mirror shows you the depths of eternal Wisdom : this is Daath, the hidden Sephirah. And, finally, the fifth symbol is the Magic Wand which confers on him who possesses it the power to work miracles. This is the Caduceus of Hermes, the crozier which symbolizes the spiritual authority of popes and prelates. And this is the Sephirah Kether.

The five symbols, therefore, are to be found on the central pillar, the Pillar of Equilibrium, and they are the gift that these five Sephirah give to the Initiate who walks the path of Equilibrium. Together, they form the pentagram. If you meditate on the pentagram, if you listen to what it says, it will reveal many, many things to you and you will also discover why it contains the smaller pentagram. It is we who are the smaller pentagram, the microcosmos within the greater pentagram. We are the smaller pentagram within the greater pentagram, the macrocosmos, because we are made in the image of the great Cosmos.

The Bonfin, 28 September 1967 (evening)

Chapter Eighteen

The Sun, Originator of Civilization — A Disciple's Clairvoyance Must Begin on the Highest Levels

As soon as the sun gets up he pours forth his light, warmth and life, and it is that light, warmth and life that encourage men and women to get up, too, and go to work. Some go off to their offices, some to factories or to the fields, others open their shops. Children go to school, and the streets are alive with the sounds of vehicles and human voices. And in the evening, when the sun goes down, people close their shops and offices and make their way home again and, before too long, it is time for bed ! Everybody knows that the daily rhythm of human life is determined by the movements of the sun, but what nobody knows is that the sun is also the originator of all civilization and culture.

We may sometimes have wondered who first taught men the arts of writing and agriculture and the use of fire and certain tools. Various names have been suggested, but the truth is that it was not a human being at all, but the sun ! Yes, the sun was at the origin of these discoveries. You will perhaps object that that is impossible, since the sun is not endowed with intelligence : he has no brain to think with and no tongue to talk with. According to you, then, human beings have a monopoly on intelligence, and the one being that has made life on earth possible is not intelligent !

No, no. As I say, the sun was the first to bring science to mankind. How ? Well, it is not difficult to understand. It is thanks to the light of the sun that we are able to see objects and distinguish shapes and sizes, colours and contrasts. It is thanks to his light that we can see where we are and where we are going, observe the world around us and compare and calculate. If there were no light there would be no science. What can you know in darkness ? Nothing !

And now, if I ask who introduced religion, those who fancy themselves as philosophers will probably say that it was fear, the fear of human beings confronted with the forces of nature. But this is an answer that betrays a very narrow outlook. Here again, it was the sun that created religion, for it was the sun's rays that gladdened men's hearts and kindled in them the need to expand, to love and adore. In the cold a human heart freezes and shrivels up ; it is incapable of love. But give a man warmth and he will feel himself relaxing and blossoming, and he will begin to love. So this is how religion first appeared : through the warmth of the sun. For many, of course, religion may begin simply as affection for another human being or even for a pet : a dog, a cat or a canary ! But that does not matter : it is a beginning ! And one day it will grow and extend all the way to the Creator and Lord of the Universe.

And finally, it is the sun that was at the origin of art, simply because he gives life. As soon as a being possesses life, he feels the need to move, work, speak and express himself through his creations, and so you have the beginning of dance, song, painting and sculpture. Art begins when life begins. Look at children : they are always on the go, shouting, screaming and scribbling. And their shouts are the beginning of music ; their scribblings are the beginning of painting ; their sand castles are the beginning of sculpture ; their little houses of twigs and cardboard are the beginning of architecture, and all their wriggling and jiggling are the beginning of dance. Yes, art begins when life begins, and life comes from the sun.

How could an artist create anything if the world were plunged in darkness ? Where would he find his models ? Who would give him notions of movement, form or colour ? I have sometimes said to artists, 'It is you who paint your pictures, but who gave you the colours ? Did you create them yourself ? No. It was the sun that put them into the minerals and plants from which they have been extracted ; do you ever think of that ?' Painters never think of thanking the sun for giving them their colours, and they rarely put the sun into their paintings.

I once knew an old man who was a famous painter ; he lived here, in the South of France, and the colours in his paintings were magnificent. He invited me to spend a few days with him and, when I got there, I was astonished to see that his house had been built in a deep hollow surrounded by mountains. I wondered how an artist, a lover of beauty, could have been so ignorant as to choose such an unsuitable spot. For him, the sun rose at ten o'clock, even in the summer, and set at four in the afternoon. I finally talked to him about it. I asked him : 'How can you live without the sun ? Your house should be lit by the very first rays, for the sun's rays are life and inspiration. They can give you everything you need !' The poor man did not know what to say to that, and when I asked him why the sun never figured in his paintings, he said that it was very difficult to paint the sun. 'No, It's not so difficult', I replied ; 'All those lovely colours come from the sun, after all. Your paintings are full of trees and flowers, but isn't it the sun that gave them life ? How can you not pay tribute to it and include it in the picture ? It is the sun that has given you all the rest and yet it is not portrayed anywhere !' I heard, later, that he had started to paint the sun !

It does not take a great deal of thought to realize that the sun is at the origin of everything that exists on this earth. Ask him to explain to you how he meditated and worked so that human beings could exist ; how he prepared just the right conditions of temperature and climate ; how he calculated just the right amounts of light and heat for life to appear. Plant life was the first to appear, followed by fish, birds, mammals and, finally human beings. It was the sun that made it possible for culture and civilization to appear ; it was the sun that was the first farmer, for it was he that distributed the various varieties of plants over the face of the earth, and caused them to grow and bear fruit. It is the sun that commands poverty and plenty, famine and abundance.

When I first arrived in France in 1937, I remember saying that in the future, men would no longer burn wood, coal or oil to produce energy ; that they would use only the sun's rays. At the time, of course, nobody believed me, but now they are beginning to see that I was right, because they know that the fuels they are using today are nearing the point of exhaustion and that they are going to have to turn to subtler energies which will never run out. In the future our houses will be lit and heated and our vehicles will be powered by solar energy. In fact, we shall even nourish ourselves on sunlight.

Without the life of the sun men could never have existed or worked or done anything at all. Without his heat they would never have experienced feeling or emotion. Without his light they would never have been able to see, and not only to see physically, but also to understand, for understanding is a higher form of sight : sight on the intellectual level. It is the sun's heat that gave birth to the things that concern the heart : all human contact and exchanges, love and friendship, marriage and the family, human society and all forms of community. If you are cold, other people will not like you and will leave you alone. But if you are warm-hearted they will come and warm themselves at your contact and be grateful to you for that warmth. Warmth is what draws human beings to each other and gives them the capacity to feel, to be moved, to be lost in wonder and to pray. The sun's warmth, therefore, is at the origin of all morality and religion.

Of course, I know that if you tell Christians that, they will be indignant because they do not recognize the importance of the sun : for them, what counts is the Mass. But then I ask, 'But if the sun were not there, how could you say Mass ? In utter cold and darkness who could say Mass ? Where would the bread and wine for Communion come from ?' I have no intention of belittling the Mass ; in fact I tell you frankly that I know much more about it than the majority of priests who have learned to say Mass, but know nothing of its deeper, magical significance. But I know what the Mass is, and that is why I have much more respect for it than most Christians, and I still say, 'If the sun did not exist who would say Mass ? And who would assist at Mass ?' The trouble is they just don't think !

And now if I tell you that it was the light of the sun acting on our physical bodies that formed our eyes, you would not believe me either ; and yet it is no more than the truth ! The sun created our eyes ; and do you know why ? So that we could see him ! In the same way it was his warmth acting on our bodies that created the organs of feeling : the heart, the mouth and, above all, the skin. He decided that only our eyes should be sensitive to light but that warmth should be felt by the whole surface of the body. You see the difference, don't you ? Isn't that interesting ?

The sun commands everything in the universe ; he is like the conductor of an orchestra or a king on his throne. When he decides something he only has to give the signal and all the spirits he has sent to earth, or to the other planets, hasten to carry out his commands. They make some slight adjustment to the atmosphere or the electromagnetic currents, and all kinds of changes ensue in the vegetable, animal and human kingdoms, in the biological, psychological, economic and social spheres. Everything that occurs on earth is commanded by the sun. Solar flares and sunspots are simply signals that the sun sends out to a vast hierarchy of intelligent beings who are there to carry out his orders.

My dear brothers and sisters, there is no need to look elsewhere : the sun is streaks ahead of anyone else. He is the first and the last, the Alpha and Omega. Like Christ, who said, 'Before Abraham was, I am', the sun existed before all other creatures, and he will still be there when the last man has disappeared from the face of the earth.

By leading you to the sun I am leading you to the Christ, the
Spirit of the sun, who said of himself, 'I am the light of the world.'
The light that lights up the world is the sun. But it is important
to understand that, above and beyond the visible light of the
physical sun, there is another light which is the veritable light of
the sun. The Bulgarian word for this light is *videlina*, from a root
which means 'to see'. I have already talked about *videlina*, the
invisible, inner light which we distinguish from *svetlina*, a word
which is derived from a root meaning 'to shine', and which
designates any visible light, whether from the sun, a fire or a lamp.
It is *svetlina* that enables us to see physical objects, but it cannot
make the invisible realities of the psychic world visible to us. For
this we need *videlina*, and to obtain *videlina* we must establish
a close bond with the sun for, even though it is invisible, *videlina*
also comes from the sun. *Videlina* is subtler and richer than visible light, it possesses an infinite variety of shades and hues
unknown to us, and it takes years and years of work, meditation, prayer and contemplation of the sun to collect even the most
minute quantity, but when we possess it, it enables us to see the
invisible world and all its inhabitants.

Very few people have ever thought about the fact that in order
to see, one has to project light. Everybody knows that if they
go into a dark cave or a forest at night, they must take a lantern
or flashlight with them, but they have never paused to think about
what that means. Physical objects are made visible to our eyes
when a ray of light falls on them, and if we wish to see in the
invisible world, we must be capable of emitting a certain kind
of light. We always expect things to be lit for us, but they won't
be : we have to illuminate them for ourselves. Actually, everything
on the astral and mental planes gives off light, but it is a light
that cannot be seen by human eyes. Man has to develop new centres within his own being, and light new, inner lamps, capable
of casting a ray of light onto the objects and creatures of the invisible world, thereby making them visible.

There are several different kinds of vision ; first and foremost that of the spirit. To grasp the meaning of something with one's intelligence is a kind of vision (In English we say, 'I see', meaning 'I understand'). This is not physical sight, of course ; in fact, people often don't realize that it is a kind of sight. And when someone receives a revelation, it means that he has cast some rays of his own light so high and so far that he is able to see the structure of the universe with its laws and correspondences. Sensation is also a kind of sight which becomes possible when we project another kind of ray onto other creatures and begin to vibrate on the same wavelength ; then we become aware of their existence, their presence and their feelings. And finally, there is a third kind of sight by which we see certain lights or entities in the etheric world. This is excellent in itself, but it is the lowest form of clairvoyance. Many people develop the ability to see etheric forms and colours, but without understanding or relating to them : they need a guide who can interpret what they see for them. This kind of sight, therefore, is not very useful and, in fact, it can often hinder a disciple in his evolution.

There are different degrees or levels of clairvoyance, therefore, and the most elevated is that which enables us to perceive and understand the divine world. This is where you should begin. Later, if you wish, you can develop your clairvoyance on other levels, all the way down to the etheric level. Etheric sight is a lower level of clairvoyance because the etheric world is closely linked to the element earth ; it belongs to the physical, not the spiritual world. According to Initiatic Science, the physical world, like all the other worlds, is divided into seven different divisions or degrees. Official science only recognizes three possible states for matter : solid, liquid and gaseous, whereas, in fact, there are four more states, and it is these that make up the etheric dimension.

There are two schools of thought in this connection. The first teaches its disciples to start from the physical level and work up to the higher levels, until they are able to see the highest, most sublime regions. This method is good, but it does have a few drawbacks which I shall show you. The other school teaches its disciples to concentrate first and foremost on the Prime Cause, the Source of Life, God Himself, and to descend into matter only later. This method is less hazardous than the first, because when you maintain very close contact with the Lord, when you love Him and work only for Him, it is He Himself who shows you how and with whom to work. He can even show you Hell and, thanks to His protection, you will be in no danger.

The great Initiates have to know everything, even Hell. If they avoided Hell for fear of its dangers they would never possess the full Science of Initiation. But it is not until they have reached a very high degree and possess true knowledge, love and power that they can study Hell and its occupants, without running the risk of soiling or burning themselves. At this stage they are protected by their aura and armed with fire and lightning, symbolically represented as a flaming sword ; even demons tremble at the sight and stay well away from them. They have to go down to Hell, so that they can see for themselves how the laws of Karma work, how faults are punished and how reparation has to be made for them. Jesus also went down into Hell. Before being reunited with his Heavenly Father, he descended into Hell and, in fact, he caused severe upheavals there and even released some souls ; all the inhabitants of Hell trembled at his passing.

The danger of beginning with the lower, etheric and astral planes in developing clairvoyance is that these regions are peopled by creatures who are not at all evolved but who are, often, extremely beautiful and seductive. Yes, even in Hell there are many very beautiful things. This is something that Christians practically never mention because they do not know what Hell is, and they imagine that it is full of nothing but filth and horrors ! Not a bit of it ! There are all kinds of pretty things in Hell, but they are illusory and false ; they are there to tempt and snare human beings.

The Devil is always represented as a monster with a fierce snout, claws, horns and hoofs, but the fact is that he assumes an appearance of the greatest charm and seduction : he is always impeccably dressed, wears the finest jewellery and even has a very impressive amount of money in the bank ! He is a smooth talker ; he knows all the best people and he strolls about, sporting a handsome moustache and a bowler hat or the plumed headgear of a cavalier, and swinging a smart little swagger-stick or a gold monocle ! Yes, yes. This is how he appears when he turns up at all the smartest social or state occasions. I do assure you : the Devil is a perfect gentleman ! And, as people think he is going to look dangerous and repulsive, they fail to recognize him so that he easily deceives them and slips in wherever he likes. Human beings have no discernment ! How could they be so stupid as to think that the Devil would appear with horns and hoofs ? He is not such a fool ; he knows perfectly well that horns and hoofs are not likely to charm anyone. This is why he assumes the most seductive disguises possible.

The danger in attempting to develop one's clairvoyance by starting on the lower planes, therefore, is that one can be seduced by the deceptive beauty of forms on these planes and succumb to the temptation to stay there. Some occultists give their disciples certain ingredients such as herbal extracts, for instance, in order to awaken the psychic centres which enable them to see the invisible world. But these methods allow them to see only the lower etheric and astral regions, no more. And if those who venture into experiences of this nature have not previously developed their self-dominance and the discernment on which I insist so much, or if they are in too much of a hurry, or motivated simply by curiosity or the desire to acquire psychic powers in order to mislead and exploit others, then they have no protection and put themselves in grave danger.

The creatures that dwell on the etheric and astral planes are not very keen on being observed by human beings ; in fact, they are often extremely hostile, and those who try to see them provoke a vicious reaction of hate. Every now and then a person who is exploring these levels will pause to enjoy the sight of something pretty and, before they know it, their desire to move on is weakened ; but then, if they dally there the inhabitants of these regions begin to torment them at night with insomnia or nightmares, in the attempt to force them to turn back. And as they are ignorant and have never cultivated the will to defend themselves with weapons of a higher order, they are at the mercy of these hostile forces. This explains how thousands of people have become helpless victims, all because of a few shreds of occult science !

In the Divine School a disciple receives a very different kind of instruction. He is taught that, before attempting to venture into invisible regions, he must have a firm foundation, strong roots ; in other words he must be attached to his Creator, to Heavenly light, by bonds so indestructible that nothing evil, no amount of hostility could ever shake or conquer him. His roots are in Heaven !

Once a disciple has gained a deeper grasp of things by working with the spirit and the highest level of intelligence, therefore, he can descend to the astral plane where he can develop kindness, love, forbearance and greatness of soul. After this he can descend even further, to the etheric plane, where he will begin to see forms and colours and nature spirits. Even those who don't like being observed cannot harm him, because they recognize that he has become very powerful ; they do not dare to pit themselves against him. In fact, they will even obey him if he gives them an order, for they sense that he speaks as one who comes from Heaven, and they are bound to obey such beings.

You see : if you are not in too much of a hurry, everything can be achieved naturally, marvellously !

Sèvres, 30 March 1968

Chapter Nineteen

The Sun Teaches Unity —
The Power of Penetration

How can I help talking about the sun ? It is so beautiful, so
pure, so powerful, so full of treasures ! How can I help talking
about God's most perfect creation ? Last summer we talked about
him for several weeks, and I revealed many aspects that you had
never heard of or even suspected. Is there anything more to be
said ? Oh, yes, indeed there is ! The subject is inexhaustible, for
this is the source of life we are talking about : it is a boundless
ocean !

In my lectures last summer, I spoke of the sun as a source
of energy, life and warmth, as the most perfect manifestation of
Cosmic Intelligence, and as the greatest of all Masters, teacher
of all human Masters. I advised you to go directly to him with
your own questions, for he always has the best answers, better
than those of any philosopher or scholar on earth. So we see that
the sun is the source not only of physical life but also of moral
and mental life. We saw this, for instance, when I spoke about
the Blessed Trinity, in which we see the Father, who is the origin
of everything, the source of life from which all the rest flows,
the Son who is the manifestation of the Father's love (warmth),
and the Holy Spirit who is the manifestation of His intelligence
and wisdom (light).

As I have often told you, the Divine Trinity can be symbolized by a triangle, and this triangle is a key which helps us to discover
a great many other triangles. Let me give you the example of
philosophy. In philosophy we distinguish three disciplines : logic,
ethics and aesthetics, and each of these three disciplines is directly
related to one of the three active principles in man : intellect, heart
and will. That is just one example for you, and you can find others
for yourselves, in other areas. But today I want to look at a certain number of questions to which the sun has the answer.

The first thing one sees when one looks at the sun, is its body,
that bright disc in the sky which is always the same shape and
size and which you can observe, measure or photograph as you
please. But when it comes to studying that which emanates from
the sun, the light that flows from the centre to the periphery ;
when it comes to determining just what it is and how far it reaches
into space, it becomes impossible. It is beyond the powers of
imagination.

And yet... And yet, a human being is built on the same lines :
he has a visible physical body with a clearly defined outline, but
what do we know about what emanates from him ? About his
thoughts, feelings and radiations ? Not very much ! People are
inclined to believe that a human being is nothing more than his
physical body, but they are going to have to revise their opinions
before very long, and recognize that Esoteric Science is the only
science that possesses the truth, for it has always taken into ac-
count the twofold reality of man : the objective, measurable,
material aspect, which must not be neglected, but also the spiritual,
living aspect, including his emanations and radiations, the nature
and power of which are still unknown.

When I said that the planets and the sun actually touched us,
you were astonished. But it is no more than the truth : the sun
does not have to move from where it is to touch us ; it touches
us with its rays. Astrology and magic both find their explanation in this : the one by the influence of the sun and planets on
the earth, and the other by the power of thought to act at a

distance and produce results without the intervention of the physical body. And, as we are built on the same pattern as the sun, we can, by means of our thoughts and our soul and spirit, project our powers far, far beyond the limits of our physical bodies. Just as the action of the sun affects minerals, metals, plants, flowers, animals and human beings, penetrating, warming and nourishing them, so can we transform, ameliorate, enlighten and vivify other beings by means of our emanations.

Unfortunately, materialistic philosophy has deprived man of his possibilities for effective action in the sublime regions, because it has shrunken and weakened him and annihilated his spiritual power. Outwardly, of course, he has more and more machines, equipment and arms at his disposal, so he seems very strong, but within himself he is mortally ill and sinking deeper and deeper into a listless stupor, because he has failed to understand the power of the spirit. When mankind finally manages to give first place to the spirit, a new religion will be born. Actually, it will not really be new, for religion has always been founded on the spirit, but I call it 'new' because, like the 'new heaven and new earth', they will be new for those who have been sleeping and who discover them when they awake.

It is not possible for a religion to be new from the point of view of the spirit. But from the cultural, philosophical, scientific and psychological points of view it will be new, because it will be built on new foundations. To put it very simply, men will recognize that they are not separate entities, but that on the subtle levels of their being they are constantly communicating and exchanging with others : that, in fact, they form a whole. And it will be their awareness of this unity that obliges them to have a different attitude towards others. The new morality will be based on a prodigious science which will enable men to see, feel and understand that every single creature in the whole universe is linked to all the others. As long as men perceive themselves as separate and apart from others they will think that they can massacre others without hurting themselves. But when they begin to develop they will be the first to feel the ill effects of what they do to others, in fact they will feel it so acutely that they will be obliged to stop hurting others.

When the new religion comes it will be founded on irrefutable laws, whereas religion today is presented in such a way that it is completely ineffectual. The fact that, for centuries, Christians have never stopped quarrelling amongst themselves is, surely, proof enough of this ? What have they understood about religion ? Do their Churches show an example of unity ? No, they are all divided. And the doctrine of division and separatism is a product of materialism, a point of view held by those who look at things from the outside, whereas Esoteric Science teaches wholeness and unity. If one looks at things from the outside, of course, one is bound to see beings as separate. But there is another way of looking at things, as I showed you when we talked about the planets : they are billions of miles apart, and yet, thanks to the tremendous range of their etheric bodies, they are in contact with each other and with the earth and, in this way, the earth is immersed in the same immense fluidic ocean as all other beings. This means that every being can influence, communicate with, give and receive from all the others, because all are one. Once you have understood this it is final : you can no longer allow yourself to be harsh or unkind !

Let me illustrate this to make it clearer. Imagine two flasks of perfume : the flasks are separate containers, but the perfumes they contain rise and blend into one in the atmosphere above them. And there you have a human being : the flask represents his physical body whereas the perfume represents his subtle dimension, his soul and spirit and his thought. This perfume, this soul, can communicate and blend with other perfumes, other souls on earth and even in distant parts of the cosmos. It seeks out those that resemble it or whose quintessence corresponds to its own, and enjoys a relationship of exchange with them and vibrates in unison with them. It is in this way that a fully conscious human being can even touch the Lord and communicate with Him : it is simply a question of resonance between them. This is the reason for prayer, meditation, contemplation and identification ; they are the means by which man can rise to such heights that he touches the Universal Soul and begins to vibrate to the same rhythm. When this occurs, there is a fusion or osmosis between them, and all the qualities, all the treasures of the Universal Soul begin to seep into the human being and gradually transform him.

There is no spiritual achievement that is impossible or beyond your reach, on this one condition : that you hold this philosophy. Those who have spurned it have, without knowing it, signed their own spiritual death warrants. Here, we are building the new religion, the new science, the new philosophy, the new life, on clear and simple foundations. Just as God created the world, we too can create our world.

Learn to look at the sun, therefore, in the realization that it is not confined to what you can see of it. Its radiance extends to the outer limits of the universe, travelling distances that astronomers measure in billions of light-years. No one knows the exact nature of the sun's rays yet, nor the power that propels them to such distances ; still less does anyone know what they contain. But I can tell you that they are the loving glances that the sun sends us. I can tell you, too, that they are tiny wagons overflowing with every kind of nutritious fare which they bestow on us before hurrying back to be refilled and return, once again, loaded with thousands of gifts. And it is not only plants, trees, insects and animals, but also stones, the earth and metals that receive nutritious elements from the sun. The whole of creation receives sustenance from the rays of the sun which fall on the earth, the ocean, the atmosphere, outer space and the other planets, and all the creatures who inhabit them.

This is why, if I may give you a word of advice, I say, 'Ignore everything else. Study only the sun's rays and you will be illuminated, warmed and strengthened.' If you only knew what power, wealth, clarity, purity and intelligence were contained in one little ray of sunlight ! Yes, there is intelligence in a ray of

sunlight. Does that surprise you ? No one on earth is as intelligent
as a ray of sunlight : no one, not even the greatest genius ! This
is why you should take them seriously ; if you yearn for them,
seek them out, love them and open yourselves to them you will
come to understand the meaning of creation, and your own life
will become creative, meaningful and splendid : you will experience absolute fulfilment. Unfortunately men are always more
interested in studying microbes, disease, crimes, poisonings,
thieves and murderers — everything, in fact, except the sun ! Is
it any wonder that the poor things are always suffering ? They
have not got enough light. Their sufferings will only come to an
end when they discover the power and intelligence of the sun's
rays. This is my philosophy : it is new, it is true and the future
belongs to it : of this I am absolutely convinced.

Religion is founded on science, that is true, but as this science
has not yet been revealed or explained, religion is only good for
those who believe with blind faith. The day is approaching when
religion will be scientific and, whether they like it or not,
everybody will be obliged to believe and work in this direction.
In the meantime, a great many of the faithful, and even priests
and religious, are so upset and confused by contemporary scientific discoveries that they are abandoning their religion and flock-
ing to science. They even use scientific terminology in their
religious writings : I have read some of them.

In fact, I once knew a pastor who had written a book that
attempted to reconcile religion with modern science, and he spoke
of God as simply a form of energy, nothing more. No, I cannot
agree ! God is energy, that is true : but He is far, far more than
that. He is also intelligence, power, kindness, love... To say that
God is energy does not really say much. It only diminishes God,
and what is the point of that ? Who will benefit from it ? Scientists ? Not at all ! On the contrary, it is they who need to be encouraged to go further, and that is what I am doing : I have great
admiration for them and their discoveries, but I am showing them
that the instruments at my disposal have allowed me to discover

far more than they have ever discovered, and one day, sooner or later, they are going to have to admit it ! Exactly the same things go on in an atom, for instance, as in human society, but in miniature : there are parties, orchestras and concerts and all kinds of jollifications. If you could only see how all those little particles love and kiss, marry and divorce, sing and dance together ! But as nobody has yet seen this they deny it and think that I'm out of my mind ! But, just as science finally had to admit that the atom was built on the same lines as the solar system, it is going to have to admit that I am right and that I am ahead of it.

For I have a key, a method which has allowed me to discover the most extraordinary truths and to see that the whole universe is governed by the same body of laws. That key is analogy. Incidentally, this is the method used by Newton : the story goes that Newton discovered the law of universal gravitation when he saw an apple fall from the tree. And I proceed in the same way, only I leave the apple to Newton, and the example I take is, for instance, the snail ! Yes, the snail shows us how God created the universe for, in doing so He applied exactly the same laws that a snail applies in forming its shell : a substance emanated from Him which He condensed and out of which He fashioned the world. And when the universe was formed, God entered it and made it His dwelling place : the universe is God's house. And we, too, have come to earth in bodies which have been formed according to the same laws ; in fact, if we knew how to enter fully into our bodies so that our spirit penetrated every fibre of our being, we could actually change them. This is what an Initiate does when he wishes to transform a human being : he concentrates and, to the extent to which a heart and soul are open to him, he introduces all kinds of transformations and improvements into them, simply because he has been allowed to enter them. When thieves enter a house they, too, change things, but differently : the house is turned upside down and ransacked ! If you learned to observe what goes on in the world below, you would readily understand what happens in the world above.

True power resides in the fact of penetration, and if the sun is all-powerful it is because it penetrates the whole universe. I am not talking about its visible rays, which are unable to pass through solid, opaque objects, but about X-rays and alpha-, beta- and gamma-rays, and many more besides, which are capable of passing through tremendous thicknesses of metal or minerals and of penetrating to the depths of the oceans to nourish all creatures. The phosphorescent fish found at great depths in the oceans are proof of this, for where do you think they get their light from ? They would have to be gods to make it themselves ! What kind of oil or petrol do they burn to light their lamps ? No, it is the sun that gives them light. Nature has provided them with the elements they need to capture certain rays and transform them and then to emit them in the form of luminescence.

Nothing has greater power of penetration than the sun's rays and, similarly, nothing has greater power of penetration than man's thought when it is identified with sunlight. Thought can penetrate anything and everything : nothing can stand in its way. Nothing can stand in its way, that is, if it is strong ; but if it is the feeble, flickering flame of a candle or a mere flash in the pan, all kinds of obstacles will vanquish it. So, as I never cease telling you : if you want to understand everything you must model yourselves on the sun. One day you will begin to believe me !

In the Emerald Tablet, the father and founder of the Mysteries, Hermes Trismegistus, says : 'This thing is the strength of all strengths for it overcomes every subtle thing and penetrates every solid substance.' The word 'penetrate' is very important. This force which comes from the sun (Hermes Trismegistus also says, 'Its father is the Sun') penetrates all things, and when man possesses it he becomes so powerful that the rays emanating from him, too, penetrate beings and objects and 'all obscurity will fly from him'. In other words, he will be freed of everything bad and harmful : sickness, unhappiness and ignorance. There is nothing very complicated here, it is all quite clear, but to understand it one has to know how to relate and combine the different elements.

This strength of which Hermes Trismegistus speaks, therefore, originates in the sun, and it is thanks to it that magi prepare their talismans, for a talisman is an object imbued with a force or light emanating from him who prepares it : it is this force that transforms a simple object into a talisman. Only those who are capable of penetrating things have the power to change them. For example, if you want to heal a diseased organ, you have to concentrate on it and send rays of light that penetrate every cell, every atom and electron, and flood it with vibrations of light, health and kindness. If you cannot penetrate into the depths of every cell, your thought will have no effect and the sick organ will not be healed. This is absolutely true : how often can one see it ! In fact, at the risk of scandalizing some of you, I would like to add that penetration is the greatest secret, the key to the creation of life. The pity is that, although human beings have been practising it for thousands of years, they have never thought about it sufficiently to draw conclusions that can be transposed and applied to other areas. And yet, the work that transcends and surpasses all others is that of penetrating the hearts and minds of men in order to enlighten, warm and uplift them. As long as one fails to penetrate hearts and minds one is powerless to change them.

I have already said it and I'll say it again : you will find the best solutions to all your problems in the sun. But as you don't know how to interrogate the sun, you just look at it and think, 'It is just a ball of light and heat ; what can it possibly tell me ?' But that is just the point ! The trinity of light, heat and life gives rise to everything else, sets in motion all plant and animal life and even humanity itself, with all its complex social, political and economic organization. In mathematics the figures 1, 2 and 3 can be combined in only six different ways. But with the living mathematics that I am talking about, you can produce an infinity of combinations : with heat, light and life you can explain everything that happens on earth. To explain it all in detail, however, would be a gargantuan task ! I sense the truth of this law intuitively, but it would take several lives to study it in detail and show how everything in life is the result of a combination or permutation of these three factors. My role is simply to provide you with the essential elements, the laws and principles, and I leave it to others to verify each detail.

Sèvres, 7 April 1968

Chapter Twenty

The Sun Teaches by Example —
The Sun, Heart of our Universe

When we look at the sun, the first thing we see, as I have already said, is the bright, shining disc which is always the same shape and size. The next thing we notice is the light that flows from it, the rays flashing from its surface as though they were angry and impatient and incapable of staying quietly in place !

So let's take a good look at this phenomenon of the sun's rays, and see what else we can learn from it. What made the sun decide to send them out into space, all the way to the farthest planets ? Did he want to worry and upset them ? I asked him about this, one day, and this was his reply : 'How can you expect those dark, murky, opaque planets to become like me and learn to do as I do, if I don't give them a good example ? I send them my rays so that they may see how I warm and illuminate others, and learn to do likewise !' And then I understood ; this is how the sun teaches : by example ; this is how he educates others. And this proves that he is the greatest of pedagogues, for he never ceases teaching by his example.

The sun has been there for thousands of years, demonstrating how to shine, how to warm and illuminate others. But human beings are so blind and unconscious that they have never understood what this greatest of all educators, this greatest of all Masters, was trying to teach them. They go rushing off in all directions to learn from others. But when, at last, they feel the need to transform themselves, they are going to have to turn back to the sun and see what he does, and learn to do the same. Look at that luminous disc, that is so tranquil and motionless : it is the sun's body. And all that glorious light flowing from it, all those bright rays, are his thoughts and ideas, his soul and spirit : it is they that go out from the centre to the periphery. Why do they do this ? Well, isn't it obvious ? They are much too hot in the sun ; they need to get away and cool off a little ! You will probably find this explanation a bit 'homespun' ! It is like the village idiot's explanation of why the days are longer in summer and shorter in winter : because heat causes things to expand and cold causes them to contract ! Yes, my explanation is rather like that : it is too hot in the sun so the rays go out to cool off. Don't we all do this ? In winter, if you sit by the fire too long, you feel the need to go out for a breath of fresh air, and once you have cooled off, you go back in to get warm again. Well, this is what the rays of sunlight do : they go out because they are too hot, and when they come back they have contracted and shrivelled up so much from the cold, that we cannot see them any more.

You must all have noticed this to and fro, this perpetual pattern of alternation in your everyday lives : there are days when we stay at home, and others when we decide to go out to work or to do some shopping, and when we have finished we go back home again. We leave the centre to go out to the periphery, and then we leave the periphery again, and go back to the centre. And when I analyze the reasons that take us out to the periphery, I find that it is either for reasons of personal gain, to earn or to steal something, for instance ; or it is in order to give, to help someone else or take them a present. Every single activity, every visit or step one takes when one leaves home, is motivated by one of these two reasons. There may be thousands of subtle distinctions, but they can all be summed up in one of two words : 'give' or 'take'.*

* See *Complete Works*, vol. 11, chap. 3.

What is the motivation behind the outward movement of the sun's rays ? What do they do it for ? One thing we can be sure of and that is that if they expected to get something out of it for themselves, they would never be so luminous and radiant. And this is a very important criterion that I learned from the sun : disinterested love makes one luminous. The sun's rays are so wonderfully hot, radiant and pure because they are impelled by their immense, ardent love to distribute the sun's abundant wealth as far and as wide as possible. And once they have discharged their burden of love, they return to the sun to replenish their supplies and return, once more, to distribute it to other creatures in the universe.

And the sun is not the only one in the universe who behaves like this ; he has his representatives on other planes, who have the same function. In our physical bodies, for instance, the sun's representative is the heart. It has the same function, the same tireless activity ; night and day, it works without ceasing because it has only one goal in mind : to help, sustain, nourish, build and repair. Its one idea is to give, to be impersonal, generous and full of love. I wonder how many human beings have ever realized that their heart is the representative of the sun in their own physical bodies !

In the same way, the rays of the sun correspond to the blood that is pumped out from the heart. Like blood, on their way out, they carry with them every sort and kind of salutary, useful element for the benefit of all creatures. When the blood has delivered its load of nutritious, invigorating, healing elements to the cells of the body, and relieved them of their impurities in exchange, it starts on its homeward journey, back to the sun, the heart. But it does not go directly to the heart ; first, it goes to the lungs of the universe to be cleansed of the impurities it has collected along the way, and the planet which corresponds to the lungs is Jupiter. Astrology generally considers that Jupiter corresponds to the liver and, as you know, the liver has very much the same function, in another area, as the lungs : it also purifies the body by ridding it of poisonous substances. The Bulgarian word for 'liver' is *cheren drob*, which means 'black lung', and the lungs are *bel drob*, which means 'white lung'. The comparison makes a lot of sense, for the task of both organs is to purify.

Although astrology attributes the role of the liver to Jupiter, I personally attribute it to Saturn. Greek mythology can help us to understand this for, to begin with, Jupiter was in the liver and Saturn in the lungs, but when Jupiter deposed his father, he took over the government of the lungs and relegated Saturn to the subterranean regions of the liver. Ever since, Saturn has led an underground life, in mines and subterranean passages, just as the liver works in the dark, poisonous regions below the diaphragm.

But let's leave all that, and get back to the sun ! As we were saying, the rays of light that pour from the sun are his blood, and once the planets and innumerable other creatures of the universe — for space is peopled with billions of creatures who also rely on the sun for their nourishment — have taken what they need from them, they lose much of their light and warmth, so they turn to Jupiter who cleanses and purifies them — Saturn and the moon both play a part in this process of purification — and, from Jupiter, they return to the sun. Then, renewed and replenished, they are sent out, once again, to carry their load of love, wisdom and truth to the farthest reaches of the universe.

So, as we can see, there is a marvellously intricate and potent circulatory system at work in the solar system. Yes, the solar system is a living organism, animated by the sun, its heart, which beats tirelessly in order to keep the whole body supplied with the nourishment it needs. And this is why the heart is the symbol of impersonal, disinterested love : because, in man, it takes the place of the sun.

Let me say just a little more about the relationship between the lungs and the heart : Jupiter and the Sun. The blood pumped into the body by the heart, has to go through the lungs to be purified before going back to the heart. A man's life depends on the relationship between the lungs and the heart. At birth, it is the lungs that trigger the action of the heart ; if a baby fails to take a first breath, the heart does not start to beat and the child dies. And at the moment of death, when the heart stops beating, the lungs stop working. This relation between heart and lungs is reflected in the astrological affinity between Jupiter and the Sun. Like the Sun, Jupiter has a generous nature ; in fact, in astrology, he is known as the planet of good fortune, for it is he that distributes wealth, glory and every form of prosperity. Jupiter does not possess the light and warmth of the Sun, of course, but like the sun he is generous and open-handed.

These little comparisons are interesting, but they are of secondary importance. What really matters for me, is to get you to understand that the light and heat of the sun come from its constant desire to give. When someone hardens his heart against his fellow men and loses the desire to help others, his face becomes sombre and loses its inner glow. Look at the face of a criminal who is hatching some dark plot, and see how tense, anxious and sombre he looks. And then, by contrast, look at someone who is on his way to take comfort and consolation to a friend in distress : his face glows and radiates a warm beauty. You must understand this language. The greater your desire to enlighten, instruct and help others, the more your inner light grows in intensity and breadth, until you are surrounded by an immense, luminous aura of radiant beauty that makes you resemble the sun. Can you see, now, that it is the sun that possesses the only valid criteria, the only genuine yardstick, the only absolute laws. I do not get them out of books. For me, the only authentic book is the sun.

From now on, therefore, try to take the sun as your model ; try to get closer and closer to him and ask him what you have to do to be like him. He will tell you, 'If you strip yourself of your selfish thoughts and desires, you will begin to radiate light and to warm your fellow creatures.' All those flawless beings who have visited the earth in order to help mankind have been like rays of sunshine. The work they accomplish in humanity is an exact analogy of that which the sun accomplishes on the earth, and without them human civilization and culture could never have existed. It is true that, in the course of their sojourn on earth, in assuming the burden of men's sins and impurities, they lose some of their vitality and brilliance, but once their mission is accomplished they return to Heaven in indescribable glory ! It is these chosen souls, these Sons of God, who are the true rays of sunlight on this earth.

And now, have you never wondered how it was possible for the sun to give and give and radiate as he has, for billions of years, without ever being exhausted ? It is because there is a law of Divine Love which says that the more you give, the more you receive. There is no such thing as a vacuum in the universe. An empty space is immediately filled by something else, and this law is operative on all levels. And if what you give is luminous, radiant and beneficial, the law of affinity also takes effect, and you receive elements of the same quality, the same luminous quintessence, in return. But if you emanate filth, your reservoirs will immediately be filled with new supplies of filth !

This explains why the sun is never exhausted : he is constantly giving, so he is constantly being refilled. He sends us his rays and, at the same time, he receives a ceaseless influx of energy from Infinity, Immensity, the Absolute. At the same time as he is sending his rays outwards to the periphery, he is drawing in nourishment from the wealth and energy of the Absolute. He explained this to me, one day, saying, 'I am permanently tuned in to the Infinite, to the Deity and, as my thoughts and desires are absolutely pure, I attract the purest and most luminous energies which pour into me. You must learn from my example how to become perfect and tireless. If you work as I do, you will see that, when you spend certain energies for the good of others, almost at once, new energies will pour into you.' Exactly how this happens is a mystery, but it is so true ! Whereas if you spend your energies in the pursuit of a goal that is too personal, it takes a long time to recuperate and get all your strength back, and if, by misfortune, you fall ill, it may take months or even years before you are well again. Those who are animated by the purest thoughts and the highest ideal always recover their health more rapidly than others.

Of course, I know very well that astronomers will never agree with the idea that the sun is inexhaustible. In fact, they have already calculated his life span : they estimate that he has a few billion years to live, and then it will be all over ! So much for the sun ; all the arrangements for his funeral have been made before he is even dead ! Yes, because they do not know that he is a living, conscious, intelligent being, capable of living as long as he needs to in order to complete his work. They would say, 'But that is animism ! It's simply childish !' What of it ? Perhaps it is children who have the right point of view. The truth is that everything is alive.

All our spiritual work is founded on the sun ; he is the conductor and we the orchestra, and we sing and play to the rhythm of his baton. You have no idea of all that will soon be discovered. If I had the sophisticated equipment I would need, I would love to record the music of the sun, for the most beautiful music imaginable pours from him and is diffused throughout the universe. One day, in fact, when scientists begin to take this seriously, mankind will be lost in wonder and delight to hear the glorious music coming from the sun.

But music is not the only lovely thing that the sun pours out on the earth. An abundance of perfumes, the quintessences of every flower in creation, also emanate from the sun. The fact that we cannot smell them is simply because our sense of smell is still inadequate. Each variety of flower on the earth chooses from amongst all the perfumes emanating from the sun that which is best suited to its own nature. It is not the flowers that manufacture their own scent ; they pick up the fragrance emanating from the sun and pass it on to us when we smell them. So it is by breathing the perfume of flowers that we discover the perfume of the sun. And this is yet another thing that will, one day, be confirmed by science. But it will be a very long time before we are capable of smelling the fragrance of the sun ; it will not be quite so long before we can hear his music.

I am leading you to the sun so that you can take him as your model. I want to convince you that he is alive and intelligent and that he is the source of every science. Yes, and besides, he is my own teacher : he is the most accomplished educator there is. Let me tell you what he said to me : 'Listen to me : you've got to abandon the old philosophy that everyone clings to. So-called educators know nothing about true education. They don't know that in order to warm others, one has to be warm oneself ; in order to illuminate others, one has to be luminous ; in order to vivify others one has to be vibrantly alive ! Educators try to impose on the younger generation moral qualities that they themselves don't possess ; they are incapable of giving an example. In these conditions, how can you expect the young not to rebel ? It is only to be expected that they should refuse to obey any longer. A true educator has to emanate the qualities he wants to teach to others ; he should be a contagious, stimulating, irresistible example. True poets and musicians stimulate others to become poets and musicians. One who is truly full of love inspires others with love. A daring, courageous general inspires courage in his soldiers and leads them to victory. Imagine a cowardly officer, shaking like a leaf and trying to get his men to launch an attack : nobody would follow him. Educators tell the young, "You must be reasonable, honest and generous," but are they reasonable, honest and generous themselves ? How can you expect the young to aspire to higher things ?'

People think that the quality of education can be improved by a bigger budget, better equipment and bigger stadiums, swimming pools and libraries. But all that is useless if there is no living example ! This is the only solution. Contemporary education in the schools only touches the surface, the periphery. True education is an education that touches the centre : if, as an educator, you are noble, fair and honest, you will not need to say a word to inspire nobility, integrity and fairness in others. Anything else comes under the heading of rhetoric and preachifying !

There you have it : this is the new culture, the 'new heaven', and it is a complete reversal of the present situation ! Those who persist in their old ways and their old conceptions are, of course, perfectly free to do so but, sooner or later, they will find that everything is crumbling beneath their feet ; they will have nothing to hang on to. Yes, tremendous upheavals in the world are going to bring man back to the truth.

And all those so-called truths of mankind : if they cannot give me love, light and warmth, I have no use for them ; they are worthless ! Truth liberates, warms, vivifies, illuminates and improves. That is the truth I want ; anything else, you can keep. I don't need it. Truth ? Once one has found truth one is never the same again. How simple it all is ! Yes, and I have never met anyone simpler than the sun.

How many of you are still full of astonishment and gratitude for the extraordinary blessing of the presence of the sun ? We should continually rejoice and give thanks for the fact that it is always there, always ready to strengthen us and give us warmth and encouragement. It is amazing ! What have we ever done to earn or be worthy of such an immense blessing ? Everybody takes the sun's presence for granted : 'It's only normal. There's nothing to get excited about !' ; and they go on eating and drinking and going to work and amusing themselves, and nobody gives a thought to the sun. Yes, all that is normal : it is my astonishment that is abnormal ! Do you know what truth is ? It is something so obvious that it stares us in the face, but that we cannot see !

Sèvres, 9 April 1968

Chapter Twenty-one

Three Kinds of Fire

Everyone has his own pet manias and, as you realize, I am no exception. Don't I keep repeating the phrase, 'That which is below is like to that which is above', for instance, or the same remarks about the great Book of Living Nature ? But at least my manias are useful, and I can prove it by showing you, once again, that this maxim of Hermes Trismegistus is a key to many doors.

I remember that when I was young — I must have been about thirteen or fourteen — I liked to try my hand at various trades. I did not stick to any of them for very long, of course, a few days or a few weeks at most. It was holiday time, school was over for the summer, and instead of going to play with the other children, I preferred to get a job and learn a trade. And that is how I became a tailor ! Oh, not for long, I assure you ! Only one day, in fact, because I must admit that I did not enjoy it much : I kept going to sleep. The only really good thing about being a tailor is the position. You know, 'tailor fashion' : legs crossed as in the Lotus position of Indian Yogis. But that did not prevent me from falling asleep because — well, sewing is not terribly exciting, is it ? It seemed endless ! And then, too, I kept pricking my fingers, so I decided that it was not for me and I gave it up after one day.

Still, there is no denying that to spend one whole day sewing,

leaves its mark on you and, ever since, I have continued to sew
in my own way, and no one is any the wiser ! I have never attempted to make money by opening a boutique, of course, but
I still continue to make my own clothes. Ah, that surprises you,
doesn't it ? Yes, I go to certain shops that I am familiar with,
choose the very best cloth and make myself beautiful clothes, the
most gorgeous tunics and coats you have ever seen. I let someone
else buy or make my external, material clothes for me, but I find
that I am the only one who can cut and sew my inner garments
exactly as I want them, so I do that myself. So, you see, I am
my own tailor. And now I shall leave you to interpret this for
yourselves !

There were several other trades which made a great impression on me. Very often, for instance, I would pass the smithy,
and it fascinated me to see how the blacksmith would hammer
a piece of white-hot iron into shape. I loved fire ; fire has always
had a great attraction for me. In fact, when I was even younger,
about six or seven, I set fire to several barns in the village ! It
thrilled me to watch them burning, and I could not understand
why everybody was in such a panic, rushing about with buckets
of water, trying to put out the fire. Yes, I admit it : you have
before you a pyromaniac ! Of course, as I got older I reformed ;
I understood that I should light other kinds of fires in men's hearts
and souls. Anyway, as I was saying, I was so fascinated with the
blacksmith's trade, that I stayed there for several weeks and en-
joyed it enormously. The main drawback was that, as I wore san-
dals, sparks kept falling on my feet and they were covered with
blisters. But I shall never forget the experience of that apprenticeship : it was my job to work the bellows, and while I pumped
I watched the smith at work. To this day I remember how the
sparks flew : it was a magnificent sight !

And now I want to draw a lesson from this experience as a
blacksmith, to show you how I use the key of analogy. Everyone
knows that if you want to forge iron, you have to put it in the
fire and wait for it to get red-hot and then incandescent. But

although everyone knows that, no one ever pauses to decipher the important initiatic truth concealed in this phenomenon. And yet this is one of the most significant pages of the great Book of Nature : how can a flame communicate its heat and even its light to a piece of iron ? What a mystery ! The iron becomes exactly like fire : luminous, radiant and burning hot. A cold, hard, dull grey piece of iron is totally transformed and acquires entirely new properties !

And a human being can be compared to a piece of metal, iron, for instance, and only the contact with fire can make him radiant, bright and warm. Obviously, I am talking about spiritual not physical fire, for there are different kinds of fire. Only mystics really know what contact with spiritual fire is : it is ardour, love, ecstasy, a very intense form of life. Yes, spiritual fire is a form of life which is capable of consuming you and transforming you utterly. Just as physical fire has the power to make iron pliant and sufficiently tractable to be given a new shape, the celestial fire of Divine Love, plunges man into a spiritual state in which he sloughs off his hard, ugly, opaque form and acquires a new one, radiantly bright and shining. This secret has always been known to true mystics, Prophets and Initiates. They knew how to find the true fire slumbering in their own souls and spirits, and how to plunge themselves into it until they became so perfectly malleable that they could hammer themselves into new shapes and, finally, temper the newly forged metal so that it would retain its form. And here, too, is a detail which very few have learned to interpret correctly : why does a blacksmith plunge a piece of white-hot metal into cold water ? So that its new form may be hard and durable.

There are several different kinds of fire, but they can all be put into one of three major categories : physical fire which consumes and devours physical objects ; astral fire which burns and torments human beings and which includes, for instance, the fire of selfish, sexual human love, and a third kind of fire : divine fire, the fire of the sun, which does not consume or cause suffer-

ing but which, on the contrary, brings light, joy and rapture and
the sublime sensation of being in direct contact with God Himself.
This is the fire from Heaven. Whereas that experienced by a
human being who cries that he is on fire is often no more than
the passing flame of passion. What is so strange is that, although
human beings become completely distraught when they are in the
grip of this kind of fire, and start suffering and weeping and losing weight, they seem to love it. Very few know how to rise to
other levels and plunge into the fire that fills the higher planes
of reality. This is the fire I am familiar with ; more than once
in my life God has granted me instants in which I have truly tasted
this heavenly fire.

   A few moments ago, I said that you did not know how to interpret the fact that hot metal has to be tempered by being plunged
into cold water. The cold water represents all the difficulties and
sufferings that come our way. Fire melts metals, whereas water
hardens them and, where the earth is concerned, the opposite is
true : water softens and loosens the soil and heat dries and hardens
it. This is just one more page from the Book of Living Nature.

   I will talk to you again, soon, about this question of water
and fire and the four elements. But today, the first thing I want
you to understand, is that if a human being wants to change his
old habits and transform himself, if he wants to remodel his
temperament, his innate tendencies and even his heredity, he must
be plunged into fire. He must call on it, draw it into himself, beg
it to descend into him ; and then he must fan the flame ceaselessly
and tirelessly, until it melts him. And, once he is sufficiently pliant
and malleable, he must call on someone to come and give him
a new form or, if he is sufficiently conscious, forge himself anew.
This is my interpretation of the blacksmith's trade and, as I was
once a smith myself, I know what I am talking about ! Yes, indeed : you see before you a blacksmith. I was even paid something
for the work I did. Not much, I admit ; in fact, if I told you how
much you would not believe me. But I was very young and very
pleased to have a few pennies to take home.

I have no hesitation in telling you how to transform yourselves, because I have verified all this for myself and I can guarantee that it works ! You begin by fanning the fire into a blaze, that is, by praying and imploring the gift of celestial fire and, when it comes, you feel the flames of such divine warmth leaping within you that you cannot help but melt. It is impossible, after such an experience, to be inwardly the same, and even physically, you will find that, little by little, you will be transformed and will begin to fashion a new visage for yourself.

When I was very young (but this was when I was sixteen or seventeen and, of course, I was very ignorant about all these things), I felt that something extraordinary was happening inside me. I felt as though a fire burned within me and I wept for joy ; I was in raptures, in an ecstasy of delight ; but as I knew nothing about these things I did not understand what it was. Thanks to my spiritual work and all the exercises I had been practising, the divine fire came and was beginning to burn me. Some time later, when I met the Master Peter Deunov, I went on with my spiritual work, and one day he said to me, 'You have changed your skin.' Even then I did not understand. I wondered what it meant, to change one's skin, and whether it was important. Years later, when I had studied the significance of every slightest detail, I understood that it was, indeed, extremely important to be able to change one's skin.

As I have said, I have experienced what I am talking about ; I have had personal experience of this fire ; in fact, I could talk about it for years. There are a lot of people who have read books on the subject, and who can talk much more eloquently than I about the raptures and ecstasies of mystics, but they have never experienced them for themselves. Whereas I have had the privilege and the immense joy of experiencing, of tasting celestial fire, and this is how I came to understand that it can melt and refashion all the old, time-hardened forms. This is why it should be your one and only desire : wish for nothing but this heavenly fire, think of nothing but this fire, contemplate this fire until it inflames and transforms your heart and your whole being. Don't rely on explanations from other people or from books : they can do nothing for you if your whole being does not vibrate and quiver with the fire burning within, if you are not like the sun : alight with a blazing fire. For the sun is fire, and that is why we should go and renew our contact with the fire from Heaven every morning at sunrise. If you forge a close bond with the sun, if, wholeheartedly, and with all the powers of your intelligence, you let the sun set you on fire, flames will begin to rise within you and enfold you. The Holy Spirit is none other than the sacred fire of the sun.

When the Holy Spirit descended on Jesus' disciples in the form of flames or tongues of fire, they received the gifts of healing, prophecy and tongues. Heavenly fire bestows gifts that no other can. This is why I say, 'Don't rely on teachers, universities or books. Rely only on the sun, for only the sun can ignite this fire in you, inflame you, make you burn and glow. Never let a day go by without a moment of conscious communication with the sun, until the divine fire that alone is capable of revealing all truth to you, dwells within you.' This is at the heart of all Initiations : you will have attained nothing in life if you do not attain this fire. This is the goal you must reach, and you need have no fear of being burned by it, because this fire does not burn, it transforms. Oh, of course, you could say that it burns, but it only burns waste and impurities ; it will not destroy that which is pure, noble and divine. Fire cannot hurt another fire ; it cannot destroy what is of the same nature as itself.

Let me say it again : I have personally experienced, verified, touched and tasted all that I am talking about. In fact, I would like to tell you about an experience that I had fifty years ago and that I have never spoken about. It happened not long before I met the Master Peter Deunov : I had got hold of some Hindu books on breathing, and for days on end, I practised these exercises from morning till night. I breathed until I nearly disintegrated ! As I had no one to watch or guide me, and being so young I had no notion of restraint, I exaggerated to such an extent that I became very ill and nearly died. But before that, one day while I was breathing, I felt something entering my lungs ; something that felt like fire, but indescribably soft and delicious ! I could feel it flooding into my whole being. I did not understand what was happening, but from that time on, all kinds of strange, unimaginable phenomena began to manifest themselves. It was at that period of my life that I heard the Music of the Spheres. Only later did I realize that the fire that I had received was a particle of the ether, of the Cosmic Spirit.

If you read Ezekiel, St John, or any of the Prophets, you will see that they all tell of how God purified their lips with a burning coal or by making them swallow a tiny scroll. The outward manifestations vary, but the reality is always the same : when we breathe air into our lungs, a spirit enters into us which, if you like, you can call the Holy Spirit. Hindus call it the heavenly Prana, others speak of it as fire or light. It makes no difference what you call it : it is a spirit that we receive from the air when we breathe. This is why some Initiatic Teachings attach so much importance to breathing. Inspiration and expiration represent the beginning and the end, God Himself, everlasting life. Life begins with the first breath, the first inspiration, and when a human being dies we say that he 'expires' : life ends with our last expiration.

A disciple must be attentive to this question of breathing, and understand how important it is. At meals, for instance, people make themselves ill because, instead of breathing correctly, they talk and gesticulate and gulp down their food. Nobody realizes it, but the nutritional function cannot happen correctly if you do not breathe correctly while you are eating. This is why it is very important not to talk while you are eating, so as to be able to breathe correctly, for through your breathing you absorb subtler elements and, in this way, build up reserves for the whole day. It almost seems as though most people deliberately choose meal times as the best moments to start arguing or quarrelling. They do not know that when they do so it has a very negative effect on certain glands in their bodies which begin to secrete poisonous substances. Yes, this question of glandular secretions has not yet been studied or understood to any great extent, and yet it is highly important.

It is possible that some of those who come here for the first time and who do not know why we respect certain rules with regard to nutrition criticize or scoff at us ; from the point of view of the education they have received, our habits are plainly ridiculous. But when they study our methods they will begin to realize how many opportunities they have been wasting. At first sight, the practice of taking a few deep breaths during a meal may seem trivial but, in fact, it corresponds to some important hidden truths. But people are so far from suspecting any of this ! So I advise any of you who are newcomers to our Teaching, not to be astonished, and not to criticize or compare our methods with what you were taught in the world. Be patient ; study this Teaching with perseverance and, one day, when the light dawns, you will be dazzled by all the wealth contained in the Teaching and its methods. They may seem insignificant at first, but, in fact, they open doors onto something entirely new and different from anything that has been known so far.   -

You must have realized by now that my philosophy does not come from books, but from my own experience. I never reveal something to you that I have not put into practice myself, for a long time. Even now, I am always experimenting, getting to know and putting into practice other truths, in the hope of passing them on to you one day, and causing you to say, with me : 'How beautiful, rich and magnificent life is !' Yes, because instead of being content with a few mingy little pleasures and joys, you will increase your range of pleasures and begin to taste delights hitherto unknown to you. So trust me, and make up your minds here and now that you are going to know the power of heavenly fire, that you are going to feel it and possess it within you. And, in order to achieve this, concentrate deeply, far more deeply, on the sun and on the fire that fills the universe. Try to understand the nature of this fire, try to understand its power to enter into us, to stir the very depths of our beings and to communicate its own properties to us. You must absorb it, let it soak into you, so that the old forms that have already hardened within you melt and can be remodelled.

In some areas we have to work with water, for water has the power to modify whatever is of earth and stone in us ; but where metal is concerned, we must use fire. One day I will talk to you about all the different exercises you can do with water when you are by a river, a waterfall or the ocean. When I was on an island in the Pacific, last spring, each morning I did a particular kind of work with the power of water. Most people have no notion of what springs, waterfalls, rivers, lakes and oceans represent. They think they are very pretty, of course, and they drink their waters, dip their hands into them or go for a swim, but that is all. They do not really work with them. Well, if they do no more than that, they can continue to spend their holidays by a lake or at the seashore for the rest of their lives, but it will not change them.

Water represents the universal fluid, the blood of the earth, and it has tremendous powers. You must learn to have the right attitude towards it, learn how to talk to it, how to create a bond with it, because it will change certain elements within you by diluting and dissolving them. Water, you see, has this power over certain substances that fire is incapable of changing. Fire does not possess every power : God has not given all powers to only one of the elements. The four elements complete and complement each other although, at the same time — in the case of fire and water, for instance — they also oppose each other, for it is water that is used to put out a fire. To all appearances fire and water are enemies. They are like man and woman, always at war with each other ; and yet they love and are attracted to each other.

So, concentrate on the power of heavenly fire. All too often, human beings allow themselves to be burned by the other kind of fire, astral fire, which produces quantities of smoke, and leaves a lot of ash. Heavenly fire produces no smoke and leaves no ashes ; it produces only light, warmth and life. Unfortunately, men and women prefer to ignite the hungry fires of the astral dimension, and then they cry out that they are burning to death ! And, of course, it never occurs to anyone to be surprised or to doubt them, because everybody knows what it is like ; it is nothing unusual ! But when it comes to lighting the inner, heavenly flame, there are not very many candidates.

As I have said, there are three kinds of fire ; or rather, there are thousands of different kinds of fire, but to simplify things, I divide them into three major categories : physical fire which burns everything and everybody indiscriminately, making no distinction between the good and the wicked. Then there is astral fire, the fire of Hell, which is particularly fond of those who are driven by passion and lust and full of evil designs. It is always ready to pounce on them and burn them up, for they are just what it needs to feed its hungry flames. But it does not have the power to harm those who remain close to God and His angels. And finally there is heavenly fire which seeks out only those who are truly pure and luminous and, when it finds them, pounces on them and sets them on fire, and they become children of God, ablaze with beauty and light like the sun.

Physical fire, therefore, does not choose ; it burns whatever comes its way without discrimination. It is not interested in knowing whether someone is just or unjust ; that is not its business : its business is to burn. But the two other fires are able to choose. Divine fire never descends indiscriminately. It is a bolt from the blue, but it is not blind : it chooses whom it will fall on. Yes, you could say that it is a thunderbolt : those who receive the Heavenly gift of grace are struck by a divine thunderbolt. The French have the expression *coup de foudre* (thunderbolt) to mean love at first sight, and when someone is struck by this *coup de foudre*, the outcome is, unfortunately, predictable : suffering and tears are in store for him. It may even drive him to murder ! Why are some people struck down by this kind of thunderbolt ? Because there are certain things they need to learn, and they can only learn them through suffering. Others are struck by a different kind of thunderbolt, the heavenly thunderbolt that also leaves them in tears, but in this case they are tears of ecstasy. Many, many saints and mystics have received this grace. Read their lives, and you will see how St John of the Cross, St Therese of Lisieux and many others, were struck by the divine *coup de foudre* for Christ ; even a few painters and poets have had this experience. To my mind, there is nothing more precious, more rare and wonderful ; no other grace can be compared to that of being struck by a flash of heavenly fire. There is nothing to surpass it.

But you must not think that, just because someone has been struck by this heavenly flash of lightning, this divine thunderbolt, he is immediately omniscient and all-powerful. Not at all. Heavenly fire does not put everything into our laps ; it simply gives us the means and the possibility of becoming a divinity on condition, of course, that we collaborate with it and work towards our own development, our own perfect fulfilment. Unfortunately, it is also possible to lose this grace again, to lose the Holy Spirit, and that is the greatest misfortune that can ever befall a human being, the most grievous loss that any man can know. Many occultists, mystics and Initiates have been in possession of the sacred fire and then lost it in one way or another. Some have managed to win it back again, but at the cost of untold suffering and tears, repentance and unflagging labours ! For heavenly fire has such a high degree of consciousness that it is almost as though it were insulted that someone should neglect it to the point of letting it slip from his grasp, and he has to humble himself, shed many tears and plead for a long time before it will consent to return to him. But once it does return, it anchors itself so firmly and puts down such strong roots deep inside him, that it can never again be uprooted !

I have studied a great many cases and gone through many personal experiences. In fact, I maintain a constant dialogue with fire. Inner fire, outer fire, inwardly or outwardly, fire is the only thing that interests me. Ever since I was born I have had a special leaning towards fire, and although, when I was young, I used to set fire to barns, later I understood that I would do better to leave physical fire alone and set fire to my own heart and the hearts of others.

And now my advice to you is this : knowing that the sun possesses the spark, the flame from which you can light your own heart, never miss an opportunity of attending the sunrise. The sunrise is like the Orthodox Liturgy of Light on Easter morning : the celebrant lights his own candle and then passes on the flame to the candle of the person next to him who, in turn, lights his neighbour's candle. In this way the flame is handed on from one to the other until the whole church is ablaze with light. From a single candle, light is spread throughout the whole church, and this is symbolic. The sun, too, is a candle from which you light your own little candle. It may take years for your candle to catch fire, because it is windy and raining within you, but one fine day it actually happens : your candle suddenly flares up and you begin to give off a tiny light of your own. And then your neighbour exclaims, 'Ah, there's a candle. I'll go and borrow some light !' and he comes and lights his candle, and then another one comes, and another and another. And so it spreads and spreads until, one day, the whole world is full of lighted candles !

Or perhaps you would like another, rather more prosaic, example : that of a man who uses a lighter to light his cigarette. It is not a very brilliant comparison, perhaps, but it serves my purpose. The sun is the flint (well, you have heard stranger things than that about the sun !), and you possess a scrap of iron. Every morning at sunrise you strike your little bit of iron against the flint and, one day, at last, you get a spark. The flint is always there, every day, but the bit of iron does not always turn up on time ! So, keep your appointment with the sun and be sure to bring that bit of iron with you and to strike it against the flint. In other words, put your will to work to produce a spark. It is up to you to do the striking.

It is always we who have to make an effort, not the sun. The sun has done all the work he needed to do a long time ago, and now it is our turn to go to him. You would hardly believe me if I told you what you gain by making the effort to get up early in the morning, especially during your holidays ; what powers you are developing by your repeated victories over sleep and laziness. You have no idea !

And now I hope that it is all quite clear to you : come up here in the morning, and light your candles at the great torch of the sun. Is it clear ? Have I given you a good interpretation of the images and symbols in the great Book of Living Nature ?

As the mornings are cold at this time of year, I advise you to drink a mug or two of hot water, before coming up here. Water is an excellent conductor of electricity, heat and life, and it will prevent you from feeling the cold. As you can see, you all have blankets except me : I never take a blanket to the sunrise because I know a few little tricks to keep me warm. Another way to resist the cold is to take a few deep breaths every now and then : take a deep breath and hold it as long as possible before breathing out again. If you repeat this three or four times, with a short pause between each breath, it will help you to resist really low temperatures. Yesterday the wind was icy ; to sit still for an hour without a blanket was enough to catch one's death of cold, so I did this exercise and wrapped myself in a fluidic coating of warmth ; after that I did not feel the wind or the cold or anything else. Practise doing this, yourselves. But don't discard your blankets from one day to the next ! It would be wiser to keep them until you have practised enough and learned how to protect yourselves ; once you are good at it you can discard your blankets.

From now on, when you concentrate on the sun, work to ignite the fire within you. Once you possess it, it will enable you to solve all the problems of life. Later, I will talk to you about air, water and earth, and tell you how to burn the wastes in your head and how to purify your lungs and heart with air. I will also reveal the mysteries of water, which washes the intestines, liver, spleen and sexual organs, and, finally, the mysteries of the earth which absorbs all the impurities of our muscles and bones.* Most people are millions of miles from anything like this, from the idea of working with the four elements in order to obtain absolute purity, the purity of the sun !

This is the science that is in store for you. The path on which I am leading you is the path of purification and true illumination ; it is the path that leads straight to the heavenly fire that will inflame you.

Sèvres, 10 April 1968

*See *Complete Works*, vol. 7, chap. 18.

Chapter Twenty-two

Making Everything Converge Towards One Goal

In a previous lecture I told you that the sun was inexhaustible because it received its energy from the Absolute. Of course,
I realize that the Absolute is a notion that is quite incomprehensible to man, but above and beyond the Sephirah Kether, the name
of which means 'crown' and which represents the Heavenly
Father, is a region known to the Cabbalah as Ain Soph Aur, which
means 'Limitless Light'. The region of Ain Soph Aur is the world
of the unmanifest Deity, whereas the Tree of Life and the ten
Sephiroth represent the different manifestations of God. The sun
receives his energy from Ain Soph Aur, and this explains how
he has been able to illuminate and warm our universe for so long
without exhausting himself. He is always in the same place ;
always bright and active, because he knows how to spend himself
and recuperate, both at the same time. He is past master at the
art. Perhaps he practises with a straw or a little tube, like
glassblowers who learn to breathe in through the nose while blow-
ing out through the mouth ! 'What a ridiculous explanation !'
you will say. But it is the truth : the sun has learned to breathe
in life from that infinite region and, simultaneously, to breathe
out blessings onto all creatures.

And this is something that you, too, must practise : you must
try to absorb or breathe in energies from the divine world at the

same time as you spend other kinds of energy in this world. If
you do not learn to do this you will soon tire. I know that nobody
will teach you this at the university, but here, in the Brotherhood,
if the brothers and sisters want to become tireless, pure, luminous
and immortal, they are going to have to learn to do this. Even
if you cannot see or feel the results for a long time, I can assure
that they are very real. Everything that we do in life produces
results.

So now, when you listen to all these lectures about the sun,
try to choose an ideal and focus everything you do on it, so as
to strengthen and sustain this one, central idea. Those who succeed will be accomplishing a great work, a great victory ; they
will be like a laser beam : instead of being scattered in every direction, their energies will stream from them in a single, narrow beam
of light, all concentrated on the same goal. Perhaps you will say,
'But isn't there a contradiction here ? You tell us that we must
shine in all directions, like the sun, and now you say that we must
focus everything in one direction.' No, there is no contradiction
in what I say, for before you can be like the sun and radiate light
in all directions, you have to make all your desires, thoughts and
activities converge towards one goal. Once you have learned to
do that then, later, you can radiate light all round. The first thing
to do is to muster all your strength, all your desires, all your passing whims, even, and put them to work to achieve a single idea.
Whatever you do, whether it be working, eating or drinking, walking or talking, reading or writing, everything must be aimed at
the accomplishment of that one idea. Nothing must be allowed
to deflect you from your purpose or weaken your resolve.

You must have only one ideal : not two, not three, just one.
Of course, you must continue with your everyday occupations,
your family and your job, but everything you do must contribute
to the nurturing of that ideal. This means that you must work
for years to free yourselves from whatever is holding you back,
and harness all those inner, scattered, chaotic forces that are pull-

ing you in all directions. You must take a very close look at your inner landscape and all it contains, and see what is harmful and contrary to your fulfillment, and what is contributing to it, and make up your mind to bend all those energies in one direction. If you do this then, yes, you will advance. So far, you have been practising all kinds of different methods without making much progress, whereas with this method, you will find that you will advance by leaps and bounds.

This is one of the great secrets of Initiation : to make everything converge in the same direction ; to convince all one's contradictory tendencies to pull together ; to impose one's will on them and, if need be, to reduce them to slavery. And when one has welded all those unknown, hidden energies into one, when one has learned to launch them all together towards one glorious, luminous, beneficial goal, then one becomes a focal point of such intense, powerful light, that one is free to send rays of light in every direction, like the sun. But before becoming a focal point of radiation like the sun, one has to practise a discipline, an asceticism which seems to be just the reverse.

Actually, when one studies things closely, one sees that concentration is a necessary prelude to radiation and expansion. If a human being, to take just one example, did not have a physical body, he would be diluted in space ; he would be nowhere. In order to manifest one has to begin by condensing. Look at the example of the sun : it is because he has a well-formed, powerful, stable body that he can radiate and project such extraordinary forces out into space.

Even God limited Himself when He created the world. He was Infinity, He was somewhere indefinable in Immensity, and then, when He decided to concentrate within self-imposed boundaries, He condensed and compacted Himself into a central point from which He projects into every corner of the Universe. This is manifestation : the first movement is one of concentration, and this is followed by projection. Concentration always goes before projection or radiation. Manifestation, therefore, is a twofold movement : the first goes from the exterior towards the interior, and the second goes from the interior out towards the exterior. The centripetal movement gathers, musters and accumulates energies, whereas the centrifugal movement throws them outwards.

Before a baby can be born on the physical plane, the living building materials supplied by the mother have to be condensed. Originally, these are simply currents, energies, subtle, spiritual forces ; and then these forces unite and condense to form the physical body of the child. Years later, all this concentration of forces begins to radiate outwards into space, and it is the beginning of life on the psychic level of thoughts and feelings, and the child becomes an extraordinarily gifted being : poet, musician or philosopher. When he was still an infant he was a little bundle of flesh, entirely absorbed in eating and drinking and grabbing everything for himself. Yes, he was obeying the dictates of centripetal forces and accumulating materials within himself. Later, he finds a balance between his centripetal and centrifugal forces. Anyone who has observed and understood these phenomena in human beings can see how they correspond to the phenomena of divine manifestation. God manifests Himself by condensing Himself, but there is always some part or aspect of God that remains unmanifested. We don't know what the unmanifest is and we call it the Absolute. Whatever is manifested is polarized into positive and negative, it has a beginning and an end ; but the Absolute has no beginning and no end, and it is not polarized.

And now for the practical aspect of all this. Ultimately, a disciple must understand his lower nature in detail, and engage in the task of dominating its every movement. He must not try to smother its instincts and appetites, but learn to use and control them. He must keep up all his normal activities, but everything he does must be done with the purpose of helping and giving, illuminating and warming others. In the eyes of Esoteric Science, this is the most important work there is. He who cherishes the ideal of becoming a perfect being, capable of radiating light, warmth, purity and life itself, may not be appreciated or thought much of by men because they will not understand him. But all the Heavenly entities will consider him a power, a unique and formidable being, and they will readily give him everything he needs. The divine world will take care of him, for such beings are very rare ! But it is not possible to achieve this without stead-fast love, a luminous intelligence and an inflexible will. With such love, intelligence and will, yes, it is possible ; it can be done.

Of course, if you do not want to adopt this point of view, you will continue to sample everything that comes along without discrimination. You will continue to get everything all mixed up, and you will be stuck eternally in the same spot without know-ing whether you are coming or going. I know very well that you are not all going to throw yourselves into this work. Very, very few, in fact, will be tempted by it, but when these few decide to broaden the scope of their understanding and devote themselves to nobler activities, in other words, to devote themselves totally to establishing the Kingdom of God and His Righteousness on earth, they will witness a radical change in their lives, for the heavenly forces set in motion by their decision will oblige the lower forces within them to submit. There is a law of hierarchy in nature according to which the lower order automatically submits to the higher order, and on earth, in the army or government offices, for instance, we find a reflection of this law. The mere presence of luminous spirits is sufficient to make the spirits of darkness tremble and keep quiet. Why do you suppose that demons obeyed Jesus ? Because of that law : because he had set in motion higher powers capable of making the demons obey. When Jesus said, 'Come out of that man !' the demon came out ; when he told the paralytic to walk, the man walked ; when he said to the sick man, 'Arise', he arose, and when he told the wind and waves to be still, they were stilled.

So if a disciple sets to work to awaken, arouse and set in mo-tion forces that are more powerful than his own weaknesses and passions, the latter will be obliged either to leave him or to submit. It is the law. But it is not possible to give orders to inferior entities and force them to obey if one is not of a higher rank ; they will simply laugh at you and say, 'Ah, we know who Christ is, but who do you think you are ?' And they will refuse to listen to you. Try it and see if you have any success. No, to succeed, you must possess the same forces as Christ. If they are not there, you could command a demon to leave someone and it might do so, but only to rush into you, and that would be even worse. So you have to know the laws.

Try to determine, first of all, which of your professional, recreational or other activities are a hindrance to realizing your ideal, and what you should do about it. Should you give them up altogether, diminish them a little, let them take up less room in your life or, alternatively, should you try to combine them with other elements so that, instead of always being weakened and im-poverished by them you become richer and stronger. That is what I mean by unification. One cannot spend all one's time praying and meditating ; one needs to do all kinds of other things as well, but whatever we do must always be aimed at the same goal, and it is in this respect that we need to analyze and know ourselves. It is an undertaking that can take a long time : several years, in fact. But when you reach the point of no longer being torn by divergent thoughts and desires, you will experience an extraor-dinary sense of lightness and freedom, strength and power. Yes, because it is the most debilitating and destructive thing possible to have one's heart, head and will all pulling different ways, each faculty working only for itself. It is the same old story of the burden carried by the mole, the eagle, the fish and the crayfish : one wants to pull it underground, the other wants to carry it up in the air, the third wants to drag it into the water and the fourth tries to pull it backwards ! This is the image of a man torn by divergent, contradictory forces : no wonder he never succeeds in what he undertakes ! Or rather, he may succeed, but not in the domain that I am talking about.

Take these ideas I have been talking about and meditate on

them at sunrise : how to unify your inner forces, how to discard anything that contradicts, hinders or opposes your ideal, and amplify whatever stimulates you and spurs you on. Go ahead : set to work ! Don't wait any longer. I know it is a very difficult, almost impossible undertaking, but I wanted to tell you this to-day. I wanted to tell you, because it is essential. The path is long and difficult, my dear brothers and sisters, but it is also very wonderful. There will be no more stagnation, no more time wasted doing nothing ; night and day, you will be full of new energies, all flowing in the same direction, towards the same goal.

Sèvres, 1 May 1968

VOLUME 11 — THE KEY
to the Problems of Existence

VOLUME 12 — COSMIC MORAL LAWS

VOLUME 26 — AQUARIUS, HERALD OF THE GOLDEN AGE — Part II

I. Forms and Principles — II. The Religion of Christ — III. The Idea of a Pan-World — IV. The Cosmic Body — V. The Kingdom of God and His Righteousness — VI. The New Jerusalem.

VOLUME 29 — ON THE ART OF TEACHING FROM THE INITIATIC POINT OF VIEW

I. On the Spiritual Work — II. On Responsibility — III. On Building the New Life — IV. On the Living Knowledge — V. On Perfection — VI. On the Reality of the Invisible World — VII. On Participating in the Work of the Universal White Brotherhood.

By the same author :
(translated from the French)

Izvor Collection

PRINTED IN FRANCE
DECEMBER 1987
EDITIONS PROSVETA
Z.I. DU CAPITOU – B.P.12
83601 FRÉJUS CEDEX, FRANCE

– N° d'impression : 1568 –
Dépôt légal : Décembre 1987
Printed in France